Impressions of I

in East Germany

Legal Education and
Legal Systems in the
German Democratic Republic

Daniel John Meador

University Press of Virginia
Charlottesville

THE UNIVERSITY PRESS OF VIRGINIA

First published 1986

Library of Congress Cataloging-in-Publication Data

Meador, Daniel John.
Impressions of law in East Germany.

Bibliography: p.
Includes index.
1. Law—Study and teaching—Germany (East)
2. Lawyers—Germany (East) 3. Law—Germany (East)—
History and criticism. I. Title.
KKA88.M43 1986 340'.07'11431 86-7756
ISBN 0-8139-1110-9

Printed in the United States of America

To Jan

Contents

Acknowledgments ix

Prologue: A Foray into East German Law and Legal Education 1

Part 1: Background and Setting
1. A Remnant from the Heart of the Reich 15
2. State, Party, and Law: An Overview 34

Part 2: The Study and Teaching of Law in the GDR
3. The Law Sections in the Universities 53
4. The Two Law Curricula 72
5. Law Teachers and Legal Scholarship 89
6. Law Students 105

Part 3: Legal Systems and Legal Careers
7. The State Courts and Judicial Careers 117
8. Citizen Roles in Dispute Resolution 140
9. Lawyers and Notaries 146
10. Procurators 154
11. Lawyers and Judges for the Economy 159
12. The Lawyers' Association 168

Part 4: Concluding Observations
13. On Law and Legal Education 177
14. On the GDR 192

Appendixes 211
A. Study Plan 213
B. The Law Curriculum (Justice), by Semester 238
C. The Law Curriculum (Economics), by Semester 241
D. Law Textbooks 244
E. Law Summaries 245
F. Law Commentaries 246
G. History of State and Law of the GDR (Table of Contents) 247

H. Constitutional Law of the GDR (Table of Contents) 253
I. International Law (Table of Contents) 260
J. Constitutional Law of Bourgeois States (Table of Contents) 269
K. The United States Constitution as Seen in the GDR 275
L. Case Exercises 302
M. GDR Laws in English Translation 306
Glossary 307
Selected Bibliography 310
Index 313

Tables
1. GDR counties and population 42
2. Justice & Curriculum Subjects 76
3. Justice and Economics curricula compared 77
4. Weekly schedule, Humboldt Law Section (1st Year, Group 1) 81
5. Weekly schedule, Halle Law Section (1st Year, Group 1) 82
6. Justice Curriculum examinations by semester 86
7. Enrollment by fields in GDR universities and higher technical institutions 113
8. FRG and GDR court structures 118
9. GDR district courts and judges 120
10. Lawyers per capita in selected countries 174

Figures
1. Germany and German universities before the First World War 16
2. The German states after 1949 29
3. The GDR and its regional administrative seats 43
4. Relationships among central state organs and University Law sections in the GDR 45
5. The machinery for the resolution of disputes in the GDR 167

Illustrations
Humboldt University, East Berlin 56
Karl Marx University, Leipzig 61
Martin Luther University, Halle 67
Friedrich Schiller University, Jena 71

Acknowledgments

From the inception of the idea for this project through the completion of this book, numerous persons have provided useful assistance. Those who have been most helpful are listed here, although at the risk of omitting others who have also contributed.

First, my wife, Jan, deserves special appreciation because she accompanied me throughout the entire mission in the GDR during the fall of 1983. Her daily assistance in getting me to interviews, managing our housing and eating arrangements, and in traveling about the country was essential. Her notes and later editorial help were also important.

IREX was, of course, indispensable. Its approval of the project, its funding assistance, and the arrangements it made under the exchange agreements with the GDR made the entire project possible. Important supplemental research assistance and funding for publication were made available by the Center for Law and National Security at the University of Virginia Law School.

Among my student research assistants at the University of Virginia Law School who assisted in a variety of ways in research and editing were Mary Nash Kelly and Nathaniel Chapman, Class of 1984, and Susan Shoenhuber, Class of 1985. Linda Perkins worked diligently on editing, typing, and assembling the manuscript. Susan Weber was helpful with proofreading and checking references. Appreciation for editorial assistance and preparation of the index is also due Andrea Fisher, a graduate English student at the University of Virginia. My son, Dan, assembled information on the GDR to prepare me for the trip, and he assisted with the German language material and in checking details in the manuscript. Professors Inga Markovits and Nancy Wolfe read the entire manuscript, and each made numerous useful suggestions. I am grateful to the Law School typing pool, under the direction of Diane Moss, for perseverance in typing and retyping the manuscript.

The maps and charts were developed with the assistance of the Department of Geography and Computer Science at the

U.S. Military Academy and the University of Virginia Printing Office. Assistance in translating German material into English was provided at West Point, New York, by Mary Ann McCausland and Nora Quigley.

Prologue

A Foray into East German Law and Legal Education

The German Democratic Republic (GDR) is little known to most Americans. The very name is unfamiliar. This territorial remnant of the German Reich is thought of by most Americans as "East Germany," a benighted land which they know only as part of the Eastern European communist bloc. Since the Second World War Americans have thought of Germany as that part of the former Reich that is now the Federal Republic of Germany (FRG), or "West Germany." But because of the peculiarities of the postwar division, and because of East-West global tensions, both West and East Germany are unusually important to international peace. In their separation we have a microcosm of our divided world. Here is the only place on earth where the armed forces of the United States and the Soviet Union directly face each other, each positioned side by side with German units. Efforts to ameliorate, and ultimately remove, the dangerous tensions in this situation may be helped by a better understanding of the East German state, including the role played by its law and legal system.

My interest in law in the GDR was initially aroused through my study of the West German courts—essentially a continuation of the nineteenth-century German legal system. This interest was intensified by several brief trips I made into the East as a tourist. I wondered what had happened to university law study and the courts in the East, where the political and social order had changed markedly since 1945. As a law professor, I was especially curious about the changes that had taken place in the study and teaching of law in universities of former renown functioning today under a Marxist-Leninist regime. I was fascinated by the circumstance that the two German states, populated by the same stock, had a common legal, social, and cultural history before 1945; yet today they are oriented in quite different directions—one modeled after the parliamentary democracies of the Western world and the other cast in the Marxist-Leninist mold stemming from the Russian Revolution of 1917. The East German state should provide a good laboratory setting for examining the effects of Marxism-Leninism on law and legal education. But I discovered that such an examination was impossible in the United States, because despite the increasing attention of American scholars to the GDR and the consequent growth of published material, there is still little available here concerning that country's legal system and virtually nothing concerning its university law faculties. The latter subject in particular seems not to have been examined by any American lawyer or legal scholar. It was to fill this void in our information and understanding that I went to the GDR in the autumn of 1983 and remained for nearly three months. This book is a report on that venture.

The trip was arranged through the International Research and Exchanges Board (IREX), the organization that administers academic exchanges between the United States and Eastern Europe. Exchanges with the GDR commenced in 1973. Approximately eighteen Americans annually have been going there under this program, but none before me had been from the field of law. In response to my study proposal, written assurances were given in advance by the GDR Ministry for Higher Education that visits for me would be arranged to the universities at Berlin, Leipzig, Halle, and Jena—the four universities where there are law faculties. But I received no such assurance concerning access to the courts and other legal organs.

This study was carried out mainly through personal interviews. Altogether I interviewed forty persons in the GDR. Most of these were university law teachers, but they also included judges, lawyers, and assorted officials. Some I talked with more than once, resulting altogether in fifty interviews. These ranged in length from forty-five minutes to two hours, averaging a bit more than an hour. To my mild surprise I was given permission by most of the individuals to tape-record the discussions. I regularly prepared written summaries of every conversation, whether or not it was taped. Also I drafted other memoranda from day to day to record observations and information gathered outside the interviews. These notes and memoranda form the basis for the text here. Social scientists would probably describe this research material as field notes with daily narrative summaries; I was what they might call a "participant-observer."

In addition to gathering data orally through interviews, I attempted to obtain a variety of documents and statistics. But here the GDR system posed an obstacle. Contrary to practice in the United States, public agencies there do not normally make such information available. Indications are that data are compiled in typically thorough German fashion by the state organs in which I was primarily interested: the Ministry of Justice, the Office of the Procurator General, the Ministry for Higher Education, and the State Contract Court. Yet I could obtain little of this in other than fragmentary form and generalized oral estimates. It was said either than it was "not available," or that "it is not secret but it is confidential." Although an official *Statistical Yearbook* is published annually, the few pages in it concerning the business of the courts convey relatively little meaningful data. In the law faculties, however, I was able to obtain more information and was even able to secure some written material, such as copies of the official curriculum and weekly lecture and seminar schedules. The availability of written matter is limited, as a practical matter, by the dearth of reproducing equipment. No law faculty has a photocopying machine; typically each university has one or two such machines and they are under close control in the central library.

I encountered two other obstacles. One was the refusal of the GDR authorities to arrange a visit for me to the University law faculty at Jena, despite their advance assurance of such a visit. No explanation was ever given. There were, however, several hints and grounds for speculation. Jena is a sensitive spot because an unusually large number of persons there apply for visas to leave the country. Also, student disturbances have apparently occurred there. Moreover, Jena is the only law faculty training persons for careers in procurators' offices, which are sensitive and important government agencies. It may also have been significant that relations between the United States and Eastern Europe were getting chillier, along with the weather, as the autumn progressed. A clamor was already underway in the GDR against the deployment of new American missiles in West Germany. Media attention to events in Lebanon was escalating, always with an anti-American coloration. Then came Grenada, raising the "American imperialism" rhetoric to a still higher pitch. Finally, news came that an East German had been arrested in Boston; he was spoken of in the GDR as a "distinguished scientist." Any lingering hope of a visit to the Jena law faculty evaporated after that event. The upshot is that although I passed through Jena twice as a tourist, and strolled through the university precincts, I was not allowed official access to the law faculty to gather information.

The other obstacle to this study was the official reluctance to allow admission to court sessions and to the central offices and buildings of several important state organs such as the Procurator General's office and the Ministry of Justice. From time to time I was told that visits to these places would be arranged, but in fact they never were. Because my inquiry into the legal system had not been expressly cleared in advance, this difficulty was not as surprising as that encountered at Jena.

Despite these obstacles I still managed to gather a considerable array of information not available outside the GDR and obtainable only by being in the GDR for a substantial time. Although denied physical access to the premises of certain state organs, I did have interviews at other locations with some of their officials. Also I interviewed the President of the Supreme Court and judges from other courts in their chambers or conference rooms. But the richest source of information was the many law teachers with whom I talked. The sensitivities surrounding conversations between GDR citizens and foreigners have led me, for the most part, not to identify persons or to cite sources of information; hence I have largely dispensed with footnoting. My chief aim here is to present a factual picture of law and legal education in East Germany, derived from an amalgam of documentary material and my many interviews. I have at times included analogies and comments in an effort to provide a more meaningful explanation for Americans. Most of these, however, I have reserved for the last two chapters where I have summed up my personal observations about the facts presented, as well as about the GDR in general—what many have described as an "Alice in Wonderland" scene.

Although I encountered some official coolness, the hospitality of the individuals with whom I dealt was generally warm. At interviews coffee was always served, accompanied sometimes by brandy or cakes.

Although some of the persons interviewed were reserved and overcautious, most were amiable, and some were even jovial. Nearly all wore the SED pin in their lapels—the membership pin of the East German Communist party, apparently an obligatory accessory for all Party members. In some interview sessions—mainly those in which several persons were present—the chief spokesman opened the session by enunciating the necessity of maintaining peace in the world, and thus of the importance of discussions between them (seemingly speaking officially for the GDR) and people from elsewhere, such as me. Most persons with whom I talked made an effort to appear cordial and cooperative, but they clearly wanted to put the best face on their system, and were careful about the information they conveyed.

People in public places were friendly, helpful, and cheerful. The atmosphere was not altogether grim. The citizens seemed adequately fed and clothed; in general they were unusually orderly and well mannered. In the city centers flowers bloomed in profusion. The streets were clean and they appeared safe even late at night. Operas, concerts, and plays were performed regularly, and they were usually sold out. The whole scene was more upbeat than it had been a decade ago and earlier. There were many more cars, a wider variety of goods in the stores, some first-class hotels that could hold their own with some in the West, and, although few could be classified as truly excellent, many restaurants were quite good.

Under the exchange agreement, the GDR Ministry for Higher Education was responsible for providing housing and a living allowance and for making all other arrangements for the project. The Ministry designates someone in the GDR as the visitor's *Betreuer*—loosely translated as "caretaker." This is the individual with whom one has personal and frequent contact, and who arranges interviews and visitations and generally deals with any problems arising during the visit. My *Betreuer* was Kurt Wünsche, a law professor at Humboldt University in Berlin, who served as GDR Minister of Justice from 1967 to 1972. He was a tall, vigorous, and pleasant man, with a cosmopolitan air. One could easily imagine encountering him in Paris or Washington. He was not a member of the East German Communist party.

On the whole, Professor Wünsche admirably filled his role as *Betreuer*. He arranged interviews for me with teachers in the Humboldt law faculty and put me in touch with the Lawyers' Association which, in turn, arranged interviews with officials in the major legal organs. He also made arrangements for my two week-long visits for interviews in Leipzig and Halle, although he was unable to arrange a Jena visit. In addition to these officially scheduled interviews I arranged conversations on my own at two other places: the headquarters of the Federation of Protestant Churches and the offices of the Association of the Blind and Partially Sighted.

The apartment provided for my wife and me in East Berlin was at Möllstrasse 4, at the corner of Hans-Beimler-Strasse—surely one of the busiest intersections in the GDR. Here, six lanes of traffic and two trolley tracks, converging from four directions, were never altogether quiet. Traffic was thunderous during the morning rush hour from 5:00 A.M. to 7:00 A.M. The apartment building was similar to many built in the GDR since the Second World War. It was eight stories tall, with a tiny balcony for each apartment. By American standards the apartment was small—essentially one room—although it had separated kitchen, bath, and sleeping areas. In the living-dining area were bookshelves, a desk, a six-foot-long sofa, several chairs, and a table of the type typically found in almost every German home and office (East and West): a combination coffee, eating, and working table. On a small radio we could receive Radio GDR, RIAS (Radio in the American Sector, broadcasting in German from West Berlin), the BBC (broadcasting in both English and German), one or two West German stations, and a French station. Only during our week in Halle did we have a televison set; on it we could receive both East and West German programs. What the Berlin apartment lacked in space was made up for in convenience of location. It was one long block from Alexanderplatz and Karl-Marx-Allee. From the apartment we could walk to all points of interest in the center of East Berlin, and our daily walks often covered as much as ten miles. This apartment was our base, the place to which we always returned after trips to other points in the GDR.

Accommodations in Leipzig and Halle were better. During our week-long stay in Leipzig we lived in University guest quarters, a modern apartment in a building some two miles from the center of the city and from the University. These living quarters were roomier and quieter than the Berlin apartment. In Halle we were quartered in the University Guest House (*Haus der Wissenschaftler*), a late nineteenth-century mansion that had been converted into twenty-five rooms and apartments for official University visitors. We had a corner suite with a huge parlor, a separate bedroom and large bath. This was our most comfortable living arrangement during the entire stay in the GDR.

From the Berlin apartment we made train trips to Rostock on the Baltic coast and to Neubrandenburg, also to the north. By rented cars—available through some major hotels—we traveled to Wittenberg, Potsdam, Weimar, Nieder Pöllnitz, and Jena. As we had done in 1969, when we spent four days driving through the southern part of the GDR, we traveled about without restraint. We had no sense of being supervised or watched. One could board a train at any time for anywhere in the GDR, and one could drive over major highways, back roads, and city streets as freely as one can in the United States. The only restraint on travel is that in order to stay overnight, one must make an advance reservation at an Interhotel. At occasional restricted military zones we encountered "no entry" signs and warnings against photography, but these seemed relatively few. Indeed, the massive Russian presence in the country was well concealed. The Red Army remains in its camps. We saw only an occasional Russian officer in the marketplace in Jena and on the streets in Weimar; it was rare to see Russian military personnel in Berlin.

On this visit to the GDR *Baedeker*'s 1904 travel guide was a constant companion, as it has been on my previous trips to Germany. That little book presents the physical scene as it was in Germany at high tide, and it has been helpful in my effort to describe the settings of the universities and their law faculties. It is surprising, in light of the destruction of the Second World War, how often one can stand at a street corner reading from *Baedeker* and see still there what it describes. On the other hand, it is not uncommon to find the scene wholly changed. It is depressing to read *Baedeker*'s description of an edifice of great architectural distinction or historical significance as one stands before weeds and rubble, a parking lot, or a styleless new high-rise structure.

Traveling about the GDR and walking the streets of its cities and towns heightened my understanding of that country and its people. My feel for the situation was aided by the hours spent walking the corridors of the university buildings, eating in faculty dining rooms, sitting in academic offices, and attending lectures and seminars. Visiting court buildings, the offices of the Lawyers' Association, and historical sites also added to my insights, as did eating at restaurants and attending operas, plays, and concerts. However, the principal focus throughout was always on the interviews—scheduling as many as possible and obtaining the maximum number of facts from each.

A visit to East Germany is necessarily also a visit to the ideological world of Marxism-Leninism. That ideology pervades all aspects of GDR life and is often mentioned in the chapters ahead. Thus, it seems appropriate to remind the reader of some of its basic features.

Marxism comes from the ideas and writings of two Germans, Karl Marx (1818–1883) and Friedrich Engels (1820–1895). Their views were combined later with the ideas of V. I. Lenin (1870–1924) to produce the ideology that has governed in the Soviet Union since the 1917 Revolution and in those Eastern European countries that have been in the Soviet sphere since the Second World War. Marx was heavily influenced by the writings of Georg Wilhelm Friedrich Hegel (1770–1830), a German philosopher who taught in the Universities at Jena, Heidelberg, and Berlin. Hegel believed that out of contradictions (thesis and antithesis) came new insights and a higher understanding (synthesis). Marx applied these Hegelian ideas to human history, seeing one social order coming into conflict with another and thereby yielding a new order. This process of "dialectical materialsm," in the Marxist view, will lead ultimately to a classless society.

Fundamental to this ideology is the proposition that a society's economic base—its means of production—determines all else. Private ownership of these means is seen as the cause of social evil and human inequality. To overcome these evils, all means of production must be brought into common ownership of the working class. To achieve this, the working class must have as its vanguard a single, ruling party within which there is no difference of opinion as to the class interest. The party acts in accordance with "scientific" theories, moving always toward the inevitable end of history—a communist society, and ultimately worldwide communism. In this world to come, property will be owned in common, and true human equality will be realized through the principle of "from each according to his ability, to each according to his need." With its focus on man and his economic relationships, Marxism-Leninism rejects religion and the existence of any divine authority as being "unscientific." Because class antagonism will be eliminated, the state will wither away, and with it, law and the traditional type of legal system, including courts.

In the meantime, socialism is considered an intermediate step. Its governing principle is "from each according to his ability, to each according to his work." Because no country has yet achieved pure communism, Marxist-Leninist regimes—

including the GDR—refer to themselves as "socialist states." In such states the means of production are in public hands, the government is controlled by a single, ruling party, and the economy is centrally planned and administered. Society is collectivized and almost all aspects of human activity are under state control, leaving little room for individual autonomy.

A distinctive circumstance in the GDR is that the Marxist-Leninist regime, unlike that in the Soviet Union, did not come about by revolution, nor did it come to power in an underdeveloped or backward society. Rather, it was imposed by external power on what had been, before 1945, an industrially and technologically advanced country with a strong intellectual tradition and sophisticated legal system. In light of this established legal system and the long tradition of law in German universities, I thought it might be especially interesting to ascertain the impact, in the GDR, of the Marxist-Leninist theory that law will wither away.

The specific questions to which I sought answers and which are addressed in the following chapters are these: What is the role of the GDR universities today in legal education? To what extent do the organization and administration of the university law faculties resemble that in the Germany of old and in the FRG? What is the curriculum for law study? Who are the law teachers and law students? What books do they use? What sorts of library resources do they have? What is the nature of legal research? Where are the law graduates employed, and what careers do they follow? How is the legal system organized and manned?

In the minds of many readers questions will no doubt arise that are not answered here. The likelihood is that those same questions arose in my own mind. Indeed, I faced a constant dilemma in the interviews. I craved to inquire into aspects of ideology and the administration of justice that would likely be of great interest to Americans, but which would also be sensitive subjects in the GDR. To pursue such inquiries, I thought, might jeopardize cordial relations and interfere with my obtaining the maximum amount of noncontroversial, factual information about legal education and the legal organs. Thus I avoided the sensitive and often more interesting questions.

In Part One of this study I present the historical background and contemporary setting of the GDR and its legal scene. The story of the German Democratic Republic is part of the German tragedy of the twentieth century, a story that has taken the German people from the heights to the depths. The years since the Second World War have brought about a situation that is truly bizarre. To understand any aspect of life in the GDR, one needs to know this historical background, and for that reason it is sketched in chapter 1. One also needs to know the major features of the governmental, party, and legal structures which have resulted from the historical events and which exist in the GDR today. Thus, those structures are outlined in the chapter following the historical summary.

Part Two then presents the information I gathered concerning contemporary legal education in the GDR. It describes the four university law faculties, the two law curricula taught in these universities, the law teachers and their work, and the law students. Part Three then describes the various types of legal work in which the university law graduates pursue careers and explains the country's two separate legal systems. In the concluding part I set forth an assortment of observations and insights derived from my stay in the GDR. The Appendixes contain English translations (prepared under my direction) of several documents and portions of texts relating to GDR legal education—none of which has previously been translated into English.

Most of the information presented here comes from what I was told by persons I interviewed. Some of it reflects my own perceptions, and some of it comes from written sources identified in the Bibliography. I have reported in this book all of the facts I collected, but I do not warrant their accuracy.

In every country there is likely to be a discrepancy between law and official policies as they appear in the books and as they operate in the system. Such a discrepancy likely exists in the GDR. In the absence of empirical research and full access to court proceedings, it is difficult to judge the extent to which the system as described in these pages corresponds to the system as it functions. And still another caveat is in order. Some of the information that was conveyed to me in interviews is documented—courses taught in the law sections, class schedules, books used, and so on. Apart from the few areas in which there is such documentation, the information reported here comes exclusively from interviews and thus conveys a picture of the GDR system as seen by those who participate in it. GDR officialdom seems extraordinarily concerned about the appearance of its system to outsiders. This extreme concern causes American scholars to regard even documentary material, such as published statistics, with skepticism.

My justification for presenting information that I cannot completely verify is that there is so little known in the United States about law and its study in the GDR that any addition to existing knowledge seems worth the risk of some inaccuracies. I look upon this work as an interim publication. One purpose it may serve is to provide for legal scholars going to the GDR in the future a head start knowing what to look for and where to go. In short, I offer here my own perceptions of university legal education and the legal order in East Germany in the fall of 1983.

Part 1

Background and Setting

1
A Remnant from the Heart of the Reich

The political entity known as the German Democratic Republic is in North Central Europe at the center of what was the German Reich. But in territory and population it is only a remnant of that nation. Created in 1949, in the zone occupied by the armed forces of the Soviet Union, the GDR is one of two German states to emerge from the chaos of the Second World War. The other, the Federal Republic of Germany, is much larger in territory and population. Other parts of the Germany dismembered by two world wars now lie in France, Poland, and the Soviet Union. Many people born in this century are unaware of the geographical, economic, and educational dimensions of Germany from its unification in 1871 until the First World War.

The geographical dimensions of Germany in that time, like much else in German history, have been obscured by the events of the mid-twentieth century. If a person had been in the cities of Metz or Strasbourg before the First World War, he would have been at the western edge of Germany. Those cities are today in France. If a traveler had proceeded from there, northeasterly in a straight line, he could have gone without interruption across German territory for some 750 miles to the cities of Königsberg and Memel. Those cities are now in the USSR. A distance of 750 miles from one side of a country to another may not seem large to Americans; it is about the distance from Washington, D.C., to Chicago. But it spans a huge swatch of Europe. To make that same trip today one would cross four international boundaries and pass through portions of five countries: France, the Federal Republic of Germany, the German Democratic Republic, Poland, and the Soviet Union.

The incorporation of this extensive territory, embracing some 209,000 square miles, into the German Reich in 1871, after the Franco-Prussian War, was followed by an outpouring of intellectual and physical energy that within a few decades brought Germany to its zenith. From 1871 to the eve of the First World War the population grew from 41 million to 65 million. The annual coal output increased over 650 percent, from 29 million tons to 190 million tons. Iron production rose from less than 2 million tons to 17 million tons annually. Railroad mileage increased fivefold. There was similar growth in the shipping, chemical, and electrical industries.

The industrial eminence of the country was matched by its academic achievements. Numerous technical schools provided training in engineering, mining, agriculture, veterinary medicine, and other fields. But it was the German universities that had the greater impact on the world of higher education. At the beginning of the twentieth century, there were twenty-one universities within German borders (see fig. 1). The oldest of these was Heidelberg (1386) and the newest was Münster (1902). All but six had been founded before 1800. The locations and origins of most of the twenty-one universities can be explained mainly in historical terms. They were the products of the separate German states. Just as each state had its own law courts, each of the larger states had one or more universities. These universities were in the front rank of the world's institutions of higher learning. Each was organized into the four faculties that had been the traditional German university structure since

Fig. 1. Germany and German universities before the First World War

the Middle Ages: Law, Theology, Philosophy, and Medicine. The only exception was Münster, which had no Faculty of Medicine. In 1908 the enrollment of these universities totaled more than 46,000 students. Of these, 12,375 were studying law.

These universities had a significant impact on American universities and colleges. Americans began to study in German universities in the second decade of the nineteenth century. About 10,000 enrolled in those institutions over the ensuing hundred years, the great majority of them coming between 1860 and 1900. This number far exceeded the number going to the British and French universities. Half of the American students studied at the University of Berlin. Leipzig and Heidelberg attracted upward of 1,000 each. Halle and Bonn came next with a few hundred each. Smaller numbers of Americans were scattered among several of the other universities. Often a student would study for awhile at one university and then move to another. Of the 10,000, about half entered the Faculty of Philosophy, which embraced all academic disciplines not included within the other three faculties. Law attracted the fewest Americans.

The evolution of the university professor into a combination researcher-teacher was a distinctively German development that provided the model for American university professors in later years. The seminar, as distinguished from the lecture and the tutorial, was likewise a German invention. The German universities in this era had an especially strong influence in the laboratory and social sciences; their influence in theology and medicine was also substantial. Many of the Americans who studied in Germany later rose to important positions in higher education, and it was through them that the influence of the German universities was transmitted to the United States, particularly in the development of graduate and professional schools.

Although law attracted the fewest American students, it was a major field of study and research in the German universities. The men who manned the German legal system as judges, prosecutors, advocates, counselors, notaries, and lawyers in government ministries all studied in the faculties of law in the universities. A law student normally spent from four to five years in a university. At the end of that time he would undergo a state examination. If successful, he became a *Referendar*, commencing a period of practical training for two to three years, rotating as an apprentice through the various lines of legal work. He then underwent a second state examination; if successful he was fully qualified to pursue a career in any of the legal fields.

The central notion in the university law faculties was that they were training men to become judges. If one was qualified to be a judge, he would be qualified to pursue any other line of legal work. From the Anglo-American perspective these judges appear to have been high-level civil servants, pursuing a career with the government, often alternating between work as a prosecutor and work as a judge. Unlike other civil servants, however, the judges were afforded a substantial measure of independence in their decision making. But the university law professors, and not the judges, continued to be, as they had been since the Middle Ages, the preeminent figures in German law.

During the last quarter of the nineteenth century these professors and other German jurists developed five codes that have had major influence on the legal systems of numerous countries. In order of their adoption these were: the Criminal Code (1871), the Criminal Procedure Code (1877), the Civil Procedure Code (1877), the Civil Code (1896), and the Commercial Code (1897). All or parts of these codes have been adopted by such geographically and ethnically diverse nations as Japan, Turkey, and some South American countries. The development of these German codes had been made possible by the unification of the numerous German states through the creation of the Reich in 1871.

This 1871 unification also made possible the creation of a nationwide legal system, superimposed upon the numerous fragmented systems. This unified legal system was symbolized by the establishment of a single court of law with appellate jurisdiction over civil and criminal cases throughout all German territory. This was the Imperial Supreme Court (*Reichgericht*), which had its seat at Leipzig. This tribunal was created by the Court Organization Act of 1877 that established the judicial structure that remains today in West Germany. It is not clear why this new supreme court was not located in Berlin, the capital. One piece of folklore is that Bismarck (Chancellor, 1871–90) believed that it was undesirable to have the judges at the seat of government, mingling with other officials, where they might be subjected to baleful political influences. This notion would be consistent with the idea of judicial independence embodied in the Act.

In any event, impressive quarters were built for the court in Leipzig and were occupied in 1895. This structure was an architectural brother of the *Reichstag* building in Berlin, which had been completed a year earlier to house the supreme legislative body. Located near the center of Leipzig, the building was four stories tall, topped by a copper dome rising to a height of 224 feet and surmounted by an 18-foot statue of Truth. In the great central room—76 feet high—were semicircular stained glass windows that revealed the richness and territorial extent of the German nation at that time. According to the 1904 *Baedeker* these windows depicted "North, Trade, with the arms of Hamburg and Lübeck; East, Agriculture, with the arms of Königsberg and Marienburg; West, Manufactures, with the arms of Cologne and Strasborg; South, Art, with the arms of Nuremberg and Augsburg."

To appreciate the importance of the 1871 unification for law and the legal system—as well as for all other aspects of German life—one must bear in mind the previously fragmented situation. The unification brought together more than twenty political and territorial entities. Each of these had evolved from various combinations of the multitudinous fiefdoms, ducal provinces, and other medieval territorial configurations. Each of these states before 1871 had its own high court, and these courts continued after the creation of the Reich, although they then formed the second level in the judiciary, just below the Imperial Supreme Court. There were twenty-three of these courts, each continuing to serve as a top court in its state. Each of these courts (*Oberlandesgericht*) had jurisdiction to review decisions coming through the two levels of trial courts below it. The higher-level trial court was the *Landgericht*. The first level of trial court was the *Amtsgericht*. But decisions of the highest state courts were subject to being reviewed by the Imperial Supreme Court in Leipzig. After unification and adoption of the codes, the same law applied, for example, in Baden, in the far Southwest, and in East Prussia, in the extreme Northeast, and a single court could ultimately adjudicate matters arising anywhere in this territory.

In each state the entire court system was under the administration of the state's Ministry of Justice. The Ministry also played a key part in the careers of the university law students and in the administration of the entire justice system of the state. The Ministry had a close relationship with the university law faculties because it administered the first state examination at the close of university law study, arranged and supervised the period of practical training, and administered the second state examination. The Ministry thus certified persons as qualified for entry into the various branches of the legal profession and made assignments of persons to be judges, prosecutors, and Ministry officials. Once appointed a judge or prosecutor, a person was moved through the ranks by the Ministry of Justice. Each Ministry was the administrator for its court system, providing logistical support, buildings, and personnel. The central Reich Ministry of Justice had relatively limited authority over legal education and the various state justice systems.

The universities, the system of legal education, the nationwide codes, and the unified court structure, as they had developed by the end of the nineteenth century, were important facets of the Germany that had only recently emerged as a major power on the world scene. From the turn of the century forward, however, this historical sketch focuses on political and military developments, because after that time these developments overshadowed other aspects of German life and led to the final catastrophe of the 1940s.

The industrial, technological, and intellectual force that was gathering momentum through the decades before the First World War could not be contained in its home territory. Between 1884 and the war, Germany acquired thirteen colonies in Africa, Asia, and the Pacific, embracing more than a million square miles and 12 million people. Such far-flung holdings led naturally to the felt need for a navy adequate to protect lines of communication and supply. Thus by the end of the first decade of the twentieth century Germany had become a serious rival to the world's leading sea power, Great Britain. The dominant military tradition in Germany, however, had been, and remained, with the army. The tradition was rooted in Prussia, stemming from the time of Frederick the Great (1740–86) and earlier. The General Staff and the Officer Corps were its heart. The army too had been growing apace in these years, and a decade into the twentieth century it was a formidable armed force prepared to fight for, or attack out of, that huge expanse of Europe stretching from Metz to Memel.

The First World War is the fundamental disaster of the twentieth century. It was essentially a civil war within the western world. It is fundamental in that from it stemmed the later chaos, destruction, and human misery of the ensuing quarter century; and from it also flowed basic alterations of political boundaries and national power in Europe and in much of the rest of the world. Concurrently with the First World War, and in part precipitated by it, came the Russian Revolution, introducing Marxist-Leninist doctrines that pose the major twentieth century challenge to Western civilization. Out of that war also came the Second World War, bringing destruction and death on a scale that had previously not been contemplated and cannot fully be calculated. So profound and far-reaching is the impact of the First World War that we find it almost impossible now to imagine what the world would be like had Germany and the other European powers been able to settle their differences peacefully in August 1914.

The war had a severe impact on Germany. Some two million Germans died in its armed forces. Under the Versailles Treaty Germany lost its westernmost piece of territory—Alsace-Lorraine (including the cities of Metz and Strasbourg)—which was turned over to France. In the East the provinces of Posen and West Prussia were made part of a re-created Poland, and Danzig was made a "free city." A large zone along the Rhine River was demilitarized and placed under the occupation of the Allied countries. Moreover, Germany lost all of its colonies.

The German monarchy ended with the war, and an era of violent and chaotic political activity ensued. The democratic government provided for in the Weimar Constitution (adopted 1919) could not seem to work. The worldwide economic depression and the burden of reparations payments caused severe economic difficulties. Both the Communist party and the forerunner to the National Socialist German Workers' party (Nazi) were founded in 1919. Each represented a new order of thinking in Western civilization. Each rejected the fundamental principles of democracy as democracy had been conceived since at least the time of the American Revolution. In this violent and supercharged political climate, real democracy and the hopes embodied in the Weimar Constitution were unlikely to prevail.

In the election of July 1932, the Communist party polled 17 percent of the vote, and the Nazi party polled 37.4 percent. Nazism may have been helped by its being indigenous and nationalistic. Communism, on the other hand, was an international movement and at the time was identified with a foreign power, the Soviet Union, although its fathers, Marx and Engels, had been German. In any event, in 1933 the Nazi party came to power lawfully through the appointment of Adolph Hitler (1889–1945) as Chancellor, although the Party never polled a majority of votes nationally at a popular election.

The course of German history from 1933 to 1945 hardly needs retelling. Increasingly, historians see the Second World War as merely a continuation of the First. The armistice of twenty-one years was a time of regrouping and rearming for Germany. The interlude was merely a "long weekend," as the English poet Robert Graves called it. The display of power and effectiveness that the German armed forces put on for the world between 1939 and 1942 had been unmatched. It was the last and most awesome manifestation of the physical energy, intellectual force, and industrial and technological power that had been welded into the German nation after 1871.

The Germany that had already been diminished after 1918 ceased to exist in 1945. Some 3.5 million had died in its armed forces since 1939. Many thousands of its civilians had also been killed. By mid-May 1945, all of Germany east of the Elbe was occupied by the Russian army. All of Germany west of the Elbe was occupied by the British and American armies. These immense forces had not had an easy time getting where they were. Germany had fought to the finish. Thus the destruction wrought by ground combat was extensive. In addition, two years of British and American aerial bombardment had left many cities in ruins. The surrender was unconditional. From August 1914 to May 1945—just under thirty-one years—Germany had come from a position in the forefront of the nations of the world to a state of ruin on a scale new to human history. It was the stated view, however, of the victorious Allied Powers that Germany was to be revived as a member of the family of nations, although with some severe surgery on its territory and with a cleansed and altogether new political order.

During the war the Allies foresaw that with the German defeat the immediate and pressing problem would be that of taking control of and administering the devastated country and its population. The commonsense notion emerged that each of the three major powers would assume responsibility for a portion of the territory. The body in charge of this planning was the European Advisory Commission sitting in London.

Designing the initial occupation zones was essentially an exercise in drawing lines on a map. The historical record is not altogether clear as to when or by whom pencil was first tentatively put to paper. Beginning in late 1943, and into the early fall of 1944, lines were being drawn, discussed, and redrawn. The German nation was on the dissecting table, with scalpels being wielded by Americans, Russians, and British.

Although it is probable that a portion of the surgery was imagined to be permanent, long-range decisions were postponed on the assumption that there would be a future peace treaty. Poland was to be revived as a nation and was probably to be given enlarged territory at the expense of Germany. The Soviet Union had territorial ambitions along its own western frontier. Pending the assumed treaty, the far eastern tip of the German Reich in East Prussia, including the cities of Königsberg and Memel, was to be placed under Soviet administration. All other parts of Germany east of the Oder and Neisse rivers were to be placed under Polish administration. This territory included the remainder of East Prussia, all of West Prussia and Posen, and large parts of Pomerania and Silesia.

The more difficult question involved the drawing of lines in the remainder of Germany to allocate zones of occupation for the three Allied Powers. As the planners conferred in London and played with lines on maps through 1944, no one could say with certainty what the military situation would be when Germany finally capitulated. By September 1944 the Americans and British were advancing in force through France, Belgium, and the Netherlands, but they had not yet reached German soil. The Soviet army was still on its own territory but steadily pushing the Germans back. At that time it was at least possible to imagine that the Soviet Union could reach and occupy much of Germany before the Americans and British moved very far into it. On the other hand, there was also the possibility that the Americans and British could overrun Germany extensively. All seemed to agree that zones of occupation should be fixed in advance and not be left to the happenstance of physical occupation of territory at the moment the war ended. The major focus was on drawing a roughly north-south line through Germany to delineate the Russian zone in the East from the American-British zones in the West.

This line-drawing exercise can now be seen as surely one of the most fateful pieces of mapwork that has been undertaken. The fixing of that line in the fall of 1944—thought simply to be one of temporary administrative convenience—was, in fact, the first step in establishing two nations on German soil and of bringing the line of communism several hundred miles westward to the heart of Europe. The line starts in the north at the Baltic Sea and meanders southward to the Czechoslovakian border. It follows no natural terrain features. Those who drew it and ultimately agreed upon it took the rather sensible course of following the boundaries of the long-existing German states. According to the London Protocol of 1944, the line runs

> from the point on Lübeck Bay where the frontiers of Schleswig-Holstein and Mecklenburg meet, along the western frontier of Mecklenburg to the frontier of the province of Hanover, thence, along the eastern frontier of Hanover, to the frontier of Brunswick; thence along the western frontier of the Prussian province of Saxony to the western frontier of Anhalt; thence along the western frontier of the Prussian province of Saxony and the western frontier of Thuringia to where the latter meets the Bavarian frontier; thence eastward along the northern frontier of Bavaria to the 1937 Czechoslovakian frontier.

The occupation zone for the Soviet Union was to be all of Germany between this line and the Oder-Neisse rivers and between the Baltic Sea and the Czechoslovakian border—with one large exception—Berlin.

The city of Berlin was treated as a special situation. Before the war it had become a huge metropolis, the largest in all of Europe. The city had developed over the centuries out of a multitude of villages, many of which had gradually grown together. In 1920 the Prussian Parliament enacted a law creating Greater Berlin out of this constellation of villages and communities. The city thus created had an area of 289 square miles, and by 1939 it had a population of 4.39 million. In territory the city was nearly three times as large as the District of Columbia. Because of its size, and its cultural, political, and symbolic importance, the planners in London deemed it appropriate to treat Berlin as a separate entity from the rest of Germany and to provide that initially it would be occupied and administratively managed jointly by the three victorious powers. Thus for the city of Berlin the London planners were faced with a line-drawing problem similar to that for Germany as a whole.

Berlin had twenty districts or precincts. Since these were existing administrative units it made sense to use them as the basis for allocating occupation zones. Likewise, it was obvious that the Russians should have the eastern precincts and the British and Americans the western precincts. Thus, as with Germany as a whole, the problem was to draw a roughly north-south line through the city that would separate the Soviet eastern zone from the western zones. Although envisaged as purely a temporary, administrative matter, the drawing of this line has proved to be, in its political consequences and impact on people's lives, as important and far-reaching as the line drawn down the middle of Germany.

The heart of the city geographically, historically, and politically, was the district known as the Mitte. Here, beginning at the Brandenburg Gate and running eastward, is Unter den Linden, the central, major street of the city, terminating at the site of the Imperial Palace. The street before the war had been flanked by the University, the opera, embassies, fashionable cafes, and shops. Intersecting it was the Wilhelmstrasse—the major government street—and Friedrichstrasse, a central business and commercial street. At first it was thought that the Mitte, being so central and so important in all respects, should itself be under three-power occupation—an island within an island. This idea seemed to make sense also because the Mitte was so positioned in relation to the surrounding districts that it did not neatly fall either on the western or eastern side of the line likely to be drawn from north to south through the center of the city. To place this district in the hands of any one of the occupying powers would make for a protrusion into the zone of another—a kind of finger sticking out one way or another. In the end, however, the Mitte was placed in the eastern zone assigned to the Russians—a circumstance of immense importance to the GDR today—although the reasons for this decision are not clear.

The line as eventually agreed upon runs from the northern edge of the city along the borders between Pankow and Reinickendorf, Wedding and Prenzlauerberg, Tiergarten and Mitte, Kreuzberg and Friedrichshain, and Neukolln and Treptow. Under the initial plan the Russians were allocated eight districts, the Americans six, and the British six. Later France was allocated a portion of the American and British zones in Berlin, as well as a portion of the American zone in southwest Germany. Thus the occupation was destined to be a four-power responsibility.

All of these occupation zones (except the French portions) had been agreed upon by early 1945 before the final push overrunning Germany. As that year progressed, the Americans and British advanced faster and farther than had been expected. On April 10, elements of the U.S. Ninth Army reached the Elbe just north of Magdeburg, approximately fifty miles from Berlin. The Soviet army was still east of the Oder-Neisse line and did not begin its final offensive until April 16.

In these circumstances a point that had been pressed by Churchill for some time took on added cogency. Churchill believed that for long-range strategic, political, and psychological reasons it was important for the Americans and British "to shake hands with the Russians as far east as possible." Specifically, he urged that Berlin not be left to be taken by the Red Army alone. In his view Berlin had a symbolic and political importance far in excess of its military value. Eisenhower, on the other hand, took the view that because of the little military significance left to Berlin the more important task was to crush the German armed forces by getting at them where they were. Also, he had to reckon with the specter of the much-rumored German "redoubt" in the mountains to the south. Finally, Eisenhower and his advisors maintained that inasmuch as the zones of occupation had already been agreed upon there was little point in expending additional lives to take ground that would promptly have to be relinquished to the Soviet Union.

With the hindsight of history it can be seen that Churchill more clearly understood the intentions and the likely course of action of the Soviet Union in Europe than any other western leader. What is less clear, however, is whether implementing his idea in April 1945 would have made any difference in the postwar world. It seems doubtful that the United States and Great Britain would have reneged on the agreed-upon occupation zones, although that was a possibility. Had the zonal lines been adhered to—as they were—then the only gain from implementing Churchill's view would have been the psychological and perhaps political one of preventing the Soviet Union from being seen as the great liberator of Berlin and the force that finally crushed the Fascist in his lair. Perhaps today there would not be the giant Soviet war memorial just west of the Brandenburg Gate. Perhaps also we would not have those photographs depicting Soviet soldiers planting the hammer and sickle atop the Reichstag and the Brandenburg Gate, and there might be no massive Red Army cemetery in Treptow, but the American and British casualty lists would surely be longer.

The fact is that the Eisenhower view was adhered to, and the Americans and English made no last push to reach Berlin with or before the Russians. Eisenhower's decision was to stop at the Elbe and to await the arrival of the Russians. The two armies met there at Torgau on April 25, 1945.

In advancing to the Elbe the Americans overran much of the territory that lay within the Soviet occupation zone, including Thuringia, a portion of Saxony, and the cities of Erfurt, Weimar, Jena, Halle, and Leipzig. The final and easternmost American line ran along the Elbe and Mulde Rivers. The Russians had taken all of Berlin. All forces remained in place from May 8, when the war ended, to July 1, some seven weeks later. Then they all pulled back to the agreed-upon zones. The Americans thereby turned over to the Soviet Army a large portion of what is now territory of the GDR, and the Russians turned over the western sectors of Berlin to the British and Americans.

Although the lines fixed in the London Protocol were viewed as temporary zones designed for administrative purposes, they have never shifted. In fact, no peace treaty has ever been agreed upon. The German territory east of the Oder-Neisse became part of Poland, except for the extreme northeastern portion which was incorporated into the Soviet Union. Königsberg is now Kaliningrad, the major Soviet naval base on the Baltic; Breslau, renamed Wroclaw, is now in Poland. All of this German territory east of the Oder-Neisse contained over 71,000 square miles (35 percent of the pre-1919 Germany), and it was populated by some eleven million Germans before the war. Several million of them had already moved westward as refugees to stay ahead of the Red Army. With the close of the war the remaining Germans—an estimated 5.6 million—were, in effect, evicted by the Poles and the Russians. These Germans moved across the whole of Germany, some 3.5 million coming to rest in the Soviet zone, and the remainder continuing further westward. This was the first and the largest of the mass uprootings and migrations of people in Germany set in motion by the Second World War. That war had brought Germany full circle from its unification in 1871 to its dismemberment in 1945.

The idea of a four-power Allied administration of Germany as a whole, and of the city of Berlin, was difficult to realize from the outset. The hoped-for reestablishment of Germany as a single political entity, with a genuinely democratic government, seemed increasingly difficult to achieve as time passed after 1945. The Soviet Union, on the one hand, and the three Western Allies, on the other, were incapable of coming together on what to the latter seemed to be a simple, undebatable proposition—that free elections were the foundation of democratic government and that only on that basis could a new government be established by the Germans themselves. The vicissitudes of those years culminated in 1949 with the creation of the two present-day German states. The western sectors of Berlin, although surrounded by the GDR, remained under western control. They became an island in the middle of a hostile political entity.

The Federal Republic of Germany covers nearly 96,000 square miles (approximately 46 percent of the pre-1919 German Reich) and has a population of 61.7 million. The German Democratic Republic covers nearly 42,000 square miles (approximately 20 percent of the old Germany) and has 16.7 million people. Both the FRG and the GDR are thus remnants of a vaster nation, but the Federal Republic is more than twice as large territorially and is nearly four times larger in population. If the GDR were a state in the American union, it would rank third in population—behind California and Texas and ahead of New York; in territory, it would rank 35th—behind Tennessee and ahead of Ohio. (Fig. 2 depicts the post-1949 German states.)

Although the GDR is but a remnant of the former German nation, it lies at its heart. Within its borders is the core of the state put together by Frederick the Great. It embraces the historical territories of Mecklenburg, Brandenburg, Saxony, and Thuringia. It includes cities that have played major roles for centuries in the history of Europe, such as Dresden, Leipzig, Weimar, Potsdam, and Berlin. It contains seven of the pre-twentieth-century German universities. It includes the sites of almost all of Martin Luther's work: Wittenberg, Eisenach, and Erfurt. The Zwinger in Dresden and the Pergamon in Berlin have long been among the world's renowned museums. Some of the towering figures of Western civilization spent their lives and did their work in what is now the GDR: Goethe, Schiller, Luther, Bach, and Humboldt, to mention a few.

The political development of the GDR began shortly after the close of the war with the formation of political parties in

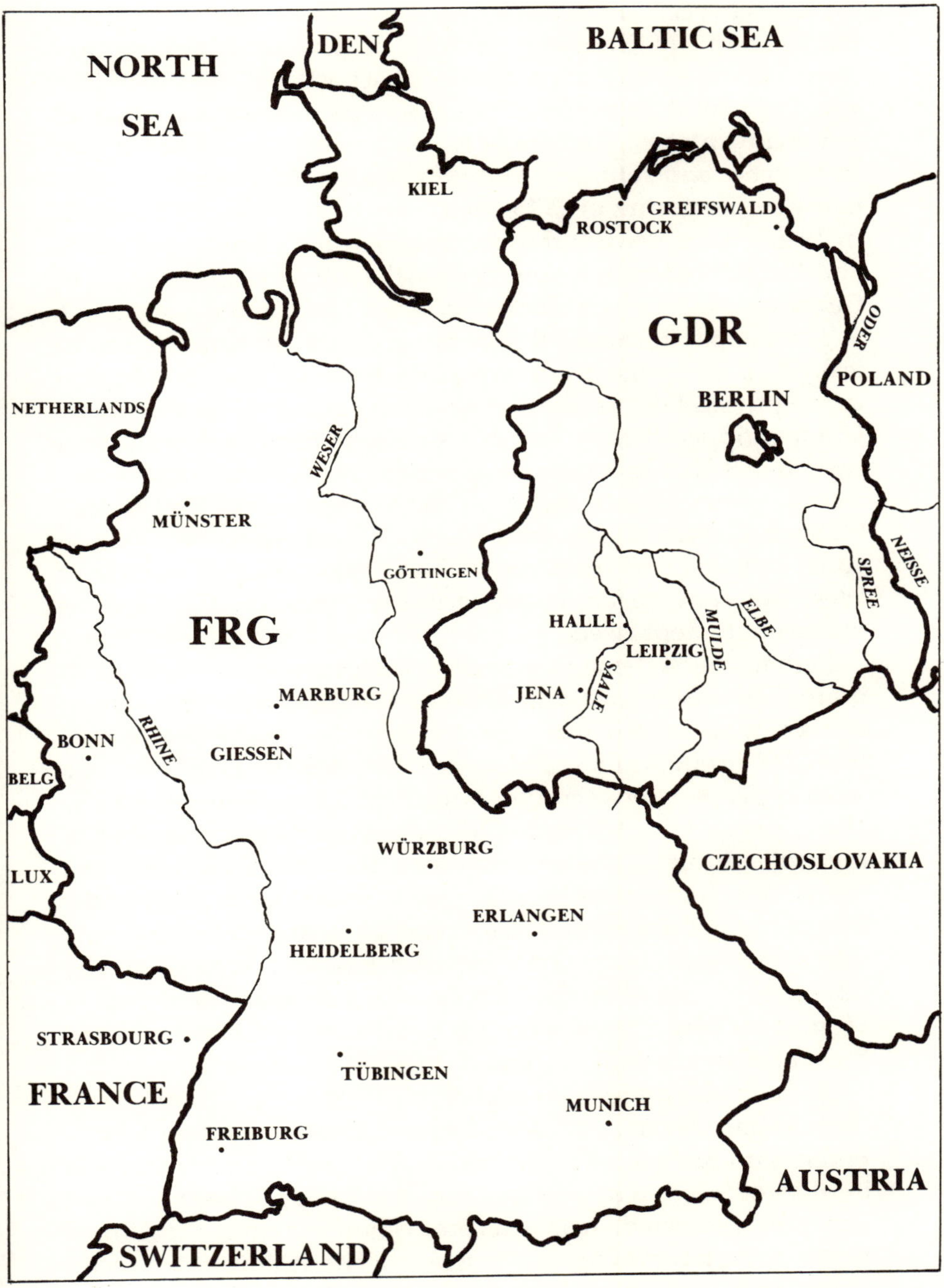

Fig. 2. The German states after 1949

the Russian occupation zone. The most important was the Communist party of Germany because of its Soviet backing and connections. Apart from it, the Socialist party of Germany (SPD) was the largest in membership. The Communist party had all of the advantages; the core of its leadership had spent the war in Moscow and returned to the Russian-occupied part of Germany in the spring of 1945 even before hostilities had ceased. In 1946 a merger was arranged between the Communist party and the SPD to form a new party—the Socialist Unity party of Germany (SED), which quickly became a Marxist-Leninist party.

The people in the GDR experienced difficult times economically and otherwise for many years after the war. In addition to the physical devastation, reparations extracted by the Soviet Union stripped the country of a sizable portion of its industrial capacity. It had few natural resources of its own, and its historical connections to the West had been severed. The United States had offered to extend Marshall Plan aid to the Russian zone, but this had been rejected. As the economic miracle of West Germany began to unfold in the 1950s, the GDR looked increasingly depressed.

Perhaps most damaging of all developments was the human drain. The earlier vast migration of Germans from the eastern territories westward was now followed by a new flow out of the GDR itself. At its establishment in 1949 the GDR had 18.8 million people; between then and 1961 2.7 million left for the West. Those who left included a disproportionate number of the well-educated, the professionals, the skilled workers, and the young. By mid-1961 the departures were equivalent to the loss of a small city every month. East Germans were streaming into West Berlin (the border between East and West Germany having been closed by the East Germans several years earlier). From West Berlin many were relocated in West Germany. Then the Iron Curtain truly slammed down.

At daybreak on Sunday, August 13, 1961, East German soldiers began sealing the sector lines between East and West Berlin with barbed wire and barricades. The United States and its allies seemed to be at a loss as to what to do. They vacillated and they protested. It is a nice question whether the United States could have done anything more. The sealing of the sector boundaries was a clear violation of the four-power occupation status of the city. The illegality of the action, however, mattered little since there was no court of higher authority to which effective resort could be had. It was a matter of self-help or nothing. Whether World War III would have erupted had the Western Allies forcibly stopped the erection of the wall within the early hours of August 13 will probably never be known. Red Army units were positioned behind the East German soldiers erecting the barricades. In any event, President Kennedy and the other leaders decided simply on a protest and a token show of force.

The GDR's closing of the West Berlin border is surely one of the major construction projects of modern times. Over 31,000 men worked to build and perfect The Wall through the center of the city and the impenetrable line of fencing and guard towers around the rest of West Berlin, shutting it off from the surrounding GDR territory. To speak of "The Wall" is actually somewhat misleading because there are really two parallel walls. Between the two is a cleared strip, at points more than a hundred yards wide. Guard towers are spaced at sufficiently close intervals to enable the entire wall to be under surveillance at all times. Probably no other wall has been so persistently reinforced by physical and human resources. Perhaps the major distinction between this and all other humanly constructed walls is that this is the first one to be built by a government to keep its own people in rather than to keep others out. Few persons have shown a desire to enter the GDR. GDR officialdom nevertheless refers to the structure as the "Anti-Fascist Protection Bulwark," and claims that it is necessary to keep out enemies. It seems clear, however, that the SED's real purpose was to stop the country's population hemorrhage.

The 856-mile-long border from the Baltic Sea to Czechoslovakia is as tightly sealed as the West Berlin boundary, although there are no solid concrete walls for any significant distance. High fences, frequent guard towers, and a wide, cleared strip of earth mark the line. At times this strip has been occupied by automatic firing devices and mines. The border clearing is so wide and so long that one can imagine it would be discernible in its entirety in high altitude photographs as a long, snaking dirt line.

The closing of the West Berlin boundary in 1961 is thought by some observers to have been a material factor in helping the GDR get on its feet economically. Persons there no longer had an option to go West if conditions did not improve; they had to make the best of things where they were. Whether that theory is valid or not, twenty years after the sealing of the borders conditions were much better economically in the GDR than they had been in prior years. Indeed, by the early 1980s there were touches of affluence. In industrial output the GDR ranked tenth among all nations in the world; it ranked first among Eastern European countries (apart from the USSR).

Politically, the GDR came into its own in 1973 when it was admitted, along with the FRG, to membership in the United Nations. Diplomatic recognition from many nations followed promptly. The United States established diplomatic relations with the GDR in 1974 and maintains an embassy today in East Berlin. The key to this development was the Basic Treaty of 1972 between the GDR and the FRG in which the latter, for all practical purposes, recognized the former. Without this agreement it is unlikely that either German state would have been admitted to the U.N.

Although the GDR is a sovereign nation in the international community, its sovereignty is peculiar and qualified. It is diluted and overlayed by external elements in a way that is unique. To begin with, in the midst of its territory—right next door to what it proclaims to be its capital city—is an island beyond its control—West Berlin, 184 square miles in area, a city of bustling prosperity containing 1.9 million persons, a cosmopolitan center of Western Europe. Then there are the air, rail, and autobahn corridors connecting West Berlin with the Federal Republic, stretching across more than 100 miles of GDR territory. Along these routes flows a steady stream of traffic consisting of West Germans, West Europeans, Americans, and indeed people from around the world, outside the Communist bloc. This traffic cannot be lawfully blocked by the GDR. Although access to Berlin was left unclear at the close of the war, these corridors today are guaranteed by the Quadripartite Agreement of 1971, implemented by the FRG-GDR Transit Agreement of 1971.

A further dilution of GDR sovereignty results from the around-the-clock intrusion of radio and television from West Berlin, the Federal Republic, Great Britain, and France. Stations in West Germany reach most of the GDR, and BBC and French radio broadcasts can be heard in many parts. However impenetrable The Wall and the border may be on the ground, these electronic waves reach most of the country.

A massive overlay on the GDR's sovereignty is the presence within its boundaries of Soviet army units having an estimated strength of 380,000 to 400,000. Indeed, the relationship of the

GDR to the Soviet Union makes the former appear to be a colony of the latter. All children must study at least six years of the Russian language in school; if they go on to a university more years are required. The Constitution of the GDR, in its opening lines, pledges the nation to perpetual friendship with the USSR. Most bookstores stock substantial quantities of books in the Russian language. Russian-language productions can be seen regularly on television, and many Russian movies play in the theaters. The Embassy of the USSR is overwhelmingly the largest embassy in East Berlin, occupying virtually an entire block in a prime location on Unter den Linden. The GDR rarely deviates in its position on international matters from that of the USSR. Many of its leaders in the years since the war have been educated or trained in Moscow. One writer has quoted a KGB agent as saying that the GDR is the sixteenth Soviet Republic.

Yet perhaps not too much should be made of this. Despite the Russian presence and influence, the GDR is German and still exhibits many German characteristics. But it is a truncated German state. In terms of both its territory and its population it is a remnant, and an artificial one at that. Territorially it has been sliced off from its natural westward affiliations; its boundaries do not result from historical evolution or from natural terrain features. Its population is also truncated in that it has lost virtually all of those who came from long-established families prominent in German history, all of those with any substantial holdings of land or industrial property, and a high percentage of university-educated and professionally trained persons. Over time, however, the GDR is gradually generating a new cadre of professionally trained persons, and there are growing numbers who are beginning to accumulate a modest amount of wealth. But it began with a base—and largely continues with that base—of persons from the lower rungs of the economic, educational, and social ladders. By comparison the Federal Republic presents a picture more in line with German history; like prewar Germany, it contains persons at all levels although now in the context of a parliamentary democracy.

The East-West world conflict is sharply focused here amidst the human tragedy of a people with a common language and a common history now divided. The vagaries of fate since the Second World War have made Germany both symbolically and actually a place of ultimate confrontation and of maximum danger. This situation is aptly captured in the name of a bar in West Berlin: "The Flash Point."

The tensions and uncertainties are heightened by an unusually tangled complex of international law perspectives. The East and the West take quite different views of the status of East Berlin and West Berlin and of the legal relationship between the two German states. These international law questions are exceedingly complicated and have been the subject of extensive writing; they will not be explored here. Whatever one's view of international law, the GDR does exist as a functioning state, one far more stable and productive than most nations in the world in the 1980s.

The last century of German history has been sketched here to show how this Marxist-Leninist state on German soil came into existence and to indicate something of its common background with the other German state to the west. Some awareness of this history seems necessary in order to grasp the peculiarities of the GDR and its institutions. Some discussion, too, of the organization of the state, the ruling party, and certain official organs will aid in understanding university legal education and the GDR's legal machinery. To those matters we now turn.

2
State, Party, and Law: An Overview

The German Democratic Republic, like other Marxist-Leninist societies, claims to function on the principle of "democratic centralism." The theory is that decisions are made through a process involving discussion and suggestions among the party membership at lower levels (the democratic element), with ultimate policy decisions being made by the central authority. Outside observers generally agree, however, that emphasis is on the second part of the principle. The truly democratic nature of the process is doubtful, but it is clear that authority is concentrated to a high degree at the top of the system. The physical location of this centralized authority is East Berlin.

Despite the four-power status of the whole of Berlin, the East Germans have occupied the eastern sector (the Russian zone) with their governmental and party offices, claiming it as their own. Foreign countries have established embassies there, some on the sites they occupied before 1939. The GDR does everything possible to enhance the image of Berlin (never "East Berlin") as its capital city, asserting this proposition in literature, on posters, and on autobahn signs. It is helped in the fostering of this image by the fact that East Berlin does embrace the heart of the old city: the historical center of the Reich government, the University, the libraries, the theaters, and the museums.

The focal point at the very heart of all of Berlin, East and West, is the Brandenburg Gate. Standing 200 feet high, with five vehicular passageways between massive Doric columns, the Gate was completed in 1791 pursuant to direction of Frederick the Great. It forms a ceremonial entranceway to Unter den Linden from the West. The London Protocol of 1944 put it just on the east side of the line dividing the city. Since 1961 a nine-foot-thick concrete wall has stood on its western side, blocking the 200-foot-wide passageway through it. The red, gold, and black flag of the GDR flutters from its top, alongside the Quadriga, its four horses facing East.

Blocked at this natural entry point, a person coming from the West must enter East Berlin through restricted access points on the north or south of the Gate, by rail on the north, or by car or foot on the south. One can also enter from the West by subway. Entering by train, one crosses an arm of the Spree and immediately passes high wire fences and guard towers before arriving at the platform at Friedrichstrasse Station. This has been a major railroad station in Berlin since the nineteenth century and is located on Friedrichstrasse about two blocks north of its intersection with Unter den Linden. Several blocks south of this intersection Friedrichstrasse runs into Checkpoint Charlie, the name given by the Western Allies to the entry point for cars and pedestrians.

Thus whether one crosses from the West by train, car, or foot he comes into Friedrichstrasse, one of the major prewar streets in the heart of Berlin. It crosses Unter den Linden between the Brandenburg Gate to the west and the site of the old Imperial Palace to the east. The 1904 *Baedeker* describes this as the "most animated point" along Unter den Linden. This point was also the center of the climactic drive of the Red Army in the battle for Berlin in May 1945. To the damage and destruction already caused by Allied aerial bombardment was added the devastation of Russian artillery, tank fire, and street fighting. Today it is difficult to imagine that devastation. Many buildings along the street have been restored to more or less their former state. But some are gone altogether and in their place are either modern structures or open spaces planted with grass, trees, and flowers. The street would still be recognizable to a Rip Van Winkle of the 1930s who came back in the 1980s, but he would surely know that all was not as it had been. It would be as though the face of a friend had been badly mutilated and had been remade through plastic surgery; one could recognize the face but would also know that it was substantially altered.

Walking west on Unter den Linden from this intersection toward the Brandenburg Gate, one passes the Embassy of the Soviet Union. Then one comes to a street marked Otto-Grotewohl-Strasse. The name is that of one of the founders of the SED. But a person with the right maps and any knowledge of history knows that this street is the old Wilhelmstrasse, the principal government street of the Reich. On it, within a block of Unter den Linden to the south, stood the residence of Bismarck. Then there was the massive new Chancellery built by Hitler. In this block momentous decisions affecting the fate of Europe were made for decades before 1945. Yet walking along it today one would think that he is in a back street in a warehouse district. Nondescript buildings and open spaces are found here now; chain link fences line the street at points, behind which are construction equipment and piles of sand and gravel. When the leaves are off the trees and one looks carefully, he can see to the west, just a couple of hundred yards away, The Wall and the weed-covered mound marking the site of Hitler's underground bunker, a part of his Chancellery complex, and the spot where he met his end. The appearance of this street suggests that the GDR authorities have decided not only to treat it with neglect, but to remove its historical significance entirely from the consciousness of the citizens. However, this centrally located, unused land is a likely site for future urban development.

Otto-Grotewohl-Strasse intersects Unter den Linden almost at the Brandenburg Gate. Here the great boulevard simply comes to a dead end. One can now stand in its center, unconcerned with vehicular traffic which in the old days would have been thundering through the columns of the Gate. Guards casually stand by as tourists mill around, photographing the scene. Flowers have been planted on either side and in the center, creating a parklike effect at this end of the street. Looking over The Wall to the west, through the Gate, one can see the tops of sightseeing buses in West Berlin pausing for their passengers to gaze into what they consider to be the netherworld of the East. Close to the Gate on Unter den Linden are assorted embassies, including those of Great Britain, France, and Poland. Just a block to the north is the American Embassy, symbolically occupying a side street and a low-key position in contrast to the Soviet presence directly on Unter den Linden.

Walking eastward on Unter den Linden, beyond Friedrichstrasse, one comes to the State Library on the left, now restored. Here the multiple rows of linden trees, stretching eastward from the Brandenburg Gate, come to an end, and in the center of the street is the forty-four-foot-high mounted figure of Frederick the Great. Years passed after the Second World War—when the statue was removed for safekeeping—before it was returned to this position, where it had been since 1851; oddly, Frederick the Great is now back in favor in the GDR. Continuing east beyond the statue one passes on the left the old University of Berlin—renamed Humboldt University—and then the memorial "To the Victims of Fascism and Militarism." At this memorial guards are changed every two hours. Their uniforms and the jackbooted, goose-stepping ceremony ironically and uncomfortably remind some observers of the Wehrmacht of the 1930s. Here, every Wednesday afternoon at 2:30 a special ceremony necessitates the closing of Unter den Linden to vehicular traffic. A band comes marching up from the direction of the Brandenburg Gate, followed by detachments of soldiers. Knots of people gather to watch the brief ceremony, after which the band and soldiers depart.

Directly across the street from the memorial is the open place where the famous 1933 book burning occurred. The restored St. Hedwig's Cathedral is set back a bit. Next on the right is the restored State Opera. A short distance further on, the street is crossed by an arm of the Spree, one of the two arms of the river forming the slender island on which are located the major museums and on which formerly stood the Imperial Palace at the head of Unter den Linden. The Palace, containing over seven hundred rooms, was badly damaged in the war, but in the opinion of many in the West it could have been restored, as were many other Berlin buildings. However, the Russians and the East Germans razed it, creating a great open space that they named Marx-Engels Platz.

Today Marx-Engels Platz is landscaped with trees and flowers, is flanked by buildings of the present regime, and is dominated by the Palast der Republik. From the upper stories of the Palast a person looking westward sees the historic buildings flanking Unter den Linden, Frederick the Great mounted in its center, and the parallel rows of linden trees leading to the Brandenburg Gate in the distance. Beyond the Gate one can see trees and buildings that to the GDR authorities mark the presence of the threatening, imperialistic Western powers. From this point The Wall is hardly visible and one has the illusion of the old, undivided Berlin in its days of greatest glory. It is easy to imagine that the ruling authorities may stand here and look westward with an envious eye, imagining all of Berlin reunited under their domain and pondering the riches that lie beyond The Wall they created.

The official function of the Palast der Republik is to house the People's Chamber, the highest "representative assembly" in the country—what those in Western democracies would think of as the parliament. In theory it is the highest organ of state power. This body and the entire governmental system of the GDR are difficult to describe because the relationship of Party and State—as in all Marxist-Leninist countries—is unlike such relationships in the representative democracies of Europe and the Anglo-American world. In the GDR the real power lies with its ruling Marxist-Leninist Party, the Socialist Unity Party of Germany, or, more precisely, in that party's Politburo and Central Committee. The state apparatus is simply a means for carrying out the policies of the Party as fixed by those two ruling bodies within it. This relationship is aptly described by the saying that the Party is the hand and the state is the glove. Thus in looking at the governmental organization, we must realize that behind it, or alongside it, is the party structure where the power is actually lodged.

The basic state structure is provided for in the Constitution of the GDR. The present Constitution was adopted in 1968 and was amended in 1974. The word *constitution* as used here can be misleading. Americans are accustomed to viewing the Constitution as law to be applied and enforced through the courts. This is not so in the GDR. The courts have nothing to do with interpreting or enforcing the Constitution. Also, unlike the United States Constitution, the GDR Constitution proclaims a political program and specifies the key state organs through which it is to be implemented. Although the 1968 Constitution had been submitted to a public vote, the 1974 amendments were adopted by a vote of the People's Chamber. This body is authorized to amend the Constitution at any time by a two-thirds vote. As this suggests, the GDR Constitution has a status only slightly higher than that of ordinary legislation.

The People's Chamber—the highest state authority—has a membership of 500. Members are elected to this body every five years. But here again one must watch terminology. The word *elected* does not have the meaning in the GDR and other communist countries that it has in western democracies. On the ballot there is only a single name for each position, plus some extra names of replacement candidates. There is a democratic element at the nominating stage (to be discussed later in connection with judges) through which the candidates who appear on the ballots are determined by the National Front, a consortium of the political parties and the mass organizations. Election to the People's Chamber seems to be a means of conferring honorary recognition on persons who have made significant contributions in other state and party institutions. Each political party and organization is allotted a specified number of seats in the People's Chamber. These do not depend on the outcome of any election; the number is fixed in advance. Inasmuch as all parties and organizations support the aims and program of the SED, this allocation of seats is not as important as an American might think. The SED is firmly in control.

Although the People's Chamber is the highest legislative body in the country, it bears little resemblance to the parliaments of the FRG and Great Britain or to an American legislature. In the first place, it meets for an average of only four to six days each year. Secondly, every measure that it adopts is enacted unanimously. The only exception to this in the history of the GDR occurred in 1972 when some members of the Christian Democratic Union (CDU) voted against a measure to liberalize abortions, and others abstained. All of this suggests that the plenary sessions of this body are not where the real policy decisions are made; rather their function is to put a symbolic stamp of approval on measures that have been worked out elsewhere.

The architecture, ambience, and uses of the Palast der Republik, where the Chamber holds its brief annual sessions, combine to underscore the fact that the People's Chamber is not the true seat of power in this regime. The Great Room in which the Chamber sits is used the rest of the year for concerts and theatrical productions. Other entertainment events take place regularly in the building, which also contains large restaurants and a bar. Music is piped throughout its lobbies. It is more an entertainment center than it is a government building. Physically it bears some resemblance to the Kennedy Center in Washington, and in function it is very much like the Kennedy Center.

Across Marx-Engels Platz to the south is the building housing the Council of State, another of the top state organs. It is a collective executive body consisting of twenty-six members. It is headed by a Chairman, the titular head of the GDR government. Erich Honecker now occupies this position. Nearby is a building housing the Council of Ministers. This is the other top state organ. It is composed of the heads of the thirty-two ministries within the government. This body bears some resemblance to a cabinet in western governments. The German penchant for specialization can be seen in these numerous ministries. There is a ministry for each area of industry and the economy as well as for numerous other spheres of human activity, such as culture, sports, and education.

Although the Council of Ministers has its own building where it holds meetings and where its staff works, each ministry has separate quarters. These ministries are located throughout the central part of East Berlin. Ministry accommodations vary in size and in prominence of location. Some ministries have small quarters tucked away on side streets. Perhaps the largest—and certainly the most prominently located—is the Ministry for Foreign Affairs, facing Marx-Engels Platz. Adjoining it in the same building is the Ministry for Higher Education, which has jurisdiction over all GDR universities and hence over their law faculties.

The Ministry of Justice occupies a building of several stories on Clara-Zetkin-Strasse, a block off Unter den Linden and only a block from The Wall. Standing in front of this Ministry, one can see the top of the Reichstag building, located in West Berlin, immediately beyond The Wall. Thus the GDR Ministry of Justice ironically is only a few hundred yards from this seat of legislative power of the former German empire.

Just down from the building housing the Council of Ministers is the real seat of power in this country. It is the building housing the Central Committee of the SED and the Politburo. The Central Committee consists of 156 members (plus 57 candidate members). The Politburo, which meets weekly, has 17 members (plus 8 candidate members). The members of the Central Committee and its Politburo hold ultimate authority over the government and society of the GDR. It is their policies that the organs of government exist to implement and enforce.

There is considerable overlap between membership in the Politburo and Central Committee and official positions in the government. For example, of the twenty-five members of the Politburo (regular and candidate), eight are also on the Council of State. Nine members of the Politburo also hold positions in the Council of Ministers. All members of the Politburo are members of the Central Committee and also hold seats in the People's Chamber. Erich Honecker, in addition to being Chairman of the Council of State, is General Secretary of the SED (the top position in the Party) and Chairman of the National Defense Council. He is clearly the top man in the GDR power structure. Willi Stoph is a member of the Politburo, Deputy Chairman of the Council of State, and Chairman of the Council of Ministers; he is the secondranking official in the country. This interlocking of party and state at the top assures SED control.

To summarize, the central state organs are the People's Chamber, the Council of State, and the Council of Ministers. The central party organs—the locus of ultimate power—are the Central Committee of the SED and its Politburo.

Below these central organs are two lower levels of government—the county (*Bezirk*) and below that the district (*Kreis*). At each, as at the top, there is a side-by-side state and Party structure. However, one should not think of these two lower administrative levels as being local government in the sense that it is known in the United States. There is no local autonomy of any significance. The purpose of these two regional administrative units is to carry out the directions and policies of the central authorities. Because the country is highly centralized in every aspect of life, there is little leeway for local options.

The counties are the principal territorial and administrative units. There are fourteen, plus East Berlin. They are somewhat analogous to counties in England. These counties were established after 1949, when the authorities abolished the historic German states within the GDR borders. Thus names such as Mecklenburg, Brandenburg, and Saxony no longer have any political or territorial significance. Each of the counties goes by the name of its principal city, which is the seat of the State and Party organs for the county. These fifteen counties (including East Berlin) with their 1982 populations are shown in table 1. Figure 3 shows the locations of these cities. Below these counties are the districts—a total of 252 in the GDR.

To return to the subjects of this study—legal education and the legal organs—we now look at five central authorities in Berlin: the Ministry for Higher Education, the Ministry of Justice, the Supreme Court, the Procurator General, and the State Contract Court.

The Ministry for Higher Education is responsible for twenty-nine of the country's fifty-seven institutions of higher education. These include the four universities in which law can be studied—the universities in Berlin, Leipzig, Halle, and Jena. Specialized institutions such as agricultural colleges and military colleges are under the ministries with responsibility for those areas. The Ministry for Higher Education is organized

TABLE 1. GDR COUNTIES AND POPULATION

County	1982 Population
Berlin (East)	1,166,641
Cottbus	884,474
Dresden	1,801,869
Erfurt	1,237,117
Frankfurt an der Oder	104,545
Gera	741,233
Halle	1,819,034
Karl-Marx-Stadt	1,913,492
Leipzig	1,398,630
Magdeburg	1,260,892
Neubrandenburg	620,975
Potsdam	1,118,519
Rostock	890,613
Schwerin	590,234
Suhl	549,098
Total	16,697,366

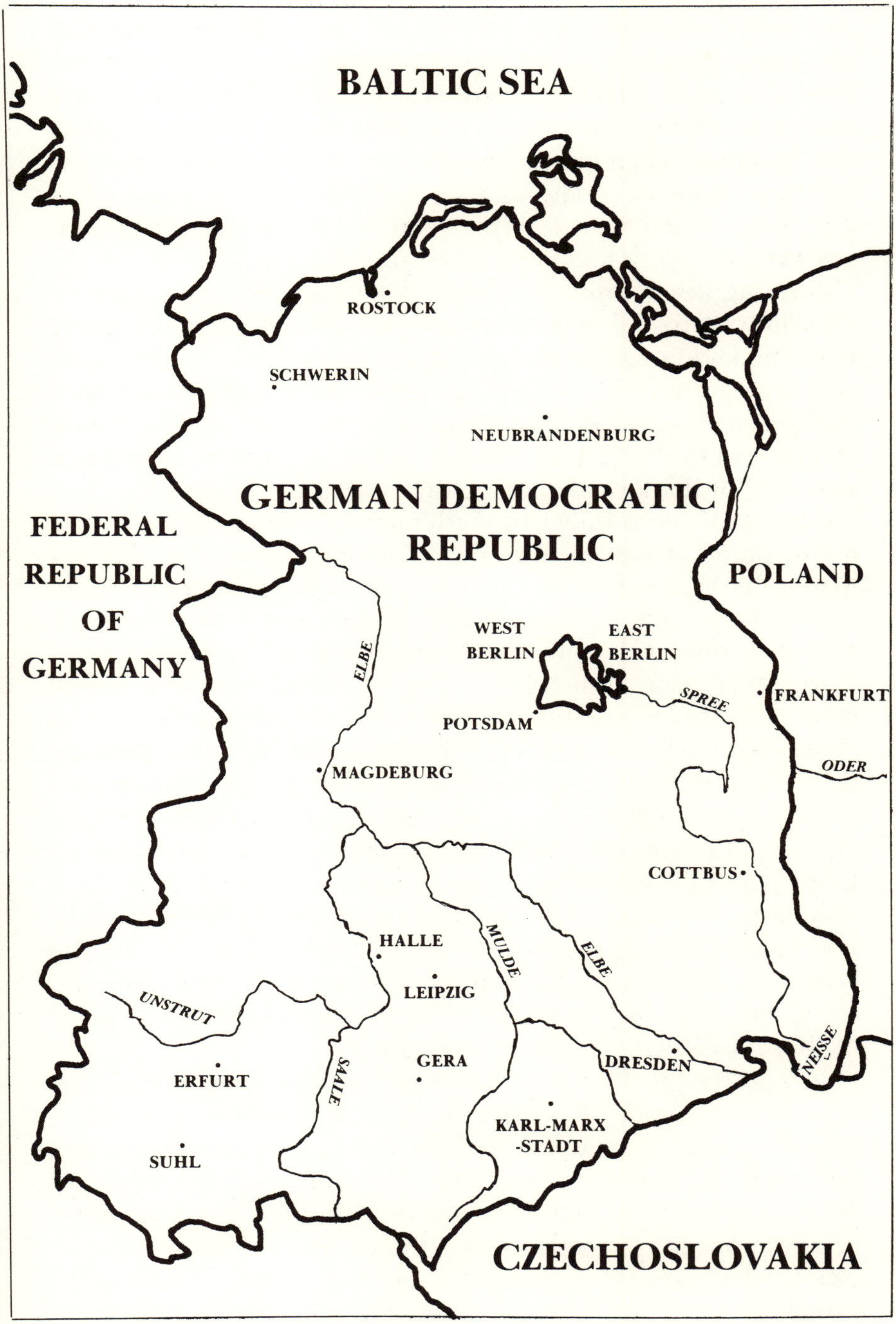

Fig. 3. The GDR and its regional administrative seats

into several departments, covering academic fields such as natural sciences, medicine, technical services, and social sciences. The Department of Social Sciences is in turn divided into several branches: libraries and museums, economics, culture, linguistics, pedagogics, and philosophical and historical sciences. This last branch includes law as well as more than a dozen other disciplines. Each branch is assigned a staff person with exclusive responsibility for that branch.

Although each university is headed by a rector appointed by the Minister for Higher Education, the Ministry deals directly with the law faculties. Among the responsibilities of the Ministry in legal education are the appointments of law teachers in the two highest grades (Professor and Docent), the establishment of the curriculum for law study, the authorization and approval of the law textbooks, the setting of the budgets, and the fixing of the number of students to be admitted each year to law study. To assist it in these responsibilities, the Ministry maintains a Council for Legal Education composed of law professors from each of the four universities and officials in legal agencies concerned with the administration of justice.

In short, the Ministry for Higher Education has overall responsibility for the four university law faculties, and each of those faculties is accountable directly to that Ministry. In addition, though, each law faculty has a special collaborative relationship with a specific central state organ, as follows: Berlin with the Ministry of Justice, Jena with the Procurator General, Leipzig and Halle with the State Contract Court. Each of these organs is considered the "practice partner" for its university law faculty. These relationships (depicted in Fig. 4), and the functions of these organs will be discussed in later chapters. Here, however, a few words need to be said about the place of these organs in the state structure.

In addition to its work with the law faculty at Berlin, the Ministry of Justice also has major responsibilities concerning the state court system. It develops the budget for this system and provides the courts with logistical and administrative support. Another important role of the Ministry is to maintain information and statistics about the court system and to recommend measures for its improvement, including needed additional personnel and changes in the law concerning procedure, jurisdiction, and structure. On court matters the Minister of Justice works with the President of the Supreme Court. Another

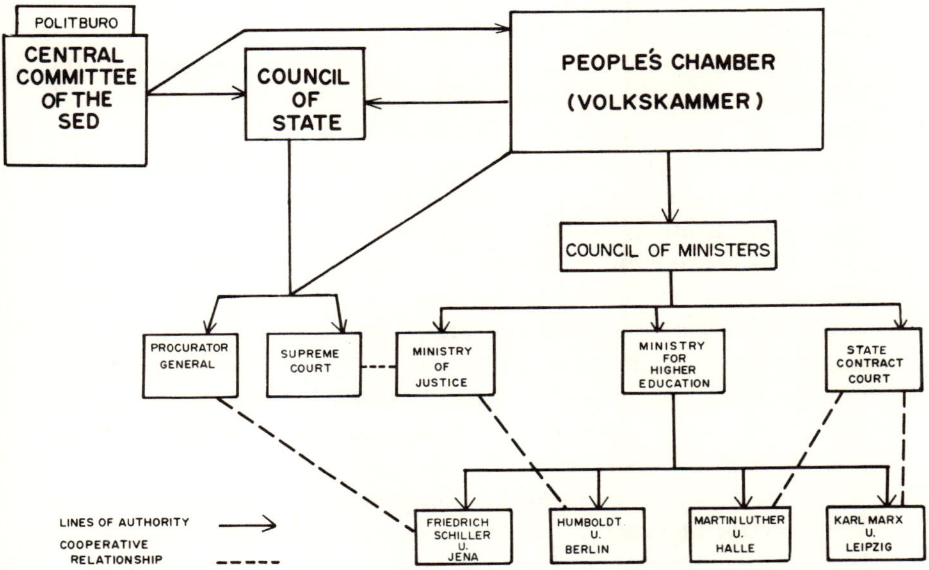

Fig. 4. Relationships among central state organs and university law sections in the GDR

important area of Justice Ministry activity concerns public education. Much stress in the GDR is placed on the importance of keeping the public informed about the law so that they will understand the system and be supportive of it. Unlike Justice Ministries in Western Europe, the GDR Ministry has no law enforcement or litigating authority whatsoever; it plays no part in the prosecution of crime.

The Ministry of Justice has two Vice-Ministers and a State Secretary. The latter is considered to be the first deputy to the Minister. Between 150 and 160 persons are employed in the Ministry, of whom fewer than 100 are lawyers. Internally the Ministry is organized into numerous subdivisions. The "main departments" are concerned with courts, information, legislation, economic law, and training and education of personnel (some of whom attend a school for court personnel at Weimar). The "departments," which apparently are smaller and less important units, are concerned with international relations, court buildings, and budgetary planning for the lower courts, the notaries, and the Justice Ministry itself. The Minister of Justice, like all other ministers, is elected to his position by the People's

Chamber. In reality, however, he is selected by the ruling authorities in the Party structure.

Partly because of its lack of law enforcement authority, the Ministry of Justice is viewed in the GDR as an agency of much less importance than the Procurator General's Office. This represents a marked change from the traditional place of this Ministry in German law and government. Indeed, it is pointed out by some in the GDR that in some of their sister socialist countries there is no Ministry of Justice at all and that one may not be necessary. In the GDR, however, there has been a Ministry of Justice from the outset, perhaps reflecting at least a measure of attachment to the traditional German arrangements. But because it does not have prosecutorial power or the power to oversee investigations, it is much diluted in its importance, at least in the eyes of many in the GDR.

These prosecutorial and investigatory powers are vested in the Procurator General, a key figure in the GDR, who is also the practice partner for the law faculty at Jena. He is elected to his position by the People's Chamber and is responsible to that body and to the Council of State. His election is based on the recommendation of the Council of State, which in turn almost certainly rests on a decision by the Politburo. In addition to the prosecutorial function, the Procurator General has a wide-ranging authority to oversee the maintenance of socialist legality. This official also is responsible for all investigatory activity. The office was copied in large part from that in the Soviet Union.

All criminal prosecutions take place in the state court system, as does litigation in the fields of civil, family, and labor law. This court system is headed by the Supreme Court and is organized into a three-tiered structure (with a subtier of informal lay tribunals called social courts) outwardly resembling many state court systems in the United States. The presiding judge of the Supreme Court is the President, who is elected to his position by the People's Chamber. He is responsible directly to that body and to the Council of State to which he submits reports semiannually. The state court system is not a practice partner with any of the law faculties; the details of its structure and its relationship with the law faculty at Berlin will be discussed in a later chapter.

The state courts constitute one of two court systems in the GDR. The other is the State Contract Court, which is the practice partner for the law faculties at Leipzig and Halle. This second court system reflects the importance attached to maintaining effective control over the economy in a Marxist-Leninist society. It is a fundamental principle in such a society that all means of production be owned "by the people" or, more realistically, by the state. This principle has been implemented to a high degree in the GDR, and today only a tiny percentage of the economy remains in private hands. The State Contract Court has exclusive jurisdiction over all disputes arising out of dealings among the multitude of state-owned enterprises. These disputes, resembling corporate and commercial litigation in the United States, are often of large economic consequence. The State Contract Court consists of two levels—county and central; these will be described in a later chapter. Their exclusive jurisdiction over enterprise disputes leaves the state court system to deal with criminal prosecutions and individual noncriminal matters of much lesser economic importance to the country.

The establishment of the State Contract Court reflects a basic reordering of the legal landscape in the GDR. In effect the GDR created two legal systems. One is referred to as the "system for the administration of justice" and covers the fields of human activity embraced by the four codes: criminal, civil, family, and labor. The governmental apparatus concerned with these fields includes the state court system, the Procurator General, the Ministry of Justice, and the Social Courts. The other legal system is embraced under the term "economic law." This is a separate body of law that has been fashioned to deal with relationships among the state-owned enterprises and conglomerates and with relationships between those economic entities and the superior state governing apparatus. The key organ in this separate legal system is the State Contract Court, functioning directly under the Council of Ministers.

This division of the legal order into two major segments came about as the means of production were brought largely under public ownership and socialism was being increasingly achieved. The society, in other words, was being divested of the remnants of "bourgeois characteristics." This necessitated a redoing of the historic German codes governing what westerners would call *private law* (a term which has little meaning under Marxist-Leninist theory). As a consequence, the 1970s proved to be an unusually active period for the rewriting of law concerning both criminal and noncriminal matters—the legal fields that come under "the system for the administration of justice," to use

GDR terminology. These rewritten laws include the Civil Code (1975), Family Code (1975), Labor Code (1977), and Criminal Code (1979). In addition, a new Code of Civil Procedure appeared in 1975; a new statute governing the Ministry of Justice was promulgated in 1976; a new law governing the work of the procurators' offices appeared in 1977; and a law governing advocates in the collegia was promulgated in 1980. All of this activity suggests a maturing of the legal system. It represents an effort to put Marxism-Leninism on a strengthened legal footing in light of the experience of some three decades as a separate German state.

These new laws spawned the writing of new texts. As the older law teachers say, after 1945 it was necessary for them to rewrite courses, lectures, and books, as well as German history in general. It was not until after 1949, however, that this process could move ahead without serious interruption. Until then there had been uncertainties about the future of Germany, and there had been at least the possibility of democratic government under a genuine multiparty system. But after 1949 hope of a united Germany dwindled and the power of the SED tightened. The new codes, statutes, and textbooks produced in the 1970s represent a significant step in the building of a Marxist-Leninist society.

In addition to holding that all means of production must be publicly owned, Marxist-Leninist dogma asserts that in any society there can be only one ruling class (ultimate power cannot be shared or divided). In order to ensure the rights of the people, and protection against economic exploitation, the working class must be that single ruling class. The will and the interests of that class are implemented through a single party; in the GDR this is the SED. To guarantee protection of the working class, that party must be in complete control. In theory, there can be no conflict between the party and the workers or between the workers and the state. This sentiment is reflected on one of the many official banners hung across the fronts of buildings: "The Program of the Party is the Program of the People." Essential to this controlled and collectivized system is the concept of central planning of all activity within the country. This, of course, includes education at all levels. Thus the universities and legal education function in a comprehensively planned and controlled environment, under the authority of the Ministry for Higher Education, as previously described. In this setting, the centuries-old German universities inherited by the GDR are maintained with flourishing enrollments. Far from withering away, law remains as a major discipline, albeit it is now taught and studied in a Marxist-Leninist context as a means of furthering socialism and collectivized life, supposedly in the interest of the working class. We move now to examine contemporary legal education in the GDR, looking first at the setting and organization of the four law faculties.

Part 2

The Study and Teaching of Law in the GDR

3
The Law Sections in the Universities

All twenty-one of the German universities before the First World War had law faculties. Seven of these were in the territory that now forms the GDR. As a result of various educational reforms, law is now taught and studied only at four: Berlin, Leipzig, Halle, and Jena. Although there is an organizational similarity to the former law faculties, law in the GDR universities today is a vastly different discipline from that studied in the universities of old.

The old and the new are both symbolized in the University at Halle. On entering the main building there, one comes into a central space rising three stories with a broad stairway leading upward. On the four walls in the upper reaches of this space are murals, one for each of the four German university faculties dating back to the Middle Ages: Law, Theology, Philosophy, and Medicine. The central figure in each of these murals is a robed woman. In each she has in her hands something of symbolic significance. In the law mural she is blindfolded and holds the scales of justice, in theology she holds a cross, in philosophy an open book, and in medicine a caduceus. On the second floor of the building, just off this great open space, is the Aula—the university auditorium. It is a huge room with murals on one wall. On another wall hang a dozen portraits of eighteenth- and nineteenth-century professors. On the ceiling are the seals of the four faculties. In the corridor outside the Aula stand the busts of Martin Luther, Philipp Melanchton, and several former rectors of the University. In this building, in the presence of murals, portraits, and busts, one senses strongly the atmosphere of the German universities of a century ago when they were approaching the peak of their renown.

But there is a sharp reminder that one is in the German Democratic Republic of the 1980s. Just across the corridor from the Aula, amidst the line of busts of the academic greats of the past, is a doorway marked "Library of Marxism-Leninism." This juxtaposition of the old and the new sets the stage nicely for a consideration of law in the GDR universities. Law is still there; the robed, blindfolded woman holding the scales of justice still stands high above students and faculty as they stream in and out of the lecture halls each day. However, law has been joined in the universities by Marxism-Leninism; perhaps it would be more accurate to say that the former has been subsumed under the latter.

For centuries, the term *Faculty of Law* was used to identify the teachers and students forming the law departments in the German universities. During 1968 and 1969 the GDR undertook a nationwide university reform. One of the changes to come out of that move was the renaming of the old "faculties" as "sections." Thus the proper name is now "Section of Law" or "Law Section." Virtually every field of study represented by a department in a typical American school of arts and sciences is also represented by a section in the GDR universities. What American universities call "schools" are also called sections, such as those of medicine, engineering, and law. In some of the other universities without law sections, and in some of the technical schools, there are individual law teachers offering courses in subjects pertinent to other fields of study. For example, courses are offered in traffic law and in maritime law in Dresden and Rostock, respectively. Those individual offerings resemble, for example, courses in business law taught in American colleges. However, the mainstream of legal education is in the four universities being examined here: Berlin, Leipzig, Halle, and Jena.

A. Berlin: Humboldt University

The University in Berlin is one of the youngest of the German universities founded before the twentieth century. Opening in 1810, it quickly rose to prominence. From the beginning its main building has been the three-story structure on Unter den Linden originally erected as a residence by the brother of Frederick the Great; three-story wings were added later, forming the present H-shaped complex. The academic eminence achieved by the institution (particularly after 1871) was fostered by its prime location on the principal street in the center of the capital city of the German Reich. The performing arts, the libraries, the seat of government, and the centers of financial power all lay within a few blocks. Today much of that is gone, but much also remains. Although the main university building was heavily damaged in the Second World War, it survived sufficiently intact to permit restoration. Today this center of the University looks more or less as it did before 1942. Across the 200-foot expanse of Unter den Linden from this main building, and beside the State Opera and St. Hedwig's Cathedral, is another major university building, the Kommode, housing academic departments and seminar rooms.

The University occupies several hundred other buildings scattered around East Berlin, although many are in the vicinity of the main building. It has a total of thirty-one academic sections and institutes and an enrollment of approximately 12,000 full-time students and 7,000 part-time students.

Entering the main university building from Unter den Linden, one passes through a gateway in a high, wrought-iron-looking fence and crosses the large open space formed by the two wings. The cobblestone central area is now flanked by trees and flowers. In former years statues of academic greats stood in this courtyard. All are still intact but have been relocated. The two Humboldts—Alexander and Wilhelm—are on the sidewalk in front of the courtyard. Helmholtz and Mommsen are on a side street. Hegel is in the rear of the main building in a plaza near the entrance to a new Seminar Building, a modern six-story structure housing classrooms.

The front entrance to the main university building leads into a large foyer, at the rear of which a broad stairway leads upward to a landing and there divides, with stairways going to the right and left. On the wall above the landing, over the name of Karl Marx, is a statement that can be translated as follows: "Philosophers have only interpreted the world, but it is your responsibility to change it."

The Law Section is located on the second and third floors of the east wing, extending toward Unter den Linden. Here are located the offices of the Section's administrators. The Section is headed by a director and has two associate directors—one for education and training and the other for research. These three administrators have a suite of rooms with a secretary; each has a private office. Their rooms overlook the courtyard and Unter den Linden, in the direction of Frederick the Great and the linden trees. On the wall of the director's office is a

Humboldt University, Berlin. Main building on Unter den Linden. The Law Section occupies the second and third floors in the front portion of the wing on the right. (Photograph courtesy of Panorama DDR)

large picture of the ubiquitous Karl Marx and a shield of the German-Soviet Friendship Society.

The teaching staff and the researchers are organized into "departments" within the Section. Before the university reforms of the late 1960s these were known as "Institutes." Thus from "Faculties of Law" containing "Institutes," the universities have moved to "Sections of Law" containing "Departments." Apart from this change of labels, the structure is essentially the same as it was historically. In the Humboldt Law Section, there are nine departments. Each department occupies two to four rooms located on the upper two floors of the east wing of the main university building. Each has at least one secretary. Each is headed by a professor. In some instances, the professor who is the department head has a room of his own. Generally, however, members of the teaching staff share rooms with their colleagues; only a few in the entire Law Section have private offices. Because of these crowded office conditions, faculty members come to this building only at times when they have lectures, seminars, or appointments; otherwise they work at home or in a library.

Departmental rooms and professors' offices are generally bare of pictures. The corridors, however, often contain exhibits of various kinds. An exhibit on Ho Chi Minh was on display in glass wall cases in the vicinity of the Law Section during the fall of 1983. For a short while a Simón Bolívar exhibit from Venezuela was on display in the main lobby of the building.

The number and the names of departments within the law sections vary somewhat from one university to another. The names of the nine departments in the Humboldt Law Section are as follows: Theory of State and Law/Constitutional Law, Criminal Law, Labor Law, Protection of Scientific and Technological Property, Economic Law, International Law, Agricultural Cooperative and Land Law, Civil Law, and Continuing and Part-time Education.

The teaching staff—totaling 115—includes approximately 17 or 18 professors and an equal number of docents (a German teaching rank, to be explained later) and 80 assistants, organized into the nine departments. Approximately a quarter of the professors and docents are women. The Humboldt law teachers reside in widely scattered locations in East Berlin; most of them commute to the main university building by public transporation.

The law library is at the front of the top floor of the east wing, overlooking Unter den Linden. It has a staff of six; its head has a law degree. Its reading room seats approximately ninety. Book shelves line the walls and contain the generally used teaching books and reference works. Newspapers available in this room include *Neues Deutschland* (the SED paper), other major GDR papers, *Isvestia, Pravda,* and *Morning Star* (the English Communist party paper). An attendant is on duty at a desk in this room. Opening off the reading room are rooms for the six members of the law library staff. These rooms also house a card catalogue; book stacks are to the rear.

The law library is the largest of the twenty-eight departmental libraries in Humboldt University. Before the Second World War it contained 150,000 volumes. At the end of the war the collection numbered 18,000 volumes. Today the law library has approximately 90,000 volumes and receives 253 periodicals. The collection is growing at the rate of about 200 items per month. The University's total library holdings are estimated to be 2,000,000 volumes, most of which are in section and institute collections. Approximately 200,000 are in the Central University Library facing Clara-Zetkin-Strasse, just west of the rear of the main building. University faculty and students also have access to the German State Library next to the main building on Unter den Linden, which has over 6,000,000 volumes. (GDR literature states that 1.8 million volumes of this library's original collection are deposited in the State Library in West Berlin.) The library at the Academy of Sciences has nearly 300,000 volumes. The library at the Supreme Court, with 300,000 volumes, is also available to members of the Law Section.

In addition to texts and commentaries on GDR law, the Section's law library contains material on political science, criminology, philosophy, economics, Marxism-Leninism, political economy, sociology, and the history of the workers' movement. There is also material on the laws of other Eastern European countries. From the Federal Republic of Germany there are periodicals, the reported decisions of the Federal Constitutional Court and the Supreme Court for ordinary civil and criminal cases, and other legal material. The law library contains little on international law; the major collections on that subject are in the central university library, the German State Library, the Supreme Court library, and the Academy for State and Law at Babelsberg. There is also scant material concerning American and English law. Decisions of the U.S. Supreme Court are available at the Academy of Sciences and in the German State Library.

Directly below the law library, at the front of the second floor, is the main lecture room for the Law Section. It seats approximately 170 students and is substantially like the lecture rooms in most universities of the world. It suffers from being directly on Unter den Linden where, when the weather is mild and the windows are open, traffic noise can be distracting. All lectures in the Law Section are given in this room. Seminars take place in the new seminar building to the rear of this main building. The law students divide their time between the main building and the seminar building. They come to the second and third floors of the main building to attend lectures in the Section's one lecture room, to use the library, and to see members of the teaching staff or administration when that is necessary.

Students whose families live in Berlin normally live at home. Others live in university-provided housing consisting of relatively modern high-rise buildings located at a considerable distance from the main Humboldt University building. However, there is good public transportation and students can reach the Law Section from their housing within some twenty minutes.

In the Humboldt Law Section 170 full-time students are admitted each year to the four-year course of study. Thus the total theoretical enrollment for the four-year program would be

680. However, there is some attrition; it is estimated that perhaps 30 students in each entering class do not graduate. In 1982, for example, the graduating class numbered 143. In a typical graduating class approximately 50 to 60 go to the state court system to become judges, 30 to 40 become notaries, 20 or more become practicing lawyers, and the remainder become research students or enter legal work with state organs.

Although at its physical center Humboldt University is heir to the home of the old University of Berlin, the spiritual and academic descendants of that University can be found several miles to the west. In 1948, as Marxism-Leninism tightened along Unter den Linden, many professors and students withdrew and created the Free University of Berlin in the American-occupied sector of the city. Today that institution is in the center of the GDR in that its seat, West Berlin, is surrounded by GDR territory. However, it enrolls no GDR students; its enrollment comes from West Berlin, the FRG, and the rest of the free world.

B. Leipzig: Karl Marx University

In the long sweep of German history the city and the University of Berlin are both relatively new. Some 100 miles to the southwest, in what was Saxony, is the much older city and University of Leipzig. In addition to its University, founded in 1409, Leipzig has been famous since medieval times for its fairs; later it became a center of music and book publishing. All of these continue to flourish today. However, the book publishing business and the fairs have diminished in international significance since the Second World War. In 1900 Leipzig had 475,000 inhabitants; today it has 559,000.

A short distance from the University is the building constructed in the 1890s to house the Imperial Supreme Court. Despite extensive destruction in the city, this impressive building survived the Second World War and today houses an art collection and a museum commemorating Georgi Dimitrov, the Rumanian communist who was tried in these very rooms for his alleged part in the 1933 Reichstag fire. One can now listen there to a recording of the heated exchange between him and Hermann Goering. The great hall, with its stained glass windows depicting four regions and aspects of German life, is closed to the public. The fact that all of the cities whose arms appear in those windows—Hamburg, Lübeck, Königsberg, Marienburg, Cologne, Strasbourg, Nuremberg and Augsburg—now lie outside the GDR impressively illustrates the truncated character of this country and the radical alterations wrought by two World Wars.

Leipzig today has much in common with many cities across Germany, West and East. Its center is a mixture of the old and the new, resulting from the devastations of the Second World War and the rebuilding that followed. The fifteenth-century Rathaus (the medieval town hall) has been restored and stands in the old marketplace, although almost all else in its immediate vicinity is postwar construction. Not far away is St. Thomas Church, where Bach held forth for twenty-seven years as choirmaster and composed much of his work. In this center of the old city is also Auerbach's Keller, which was frequented by Goethe and which served as the setting for a portion of *Faust*.

A few hundred yards from the old city center are the main university buildings and two other venerable Leipzig institutions—the Opera House and the concert hall known as the *Gewandhaus*. But all these structures are new from the ground up. The nineteenth-century buildings housing all of these stood here on what was formerly known as Augustus-Platz. The main post office also stood here. The idiosyncrasies of modern aerial bombardment are such that all of these buildings and the great fountain in the center of the platz were destroyed beyond reconstruction, while nearby St. Thomas and the Rathaus survived. Rebuilding commenced in the 1960s. The Opera House was the first new structure to be completed in its old site. New university buildings were completed in 1973. The last of these historic institutions to be physically re-created was the *Gewandhaus*. In the 1960s an Interhotel was constructed on the Platz across from the University. The main post office has also been rebuilt. A new and impressively splashing fountain has been created in the center on the site of the old, and the area has been renamed Karl Marx Platz. GDR flags and red banners flutter here in profusion.

The configuration of the streets in this center of Leipzig is as it always was, and there is still a park and a small lake behind the Opera House. From here it is only a few yards to the narrow streets of the old city and some of the medieval structures. Here the 1904 *Baedeker* is still a reliable guide. In the newness of Karl Marx Platz, however, one can physically sense the claims of

Karl Marx University, Leipzig. The twenty-seven-story "High Building" from Karl Marx Platz. The Law Section occupies the sixteenth floor. The three lower university buildings are obscured. The building at the left is the Gewandhaus (Concert Hall). (Photograph courtesy of Panorama DDR)

the GDR that a new society is being created, that a new order has arrived. The clean break with the past is vividly dramatized through concrete, steel, and glass.

The reconstructed University on Karl Marx Platz consists of a group of four buildings, forming a quadrangle. Three of these are five or six stories high. The fourth has twenty-seven stories; it is the tallest building in Leipzig by a good measure. Some refer to it as "the Great Finger," others call it the "High Building." It is constructed in a triangular shape resembling an opened book. Like almost all new construction in the GDR, these buildings are white—or nearly so—and are glass and concrete. One of the three lower buildings houses the administrative offices for the University. Another contains seminar rooms. Another contains lecture halls and the University's central library. The tall building houses the offices of most of the academic sections. Medicine and a few other sections occupy buildings in other parts of the city. The University has a total of twenty-three academic sections and institutes and an enrollment of approximately 14,800.

Of the four universities, Leipzig is the only one in which the Law Section does not occupy, at least in part, university buildings from the eighteenth and nineteenth centuries. Here the Law Section is on the sixteenth floor of the "High Building." Along a V-shaped corridor, following the design of the building, are located the offices of the director, the two associate directors, and the members of the teaching staff and secretaries.

The teaching staff here includes sixteen professors, sixteen docents, and a large number of assistants. All these are organized into nine departments: Constitutional and Administrative Law, Theory of State and Law, History of State and Law, Civil Law, Criminal Law, Labor Law, Economic Law, International Economic Law/Protection of Scientific and Technological Property, and Land Law.

In the usual pattern, each department has space of its own. However, as is also typical, few members of the faculty have private offices; some rooms are occupied by two or three persons. As many as twelve young assistants share the same room. The result of this shortage of office space, here, as in the other universities, is that the members of the teaching staff tend to come here only around the times they have lectures, seminars, or conferences. Otherwise, they work at home or in the library. Students appear to come rarely to the sixteenth floor. The only occasion for their coming here would be to talk to a member of the faculty or to attend to administrative matters.

Faculty members in the Law Section present their lectures in one of three lecture rooms allocated to the Section in the building housing the University library. These rooms seat 120 students each. (Other lecture rooms in this building seat between 60 and 300 students each.) Law seminars are conducted in the adjacent seminar building in rooms seating between 20 and 40 students each.

Here, unlike in Berlin, there is no separate law library. Law books are housed in the central University library, which contains mainly social science material. Collections in other fields are housed in other locations. The main floor of the central library contains a circulation desk, card catalogue, and a reading room with newspapers and periodicals. Newspapers from some Western countries are received by the library, but access to them can be had only with a special card. On the second floor of the central library are two reading rooms seating over 140 students. These rooms contain books on open shelves. Many of the law books are shelved together in one stack area, and it is there that law students mainly work. The collection contains only a few, mostly out-of-date books in English about American law. There are many law books in braille.

Leipzig is relatively rich in library resources. In addition to the University's total library holdings of 3,000,000 volumes the German library (Deutsche Bucherei), founded in 1912, contains 7,000,000 volumes. Also in Leipzig is the Central State Library for the Blind, established in 1894, which produces several hundred books annually in braille and on tape.

The Law Section admits 100 full-time students annually. Of these, 95 usually complete the four-year program and graduate. Thus the total full-time enrollment approaches 400. The attrition rate at Leipzig is less than one third of the attrition rate in the Humboldt Law Section.

Leipzig is a GDR center for foreign students pursuing various fields of study. The University has special language and other programs for these students. Many come from Africa and Asia; others come from Eastern Europe and Cuba. In the Law Section, 20 percent of the students are foreign; the largest foreign enrollment of any of the four law sections. In the fall of 1983 these students came from Vietnam, Campuchia, Afghanistan, Yemen, and Bulgaria.

Student housing is in new, multistoried buildings located about a 20 minute walk or a 10 minute trolley ride from the central University buildings. This student housing is in the vicinity of the old German Library. Nearby is the Bayerischebahnhof (Bavarian railroad station); whistles can be heard as trains come and go. (The main railroad station is still on the Ring in the center of the city.) From the vicinity of the student housing one sees also to the south the massive monument to the "Battle of Nations," commemorating the victory here over Napoleon in October 1813. This monument was the scene of the last engagement between German and American forces before the American army occupied Leipzig on April 19, 1945.

The University in Leipzig claims a continuity with the past. In 1984 it celebrated its 575th anniversary. Yet its starkly modern buildings, with its soaring "Great Finger," make it difficult to relate to the renowned university that formerly stood on this spot. There are only two physical reminders. One is a portal at the entrance to the quadrangle taken from the front of one of the old university buildings, one of the few portions not destroyed. The other is a statue of Leibniz (1646–1716), moved from its original site a few blocks away and placed in front of the new university buildings where it now stands near a bust of Karl Marx. The whole scene, including the red flags flapping around the fountain, seems designed to signify a new direction in German affairs.

C. Halle: Martin Luther University

Just under an hour's drive to the northwest of Leipzig is the city of Halle. Situated on the Saale River, it, like Leipzig, dates from the Middle Ages. In 1900 Halle had a population of 157,000; today its population is 233,000. Moving from the Leipzig Law Section, in its modern high-rise building in a university named for Karl Marx, to the Law Section in the University at Halle, named for Martin Luther, imparts at least superficially the impression of moving backward in time. The city of Halle and its University hold much more of the flavor of the nineteenth century than one finds in the precincts of the University in Leipzig. The Market Place in Halle imparts a sense of the old city. There stands the sixteenth-century church where Martin Luther occasionally preached. Adjacent to it stands the old clock tower, 276 feet high, a Halle landmark. Not far away are the ruins of the Moritzburg, a castle dating from the Middle Ages. On one of the nearby winding streets is the boyhood home of George Frideric Händel, whose statue remains in the Market Place.

However, Halle does have its contemporary elements. In the southeastern section of the city is a great new Platz, named after Ernst Thälmann, Chairman of the German Communist Party just before the Nazis' assumption of power in 1933. He died in the Buchenwald concentration camp and has become a GDR martyr. Here everything is new and motor vehicular traffic is intense. A monument in the massive Soviet-communist style, with multiple raised fists, commemorates various workers' movements and uprisings.

The central buildings of the University, dating from 1834 and located on University Ring, are but a short distance from the Market Place. As one moves away from these buildings on Geiststrasse and Bernburgerstrasse, he is in an area that seems relatively unchanged since the turn of the century. Those streets lead to the University Guesthouse—Haus der Wissenschaftler—a large, three-story, late Victorian mansion, complete with corner towers and turrets.

Halle today is in the center of an area of intense chemical manufacturing. The Leuna Works, one of the largest in Europe, is just to the south. At times odors and fumes permeate the air and fog occasionally covers the city. This combination of natural fog and chemical-industrial fumes can create a smog so thick that even automobile headlights do not penetrate. At such times people must walk or take a trolley. Fortunately such days are infrequent.

Automobile traffic here, at least between the central University buildings and the Guesthouse, is less intense than in Leipzig and Berlin. On most evenings after 7:00 or 8:00 P.M. automobiles disappear altogether. A silence sets in that can only be described as dead. Even insect sounds and the rustling of leaves are absent. Although lined with shops and densely inhabited row houses, in the evening these streets are devoid of human life. This unreal silence is punctuated at intervals by the distant whining of a trolley, with steel wheels screeching on steel tracks as it rounds turns. When it comes to a stop its motors continue and then the whining and screeching resume as the trolley pulls away, finally passing out of hearing altogether, leaving again a sound vacuum and a deserted scene. Here, among relatively unchanged buildings, one can imagine that he is walking the same street in 1939 or even in 1914.

The University at Halle was founded in 1694. In 1817 it merged with the University of Wittenberg, which had been established in 1502. With the merger the latter closed and its faculty moved to Halle. Wittenberg is a small town on the Elbe, some forty miles to the northeast, between Halle and Berlin, made famous as Martin Luther's home and the place where he did most of his significant work. In 1933 the University was formally named "The Martin Luther University of Halle/Wittenberg," and it retains that name today.

Among the central University buildings on University Ring, perhaps the most important is the "Lion Building," so called because of the pair of large stone lions flanking its main entrance. Completed in 1834, it was designed by the architect Schinkel, who also designed the Altes Museum in Berlin and other important buildings in Germany. It contains lecture rooms and the University Aula, the 500-seat auditorium described earlier.

Nearby is a large L-shaped building. A portion of this building has on its pediment the name of Christian Thomasius; the Law Section is located here. The other portion of the building, housing other academic sections and seminar rooms, carries the name of Philipp Melanchton. One of the interesting features of the GDR is its selection of heroes and persons from the past to be honored. Melanchton was a colleague and supporter of Martin Luther. With Luther's having been refurbished as a progressive folk hero during the 1983 celebrations of the five-hundredth anniversary of his birth, Melanchton should be reasonably secure. Thomasius, who is obviously well regarded among the Halle Law faculty today, began his career in the Leipzig law faculty in the late seventeenth century but encountered difficulties there because of his unorthodox theological views, a circumstance likely to attract official admiration in the GDR. When the University at Halle was founded he was appointed to its first law faculty and in 1710 became its Rector. Thomasius is the only former law professor whose portrait hangs in the University Aula.

The main University library, housed in a nineteenth-century building, is a block away from the Thomasius-Melanchton building and the Lion Building. Its collection numbers over 3,000,000 volumes. Nearby on University Ring is the University's "Theater of Peace," a large modern concert hall and theater. Approximately one hundred other buildings throughout the city of Halle are occupied by various sections and offices of the University. The University has a total of twenty academic sections and institutes and an enrollment of over 8,000 students.

The Law Section occupies all four floors in the Thomasius building. The lower floor, a semibasement level, houses the law library and its staff offices. The main level of the building—the floor one enters from the outside—houses only the Civil Law Department. That Department has a central office with several adjoining rooms. A large stairway leads up to the second floor, on which are located the offices of the Director, the two Associate Directors, and some of the departments. The top floor houses other departments.

Here one notices an idiosyncratic variation in security arrangements. In Berlin and Leipzig, in order to gain access to the law sections one must enter the main university buildings by passing through a guarded entrance and showing an official pass issued by the University. In Halle, however, the law section

Martin Luther University, Halle. The Melanchton building from the front entrance of the Lion building. Not shown, to the right of the street lamp, is the Thomasius Building, housing the Law Section. (Photograph courtesy of Panorama DDR)

building and Lion Building have no guards, and anyone off the street may freely enter, without a pass. Indeed, in the spring of 1982, I and one of my law faculty colleagues drove into the University, parked outside the law section building, walked into the building with no prior arrangements, and had a conversation with a law teacher whom we had never met before. This would have been impossible at Humboldt and Karl Marx Universities. The setting in Halle is distinctly more American in this respect.

The Law Section has a total of ten departments: Civil Law, Criminology, Labor Law, Theory of State and Law, History of State and Law, Land Law, Agricultural Cooperative Law, Economic Law, State and Administrative Law, and International Economic and Finance Law. The last three of these are housed in buildings a few blocks from the old University buildings. All others are in the Thomasius building.

The Law Section has fifteen professors, six docents, and twenty-six assistants, for a total teaching staff of forty-seven.

Of these, almost one-third are women. As in the other universities, the Law Section has an Associate Director for Education and Training and an Associate Director for Research. Likewise, as in the other universities, there is a shortage of rooms to house the teaching staff. Only a few professors have private offices; the others share rooms and do most of their work either at home or in the library. Most of the lectures and seminars are conducted in the adjoining Melanchton building or in the Lion building, just a few steps away. The three departments that are located several blocks away hold lectures and seminars in their buildings.

The Law Section in Halle admits 100 full-time students every year. This means that there is a potential total enrollment of 400, although the actual enrollment is smaller because of an attrition rate of about 10 percent. This attrition rate is double that of the Leipzig Law Section but is little more than half of the rate in Humboldt. Approximately 60 percent of the Halle students are women. In the fall of 1983 the Section had twenty-four students from Vietnam, one from Laos, and one from Greece.

Student housing is provided in new buildings in Halle Neustadt, a new city adjacent to Halle, about a fifteen minute trolley ride from the center of the University. A student center for recreation and meetings has been created in a section of the Moritzburg, the medieval castle only a short distance from the main University buildings. Much of this structure is in a state of ruin, but a portion has been restored to provide for this center of student life.

Of the students graduating annually at Halle—and at Leipzig as well—approximately 80 percent enter legal work with the various state-owned enterprises, 10 percent go to county contract courts, and the remainder enter legal work with state administrative organs.

The Section's law library contains approximately 110,000 volumes. Most of these seem to have been assembled since the Second World War. According to a staff member, during the war 30,000 volumes belonging to the library were moved westward to Marburg for safekeeping and they have never been returned; their present location is unknown. The law library has the usual material found in all four of the universities. It receives approximately 1,500 new titles annually. It has very little Western and American material. Law library offices for the staff of five, the catalogue, and most of the books are located on the bottom floor of the Thomasius building, a semibasement. The reading room is on the second floor. It contains fifty study places, copies of all law textbooks, miscellaneous other books, and GDR newspapers and periodicals. The library receives approximately 140 periodicals published in the GDR, other eastern European countries, the Soviet Union, and the FRG.

On the top floor of the Law Section building there are two rooms housing old books. One contains between 1,000 and 2,000 volumes on German legal history. Although these belong to the law library, they are in the charge of a professor who is a legal historian and who works with them constantly in the room where they are located. Another room on the top floor contains a smaller collection of old German legal material—perhaps a few hundred volumes—all said to have been published before 1700.

In Halle, as in Berlin, the law faculty carries on today in a physical setting that is essentially the same as that in which the law faculty held forth for many decades through the nineteenth and early twentieth centuries. Unlike Berlin, the main University buildings in Halle escaped altogether the damage of the Second World War, as did much of the surrounding city. American army units occupied Halle on April 19, 1945, in their final drive eastward and remained there until July 1. Unlike Leipzig, Halle is not a great historical or contemporary music center, and it has seen few Americans since that date. Here in the University, except for the Marxist-Leninist trappings, one can feel much more the atmosphere of the nineteenth-century German university than in Berlin, where one is surrounded by the signs and symbols of the new order, and, of course, more so than in Leipzig where there is no longer any physical trace of the University of old.

D. Jena: Friedrich Schiller University

To the southwest of Halle and Leipzig, just inside Thuringia, is the city of Jena. Its University was founded in 1548, and has long played a prominent part in the German university tradition.

Jena is in historic country. Some fifteen miles to the west is the town of Weimar, rich in its associations with Goethe, Schiller, and Liszt. It gained twentieth-century fame as the site of the Constitutional Convention of 1919, which framed Germany's only authentically democratic constitution before the Second World War. To its north is a more jarring twentieth-century note, the site of the Buchenwald concentration camp. Five miles to the north of Jena is the site of the battle of October 14, 1806, between Napoleon's forces and the Prussians.

The town of Jena itself, however, is most famous for its University and, in recent decades, for the Carl Zeiss Optical Works. In 1900 it had a population of 21,000; today it has 105,000 inhabitants. Whereas Halle and Leipzig are the chief cities and the administrative seats for their counties, Jena is not; the chief city of its county is Gera, some twenty-two miles to the southeast. Jena has a market place characteristic of most German towns, with a Rathaus and a principal church. In the center of this open space stands a statue of John Frederick the Magnanimous, credited with founding the University. Looming high above the town, somewhat incongruously, are two tall, modern structures. Atop one is the name of Carl Zeiss, the old optical firm still actively in business, now as a state-owned enterprise. The other, a round structure over twenty stories tall, was originally built for the Carl Zeiss works but was later found to be unneeded and was turned over to the University.

The old University buildings, dating from the nineteenth-century and earlier, line a street just a short distance off the central Market Place. Here in the late eighteenth century—an academic golden age for the University—Schiller lived and taught. He is still among the heroes of the GDR, and the institution has been renamed "The Friedrich Schiller University." The line of old University buildings is set back a few yards from the street, with small plots of grass and shrubbery in front. Some half-dozen busts of distinguished nineteenth-century professors rest on pedestals placed at intervals facing the street along this row of buildings. Apart from its contributions to learning over the centuries, the University here is noted as the place in which the tradition of fencing among German university students began. Today the University in Jena has a total of nineteen academic sections and institutes and an enrollment of approximately 4,700 full-time students and 600 part-time students.

The Law Section in Jena is housed in the new, tall, round tower taken over by the University from Carl Zeiss. Some persons refer to this building as "The Cigar." The Section has two floors in the structure, approximately halfway up. This is the

Friedrich Schiller University, Jena. Main building. The Law Section is housed in a modern high-rise building nearby. (Photograph courtesy of Panorama DDR)

smallest of the four law sections in the GDR universities. It has six departments: Theory of State and Law, Constitutional and Administrative Law, Criminal Law, Criminology, Civil Law and International Law. The Law Section has ten professors, five docents, and twenty-five assistants. It has the usual director and two associate directors—one for education and training and one for research.

Lectures and seminars for the Law Section are conducted in the old University buildings a short distance from the new high-rise office space. There is no separate law library; law books are housed in the general University library which contains altogether about 2.5 million volumes.

The Law Section admits 60 full-time students each year, making a potential total enrollment for the four-year program of 240 students. Almost all of the Jena law graduates enter careers as procurators under the authority of the Procurator General.

Much less information about the Law Section in Jena is reported here and in the following pages than is reported about the sections in Berlin, Leipzig, and Halle because of the GDR Ministry's refusal to arrange access to the Director and faculty in Jena. The facts that are presented here are derived from the estimates and opinions of persons elsewhere in the GDR.

As suggested by the foregoing descriptions, in terms of teaching staff, enrollment, library resources, and physical facilities, law is a well-established discipline in these four GDR universities. We proceed now to examine the curriculum pursued in the four law sections. It is in the subject matter of the discipline that "Law," as now taught and studied in these universities, differs most markedly from the discipline of the same name in these same universities in bygone decades.

4
The Two Law Curricula

Legal education in the GDR universities is a four-year program for full-time students. For part-time students it is a five-year program. On either basis the course of study leads to the award of a university degree called *Diplom jurist*. The focus here is on the full-time, four-year curriculum.

The most distinctive features of university legal education in the GDR are these: (1) The curriculum is officially promulgated by centralized authority—the Ministry for Higher Education. (2) This centrally promulgated curriculum rigidly fixes the subject matter and sequence of all courses, the amount of time devoted to each, and the nature and timing of all examinations, leaving little room for law faculty variations. (3) The curriculum is grounded exclusively on, and is pervaded by, Marxist-Leninist principles. (4) The curriculum is organized into two tracks, one concentrating on the administration of justice and the other on the economy. Thus there are really two law curricula. (5) University legal education is specialized on the basis of the two curricula, with two universities concentrating on each. Collectively these features serve to distinguish legal education in the GDR from that in the FRG and other Western European countries.

The two curricula, which are quite similar, have been developed and are revised from time to time through a process of consultation with law professors and government officials. This process is described in the next chapter. Once it is fixed by the Ministry for Higher Education, however, the curriculum is binding on the law sections. No law section as a whole, or any individual teacher within it, has authority to deviate from this official curriculum. Normally a curriculum stays in force for several years before being revised. The present curriculum was first formulated in 1974 and was modified slightly in 1982. It is unlikely to be tinkered with again for a few more years.

The law curricula are set forth in a printed booklet of twenty-nine pages known as the *Study Plan*, issued by the Ministry for Higher Education. This booklet contains a statement of the purpose of law study and a brief description of each subject to be taught. It presents a detailed listing of the courses to be offered in the two curricula, in each of the eight semesters during the four-year program, with the number of hours allotted each course and the points at which examinations are to be given. (An English translation of the entire booklet is set out in Appendix A.) It is an extraordinarily detailed document, especially when one considers that it is centrally promulgated for all four universities. All that is left for decision by each law section is the daily and hourly schedule for the lectures and seminars. However, the *Study Plan* does provide for Special Section Time in each semester after the first, during which each section can offer some lectures of its own choosing. Such lectures afford the student his only opportunity for curriculum choice, since all subjects specified in the *Study Plan* are mandatory. The student does have a choice of a topic, within limits, for a paper to be written during the fourth year.

The Marxist-Leninist orientation is clear and explicit throughout the curriculum. This keynote is sounded at the outset of the *Study Plan* and it runs through the course descriptions like an unbroken thread. The full flavor of the theme, as well as the explicitly political nature of law study, is imparted in the opening paragraphs of the *Study Plan*:

> In realization of the historical mission of the proletariat, the historically inevitable legal leading role of the working class and its Marxist-Leninist party grows through ongoing construction of the already developed socialist society and the establishment of basic prerequisites for the gradual transition to Communism. Connected with this is the universal strengthening of the socialist state of workers and farmers as a form of dictatorship of the proletariat which represents the interests of all the people of the German

> Democratic Republic and guarantees freedom and human rights, further development and improvement of the socialist democracy, and the consistent realization of democratic centralism.
>
> Inseparably bound up with the universal strengthening of the socialist state are the systematic improvement of the socialist judicial system and the guarantee of socialist legality. Socialist law serves as an expression of the power of the proletariat, the realization of the interests of the workers, the protection of the socialist order and the freedom and human dignity of the citizens.
>
> Accordingly, high and constantly improving standards have to be set for the political and ideological education and for the theoretical and practical training of the students who enroll in the GDR university courses of political science and law. The student's training and education is aimed at the attainment of a firm class-consciousness and stresses that all their future activities are perceived as political functions. The student is to develop into a socialist lawyer working within the socialist apparatus of state and economy. He must become a political functionary and public leader who is able and determined to protect the socialist order of state and society, to apply socialist law in the service of social progress, and to preserve the rights and interests of the people. This requires also the student's training in loyalty to the socialist fatherland, to proletarian internationalism, and especially to a firm friendship with the Soviet Union and with the other socialist countries. In conjunction with this the student is to be instructed in the ability and preparedness to represent at all times the policies of the party and of Marxism-Leninism and also to aggressively dispute the bourgeois ideology and the policies of imperialism.

In these paragraphs are the words and themes that repeatedly appear throughout the *Study Plan* and indeed in all official writing in the GDR. Some of the key words and phrases are "party of the working class," "class consciousness," "socialist," and "imperialism." The combination of "practical and theoretical" training is emphasized in all areas of education. The linkage internationally to other socialist countries and friendship with the Soviet Union are points made in all spheres of GDR life.

Although Marxism-Leninism is pervasive, in some courses the concentration is more intense and direct. These include subjects such as Dialectical Materialism and Classics of Marxism-Leninism. Subjects such as Theory of State and Law and History of State and Law are essentially courses in Marxism-Leninism. In subjects that might otherwise appear to be neutral, such as Family Law and Civil Law, Marxism-Leninism is a constant point of reference. It provides the premises on which all subjects rest. Indeed, it is perhaps not too much to say that no offering in the curriculum is free from or outside this central and dominant theme. It is probably inconceivable that any subject could be dealt with from any other point of view.

The subjects described in the *Study Plan* are pursued in both curricula. The academic track focused on the administration of justice will be referred to hereafter as the "justice curriculum." The one concentrating on the economy will be referred to hereafter as the "economics curriculum." Both are set out in the *Study Plan* with the same degree of detail, semester by semester. Both cover the same subject matter; the difference lies in the varying amounts of time devoted to some subjects and the order in which they are studied. A list of the subjects in each of the eight semesters, with the time to be devoted to each, is set out in Appendix B for the justice curriculum and in Appendix C for the economics curriculum. These two curricula are keyed to the two legal systems previously described.

The justice curriculum is designed to train persons to work in what is referred to as the "system for the administration of justice." This system involves the state court judges, procurators, practicing lawyers, notaries, and lawyers in various state organs. This curriculum is followed in the Universities in Berlin and Jena. The economics curriculum is designed to train persons to enter legal work in various facets of the economy. These positions include those of judges on the State Contract Court, lawyers for the many state-owned enterprises, and lawyers for the various state organs and agencies concerned with the economy. This curriculum is followed in the Universities in Leipzig and Halle.

The justice curriculum, which can be used for illustration, contains a total of thirty-three academic subjects plus sports. These subjects, spanning the four years, are listed in table 2 with the total number of lecture and seminar hours allotted to each.

These subjects are also contained in the economics curriculum but with varying amounts of time devoted to them. In order to compare the justice curriculum with the economics curriculum, table 3 combines these thirty-three subjects into several broad categories and shows the total number of hours for each category in the two curricula. The major differences between these two curricula are revealed by this table. The justice curriculum devotes over twice as much time to criminal

TABLE 2. JUSTICE CURRICULUM SUBJECTS

Subject	Lecture and Seminar hours
Dialectical and Historical Materialism	120
Political Economy of Capitalism and Socialism	165
Scientific Communistic Fundamentals of the History of the Workers' Movement	144
Special Courses on Selected Problems of Marxism-Leninism	30
Special Seminar on Classics of Marxism-Leninism	30
Marxist-Leninist Theory of State and Law	150
History of the Perceptions of the Theory of State and Law	48
History of State and Law	120
Constitutional Law of the GDR	60
Constitutional Law of the USSR and other Socialist States	45
Constitutional Law of Developing Countries	15
Constitutional Law of Bourgeois States	30
Administrative Law	60
System for the Administration of Justice	45
Economic Law	84
Scientific-Technical Protection Law	45
Labor Law	90
Agricultural Cooperative Law	45
Land Law	60
Environmental Law	30
Civil Law	180
Civil Procedure	60
Family Law	45
Copyright Law	15
Criminology	30
Criminal Law	210
Criminal Procedure	60
International Law	60
Private International Law/International Economic Law	50
Forensic Science	42
Introduction to Psychology	30
Russian Language	75
Other foreign language	75
Total	2,348

TABLE 3. JUSTICE AND ECONOMICS CURRICULA COMPARED

Category of subject	Justice	Economics
Marxism-Leninism	807	831
GDR Constitutional and Administrative Law	165	165
Criminal Law and Procedure	372	165
Civil/Labor/Family Law and Procedure	375	350
Economic Law	144	410
Land and Environmental Law	135	135
Foreign Law	90	75
International Law	110	174
Foreign languages	150	150

law subjects. Not surprisingly, the economics curriculum devotes almost three times more attention to economic subjects. The economics curriculum also gives more time than the justice curriculum to international law subjects, with an emphasis on international finance.

The category of "Marxism-Leninism," which includes the first eight of the thirty-three subjects listed in table 2, accounts for more than one-third of the lecture and seminar hours in both curricula during the four years of study. These courses deal with the doctrines embraced by Marxism-Leninism from a variety of perspectives. For example, the Marxist-Leninist historical approach is revealed by the table of contents from the textbook used in the course on History of State and Law, set out for illustration in Appendix G.

To identify only eight of the thirty-three courses as being in the category of Marxism-Leninism may be somewhat artificial and misleading. As pointed out earlier, these concepts dominate the entire curriculum, as can be seen from the course descriptions contained in the *Study Plan*. The description of the course in Criminology provides a good example:

> Criminology deals with criminality as an acknowledged social and historical occurrence. . . . It shows also in this the superiority of socialism and communism as compared to all other social structures. The basis for understanding the problems and possibilities of socialist criminal law and the gradual elimination and final conquest of crime through the historical process of constructing a socialist society and subsequently a communist society is the discovery of a strategy built upon the perceptions of Marx, Engels

> and Lenin. . . . In the analysis of imperialistic teachings and other bourgeois views about criminality, the students affirm their own Marxist-Leninist positions and can then further develop their abilities to differentiate between these concepts.

The offering of a course in Criminology points up an aspect of the GDR law curriculum that would be admired by many American legal educators, if they could put aside the Marxist-Leninist doctrines (a big *if*). This is the interdisciplinary character of the curriculum. In addition to courses in criminology and forensic science there are courses in psychology and economics (domestic and international), as well as in history and philosophy. Another aspect of the curriculum that might excite American admiration is the substantial amount of time devoted to foreign, international, and comparative law. These courses account for almost 10 percent of the lecture and seminar hours. They expose students to the legal and governmental systems of the Soviet Union, United States, Great Britain, France, Italy, Japan, the Federal Republic of Germany, and some developing nations. Twelve hours of lectures are devoted to the United States Constitution, accompanied by seminar meetings on the subject. Students study the United Nations organization as well as other aspects of international law. Few American law schools offer this array of instruction in these areas, and, if they do, such subjects are electives. In the GDR all of this subject matter—indeed the entire curriculum—is required of all law students. Again, however, this material is presented from a Marxist-Leninist viewpoint.

To illustrate this perspective, English translations from two of the teaching books are set out in the appendixes. Appendix I contains the table of contents from a book on international law. Appendix J contains the table of contents from the textbook on the constitutional law of bourgeois states. The chapter in the latter dealing with the United States Constitution is reproduced in its entirety in Appendix K. Through that text Americans can see themselves as they are seen from the Marxist-Leninist point of view.

Required foreign language study is another distinctive feature of the curriculum. Each law student must pursue the study of Russian through the first three semesters in the university and also the study of another language of his choice. Before entering the university he will already have had eight years of Russian in school. After three semesters of Russian the student undergoes an examination in that language, focusing on legal material. To pass, a student must demonstrate a reasonably fluent reading capability so that he can read a standard Russian legal text without missing many words and within a reasonable time. If a student fails the test, he can take it again at a future date. If he fails then, he may be excluded from the university. There is no required proficiency test in the second foreign language. The most popular choice of a second language appears to be English, although French and Spanish are frequently chosen.

Each student is required to participate in sports each week throughout the four years. A wide choice of sports is available. The possibilities include all of the standard sports, such as soccer, swimming, and tennis. There are men's groups and women's groups and some mixed groups. Some of the sports groups participate in interuniversity competition. A student can shift from one sport to another as he progresses through the university, although a common pattern appears to be for a student to stay with the same sport throughout the four years in order to become proficient and hence to be a more effective participant in the interuniversity competition. Failure to participate in the requisite number of hours of athletic activity during a semester will result in a student's being ineligible to take examinations in his legal subjects. Reports are made periodically to the law section by the sports instructors.

The Special Section Time authorized by the official curriculum allows each law section a certain number of hours per week (after the first semester) which the section can use to present lectures relating to its specialty. For example, in Leipzig lectures are presented on legal aspects of the economy; in Berlin lectures are presented on aspects of the administration of justice; in Jena special instruction in rhetoric is offered, designed for future procurators. The time allotted for such lectures varies from two hours per week in some semesters to as much as eight to twelve hours per week in the advanced semesters. Students must attend lectures during these times, but they have some options as to the subject matter.

A law student in the GDR universities spends a substantial number of hours per week in the classroom, attending either lectures or seminars. Required activities for first-year students total about thirty hours weekly; for fourth-year students the total is about twenty hours. Moreover, the days can be long, beginning sometimes at 7:00 A.M. and ending at 6:00 P.M. For illustration, table 4 shows the weekly schedule of a first-year law student at Humboldt University. This is the schedule for one of the seven seminar groups into which the first-year class is divided. Not including sports and foreign language study, this schedule requires a student to spend a total of twenty-four hours per week in the classroom. Sports adds another four hours, and foreign language study (not shown on this chart) adds several more.

The Humboldt weekly schedule shown in table 4 is under the justice curriculum. For comparison with the economics curriculum, the weekly schedule of a first-year student in Halle is set out in table 5. The Halle weekly schedule involves slightly less than twenty-two hours in the classroom, not including foreign language study and sports. The schedule shown here is for one of the four groups into which the first-year law class at Halle is divided. According to this schedule five hours per week are required for language study and four and a quarter hours for sports, thereby adding a total of more than nine hours to the weekly academic schedule.

These first-year weekly schedules at Berlin and Halle do not clearly reveal the previously mentioned differences between the justice curriculum and the economics curriculum. As pointed out earlier, the subject matter of the two is substantially the same; the differences are largely in emphasis, revealed by looking at the course offerings in both four-year programs, as shown in Appendixes B and C.

In the major subjects the general format of instruction combines lectures with seminars. Typically there is one lecture period per week and one seminar session per week in each major subject. In this format the kinship of GDR legal education with German and European education generally can be seen.

The lecture is a set piece. It is literally read by many professors. Each lecture period is two hours, but this does not mean that the professor speaks for two hours. The normal procedure is for the lecture to commence 15 minutes after the announced hour of beginning. It then runs for 45 minutes with a 15 minute break followed by another 45 minutes of lecture. The lecturer is thus talking for a total of an hour and a half out of the two hour period. The lecturer typically lays down general principles and provides a systematic, comprehensive framework. To an American the lectures would likely appear to have an abstract

TABLE 4. WEEKLY SCHEDULE, HUMBOLDT LAW SECTION (1ST YEAR, GROUP 1)

Hour	Mon.	Tues.	Wed.	Thur.	Fri.
0900	*Sem.* Philosophy (0900–1100)	*Lec.* Political Economy (0900–1100)			
1000					
1100	*Lec.* Criminology (1100–1300)	Sports (1100–1500)	*Lec.* Theory of State and Law (1100–1300)	*Lec.* Philosophy (1100–1300)	
1200					
1300			*Lec.* History of State and Law (1300–1500)		
1400	*Sem.* Political Economy (1400–1600)				
1500				*Lec.* Constitutional Law (1500–1700)	*Lec.* History of State and Law (1500–1700)
1600		*Sem.* Constitutional Law (1600–1800)			
1700				*Sem.* History of State and Law (1700–1900)	*Sem.* Theory of State and Law (1700–1900)
1800					
1900					

TABLE 5. WEEKLY SCHEDULE, HALLE LAW SECTION (1ST YEAR, GROUP 1)

Hour	Mon.	Tues.	Wed.	Thur.	Fri.
0800	*Lec.* Constitutional Law of GDR (0800–1030)		*Lec.* History of State and Law (0800–1115)	*Lec.* Philosophy (0800–0930)	*Lec.* Political Economy (0800–1100)
0900					
1000	*Lec.* Civil Law (1045–1215)			*Sem.* Political Economy (1000–1130)	
1100		*Sem.* Civil Law (1115–1300)			
1200					*Sem.* Philosophy (1200–1330)
1300	Language (1300–1800)	Sports (1345–1800)	*Lec.* Theory of State and Law (1300–1500)	*Sem.* Theory of State and Law (1315–1500)	
1400					*Sem.* Constitutional Law of GDR (1415–1545)
1500					
1600					
1700					
1800					

quality. They do not deal with specific cases or with concrete illustrations to any great extent. Lectures are usually given to the whole class at once: in a first-year subject to the entire first-year class, in a second-year subject to the entire second-year class, and so on. At the conclusion of each lecture the students applaud German style, knuckle-rapping on desk tops.

Most lectures seem to be structured along the lines of the teaching books on the subject. Thus one can get an impression of the scope and organization of a series of lectures by examining the table of contents in the teaching book for that subject. The contents of four of these books are set out in the appendixes: *History of State and Law of the GDR* (Appendix G), *Constitutional Law of the GDR* (Appendix H), *International Law* (Appendix I) and *Constitutional Law of Bourgeois States* (Appendix J). In each of these subjects lectures are given over a period of weeks with a coverage substantially similar to that shown in these tables of contents.

The seminars in the law sections of the GDR universities are not like American law school seminars. They are also unlike most seminars in West German law faculties. In the latter a seminar typically consists of presentations and discussions almost entirely in the hands of students, each of whom is writing a substantial paper. The GDR seminars resemble typical American law school class sessions. Each class year—that is, first year, second year, and so on—is divided into seminar groups. Each group consists of twenty-five to thirty students. At Humboldt University, for example, there are seven seminar groups in the first-year class; in Leipzig there are four. Each seminar group has its own weekly schedule. The weekly schedules shown in tables 4 and 5 are for Seminar Group 1 in Berlin and Seminar Group 1 in Halle. The lectures will, of course, be the same for all first-year students, but the seminars meet at different times and in different rooms and with different instructors. Thus, each seminar group has a slightly different weekly schedule. Seminar rooms are usually designed to hold two to three dozen students. The students sit in rows behind tables or desks in the usual American classroom fashion. They do not sit around a single large table of the sort often used in American law school seminars.

These sessions often do not deal with problems or cases in the collegial style of discussion usually associated with American seminars. Again, they are more like an ordinary American law school class, with the instructor standing in front proceeding through a mixture of lecture and questions. Questions are raised and answers are sought voluntarily from the students. The style would be familiar to an American law teacher. The answer of one student is often followed by a slightly different answer given by another. Sometimes the instructor comments on the answer or asks other questions based upon it. However, there does not appear to be the same degree of argumentation or of directly conflicting viewpoints that one often hears in an American law school class. The questions tend to seek generalized and abstract definitions, concepts, and principles.

Sometimes, however, problems are distributed to the students in advance and they form the basis for seminar discussion. "Case Exercises" used in the Seminar in the System for the Administration of Justice at Humboldt are set out in Appendix L. In the International Law Seminar at Humboldt the students are assigned one chapter each week in the teaching book (see table of contents in Appendix I). They are also given a weekly problem for discussion. One such problem, for example, concerns the appropriate steps to remedy violations of U.N. Security Council action on South Africa.

In both the justice and economics curricula there is an item in the *Study Plan* described as "civil defense." It occupies a full month of each student's time during the second year in the university. The time of year varies. At Humboldt, for example, this training period occurs in the spring, whereas in Halle it is scheduled in the late fall. During this month the male students go away to one camp and the female students go to another. According to the *Study Plan* this training is designed to teach the students "basic principles and preventive measures to protect the workers and the economy against weapons of mass destruction, sea disasters, and other catastrophes." Civil defense is also treated in lectures in the courses in the Constitutional Law of the GDR, the Constitutional Law of Bourgeois States, Administrative Law, and Economic Law.

In all aspects of higher education the GDR authorities stress the importance of welding together theory and practice. The premise is that education is designed to equip persons to serve society in useful ways. To prepare students for effective service, so the reasoning goes, they must get to know the citizens for whom and with whom they will be working after graduation, and they must gain an understanding of the situations in which they will function. Thus in the law sections there are two periods of required practical work during the four years. The first occurs at the end of the second year and is for a period of four weeks. The next occurs at the end of the third year and is for a period of twelve weeks. Each of these work periods is known as a *Praktikum*.

During these periods the students are placed in agencies and activities related to their future work. Thus students in Leipzig and Halle work in enterprises or in state organs concerned with the economy. Students from Jena work in procurators' offices or in other state organs concerned with the administration of justice. Students from Berlin work chiefly in the state courts and other agencies in the justice system. During the second *Praktikum*, at the end of the third year of law study, efforts are made to assign students to work in the precise locations where they will work after graduation. Generally students will have ascertained by that time where they will go at the end of their studies.

The *Praktikum* at the end of the third year is also designed to provide the basis for a paper which must be written during the fourth year. That paper should be derived from some aspect of the student's work experience during the preceding summer. This is a substantial paper of perhaps fifty double-spaced typed pages. At the end of the fourth year the student is examined orally on the paper and must defend it before two or more members of the law faculty.

Unlike American law schools, the law sections do not administer examinations in each course at the end of each semester. During the semester, however, the teacher may administer a written exercise to be done by the students during a lecture or seminar period. These exercises resemble questions on an American law school examination. It seems to be common for teachers in the major subjects to have two of these exercises in each semester.

Although these classroom exercises are at the discretion of the teachers, all other examinations are specified in the *Study Plan*. (For a listing of the examinations by subject and semester see Appendix A.) Three types of examinations are required in all law sections: intermediate, final, and comprehensive. Table 6 shows the semesters in which these three types of examinations are administered in the justice curriculum and the number of each type in each semester. In the economics curriculum the

TABLE 6. JUSTICE CURRICULUM EXAMINATIONS BY SEMESTER

Semester	Intermediate examinations	Final examinations	Comprehensive examinations
1st			
2d	3		
3d		2	
4th	2	1	
5th	1	2	
6th		3	
7th		1	
8th		1	5

examination schedule is not significantly different. In some subjects the *Study Plan* requires no examination at all. Instead a "certificate" is awarded, evidencing that the student has attended the required instructional sessions.

Most of the subjects of the intermediate examinations are dealt with again in the comprehensive examinations—hence the name "intermediate." The comprehensive examinations come at the end of the four years in the university and are the final step toward graduation. These examinations concentrate heavily on Marxist-Leninist doctrines. In the justice curriculum they concentrate also on civil and criminal law; in the economics curriculum they focus instead on economic subjects. The "final" examinations are administered in those courses where the subject matter is not included in the comprehensive examinations. A final examination can be taken as many as three times by a student, if necessary; apparently many students do repeat examinations one or more times before passing.

All three types of examinations are oral. They are typically conducted before panels of two or three members of the law teaching staff. Practices vary from one law section to another. Sometimes the students are examined individually. On other occasions they are examined in groups of two or three. The examining teachers give the student a mark on his performance at the end of the oral proceeding. Conducting the comprehensive examinations and hearing the fourth-year students' defense of their papers constitute a substantial task for the law faculty every summer. Several weeks during July and August are consumed in this process.

A student representative may also be present at these examinations. This student is a member of the Free German Youth (FDJ), the only student organization in the GDR universities. This is a countrywide youth organization and includes persons from age fourteen through twenty-five. It has a chapter or unit in each university. Apparently it is considered a matter of right for an FDJ representative to be present at an oral examination, although one is not always present. The subjects that usually attract an FDJ representative are those that focus most directly on the principles of Marxism-Leninism. The role of the FDJ representative is one of listening and later making observations about the examination to the teachers. This student apparently plays no role in assigning the mark given on the particular examination. Rather, the student's concern appears to be with the technique and style of examination and with the general quality of the answers, all said to be directed toward improving the process for the future.

The basic textbook in each of the major legal subjects is the *Lehrbuch,* written under the aegis of the Ministry for Higher Education. In seventeen subjects there is such a textbook available. In two subjects—Civil Law and International Law—this is a two-volume work. In all others it is a single-volume text or treatise. The book presents a comprehensive and systematic treatment of the subject. The book serves not only as a basic text for students in the universities but also as an authoritative text for practitioners and officials. A list of textbooks available for the seventeen major subjects is in Appendix D. Not only are these textbooks the authoritative works, they are also (with the exceptions noted below) the only comprehensive texts available for use in law teaching in all four universities. In other words, there is no array of books from which a law teacher can choose; the principal book in each subject has already been written, published, and selected for him. The process through which these books are written is described later.

Although these books are on sale in the bookstores in the vicinity of the universities, many students do not acquire personal copies. Cost is probably one reason for this. Another may be a shortage in the supply. Inquiries at several bookstores near the universities at Halle and Berlin revealed that no bookstore had in stock a complete set of the textbooks, and most had fewer than half on hand. The libraries in the law sections stock numerous copies of each *Lehrbuch* for student use. Students are expected to read in these texts the material that goes along with the lectures and seminars.

Another type of publication used in legal education is known as the *Grundriss,* meaning summary or outline. Such a book is available in seven subjects. Unlike the textbook, a summary is not an official or authoritative publication. It is sometimes said that a summary is a would-be textbook, or a manuscript that did not quite make it as a textbook. A summary is what its name implies—a summarized presentation of the subject. In general, summaries have fewer pages than textbooks, although there are exceptions to this. Summaries are thought to be of sufficient value and quality, however, to justify printing and offering for sale. Apparently students often find these publications more useful than a textbook. Some teachers agree with this view. Moreover, there are legal subjects on which there is a summary but no textbook. A list of the summaries appears in Appendix E.

Still another kind of legal publication used in law study and teaching is the "commentary." This type of work has long been associated with the civil law tradition. Commentaries have been published on four of the major GDR codes: Civil Law, Family Law, Criminal Law, and Criminal Procedure. There are twelve other commentaries on specialized legal subjects. A list of these publications appears in Appendix F.

Most of these textbooks, summaries, and commentaries have been written since the early 1970s, the period during which many of the codes were revised. These books form a large and important part of the writing and research done by law teachers in the universities at Berlin, Leipzig, Halle, and Jena. The next chapter presents a description of those teachers and their work.

5
Law Teachers and Legal Scholarship

The role of the law teacher in the GDR is in some respects similar to that of law teachers elsewhere. In other respects, however, it differs markedly from that of a law teacher in the United States and in other Western countries. Because of the centrally prescribed law curriculum the teacher has at best only an indirect role in shaping the academic program in which he works. He has limited choice as to teaching books. As just discussed, in each subject he has only the textbook, possibly a summary, and in some instances a commentary. Moreover, the premises, principles, and concepts embraced by the subject he teaches are all uniformly and precisely defined within the Marxist-Leninist framework. Thus the role of the teacher is essentially that of implementing a specific academic design, using a relatively fixed set of teaching materials. In addition to this task, however, a GDR law teacher participates in certain administrative policy decisions concerning the work of the section and undertakes research and writing. All of these activities of the law teachers will be discussed below.

There are four ranks in the GDR university faculties. From the lowest to the highest these are: Assistant, Higher Assistant, Docent, and Professor. The two lowest ranks are referred to collectively throughout this book as "assistants." Appointments to the two lowest ranks are made within the university. The rector formally makes these appointments, but he does so on the recommendation of the director of the law section, who in turn must have the concurrence of the executive of the trade union organization in the university. Persons in these two ranks are the most numerous among the law teachers. They do not all progress higher. In this respect they are analogous to associates in some large American law firms where some will make partner, others will stay on for years as senior associates, and others will leave.

Appointments to the two highest ranks, Docent and Professor, are made by the Minister for Higher Education. He fills each vacancy from a list of three recommendations submitted by the law section through procedures described hereafter. Although most Docents are appointed from the ranks of the Assistants and most Professors from among the Docents, Docents and Professors are sometimes selected from persons whose legal careers have been outside the universities.

The academic rank of Docent, quite old in German universities, has no exact counterpart in American academic life. It is a more important and a more senior position that that of an associate professor in an American law school. The position is sometimes equated to that of a Reader in Law in the English universities. Not every Docent is promoted to Professor. The rank of Professor in the GDR still carries, although in diluted form, something of the prestige of that position in the Germany of old. Persons typically become professors between the ages of 35 and 40. The department heads are selected from among the professors in the section, as is the director. In addition to their full-time teachers, the law sections employ "honorary professors." These are persons engaged in other legal work who lecture part-time.

Individual teaching loads seem to vary considerably. The usual pattern appears to involve the giving of one lecture per week and teaching from two to six hours weekly in seminars. However, teaching loads of ten to twelve hours a week are not unknown, although they are considered to be unusually heavy. Not all courses run throughout the fifteen-week semester, so a teacher's lecturing and seminar instruction can be bunched into a period of a few weeks. Some members of the faculty do all of their teaching in one semester, devoting their entire time in the other semester to research.

Law teachers are paid on a compensation scale that is fixed centrally, like all other pay scales in the GDR. The beginning monthly salary for each rank is as follows: Assistant, 900 marks; Docent, 1,500 marks; Professor, 2,400 marks. The amount is increased periodically on the basis of length of service. In comparison, in 1981 the average compensation for workers and farmers in the GDR was between 1,000 and 1,200 marks per month. A judge on the Supreme Court—the highest court in the GDR—receives approximately 2,700 marks per month.

A young law graduate aspiring to pursue an academic career would normally begin by becoming a "research student" shortly after receiving his *Diplom jurist.* Students are normally elected to this position by the faculty during their third year of law study. This position gives them the status of students in the university with time to work on the dissertation that will be the basis for their receiving the degree of *Doktor jurist* (*Dr. jur.*). This is sometimes referred to as the first dissertation or as Dissertation A. A research student also assists in teaching. He typically has one or two seminars weekly under the supervision or tutelage of a more senior member of the faculty. These research students appear to be similar to graduate teaching assistants in the arts and sciences departments of American universities.

Obtaining the degree of *Dr. jur.* is an essential prerequisite for an appointment to the position of Assistant in a law faculty. It typically requires two to three years of work. The dissertation is supposed to be a substantial piece of scholarship, and it must be defended orally before a faculty committee. Not all persons who obtain this degree remain in academic work; indeed, numerous persons in other lines of legal activity have the degree of *Dr. jur.*

Once he is appointed an Assistant, the young scholar may progress into higher academic ranks without any other degree. However, his chances for ultimate appointment to the upper ranks are probably enhanced if he pursues the second doctorate by undertaking a second dissertation—Dissertation B. This is supposedly a much more substantial piece of scholarship than Dissertation A, and it usually requires more than two or three years of work. If the dissertation is completed and is satisfactorily defended, it leads to the award of the degree of *Doktor scientiae jurist (Dr. sc. jur.*). This period of research, at least in name, has replaced the old *Habilitation,* the traditional period of advanced scholarly research in the German universities. The term *Habilitation* (still used in the FRG) has been formally dropped in the GDR but one occasionally hears it among the older GDR academicians.

The possession of two doctorates by a senior scholar or teacher has long been familiar in the German academic scene, and it is no less familiar in the GDR today. The apparent attraction of academic titles and the formal use of all such titles also continues in the GDR. A person with two doctorates is usually referred to, at least in writing, as "Dr. Dr." For those lawyers interested in economics or in working in various aspects of the economy, the second doctorate can be and sometimes is the Doctor of Economics (*Dr. sc. Ök.*).

The educational backgrounds of the older law teachers in the GDR differ from those of the younger teachers. The most senior professors still active in the early 1980s received their legal education and training in the years immediately following the Second World War. They studied either in the Academy for State and Law or in a university law faculty. It is likely that no person still actively engaged in law teaching in the GDR in the 1980s received his legal education before 1945. If there are any, they are exceedingly few. To have been old enough to have pursued university law study before the collapse of Germany, one would have been at least well into his sixties, by the early 1980s.

The university law faculties in East Germany continued for several years after 1945 with the traditional German structure for the study of law, as described in chapter 1. This involved four to five years in the university, followed by the first state examination, and then two or three years of practical training. On passing the second state examination the student was then qualified to enter the judiciary or any other branch of the legal profession.

Although that traditional program of legal education was continued, the period from 1945 to about 1950 was one of considerable upheaval and uncertainty in higher education. Most of the law professors who had clearly identifiable Nazi affiliations left the universities then in the Russian occupation zone. Others who were not Nazis, and who were also not Communists, had an increasingly difficult time as the pressures of Marxist-Leninist ideology mounted. Many of those also left. It was this movement that resulted in the founding of the Free University of Berlin. To listen to many of the law teachers in the GDR today who were students in that time one would get the impression that all university teachers who left for the West were Nazis. However, that is not the case. It does seem to be the case that virtually none of the pre-1945 faculty members were left in the GDR universities after about 1950 unless they embraced Marxism-Leninism.

The shortage of university law teachers immediately after 1945, and the "unreliability" of some of those who remained, was one of the factors responsible for the establishment of a program of legal education in the Academy for State and Law. The purpose was to provide crash programs of legal training for persons to man the legal system in place of those who had been removed because of Nazi affiliations. At a later date the Academy undertook more extensive programs of legal education. Its graduates appear to stand on equal footing with the university law graduates. Some of the senior law teachers today received their training in the Academy and not in a university. That role of the Academy, however, was discontinued some years ago. More is said of this institution later.

As described earlier, the law teachers in each of the university law sections are organized into departments, grouping together teachers in the same subject matter or in closely related fields. This plan of organization is unknown to American law schools. It makes for a rather rigid academic career. Normally a young teacher remains in the department in which he begins. Switches between departments do occur but they are relatively rare. Physically each department has its own rooms. There is typically a departmental secretary who sits in an office adjoining the room of the Professor who is the department head. As mentioned before, there is seldom enough space for anyone other than the department head to have a private office.

In theory each law section aims to staff its own curriculum. That is, the objective is to have all subjects in the curriculum taught by permanent members of the law section. But this is not completely achieved. The foreign language courses, required of all students during their first two years, are taught by members of the Section on Foreign Languages. Sports are in the hands of sports instructors. Even in the strictly legal subjects, sections sometimes call on others. In Leipzig, for example, International Law is taught by teachers from the Section of International Relations, and Marxism-Leninism is taught by instructors from the Section of Marxism-Leninism. Also, Leipzig calls on Halle for an instructor in International Finance Law. In Berlin, Constitutional Law of Developing Countries is taught by a professor from the Academy for State and Law.

Each law section has a council. This is, in effect, the governing body of the section. It has a variety of policy-setting functions and serves as advisor to the director. At Humboldt, the Law Section Council includes all of the Professors and some representatives from each of the lower teaching ranks, elected by those in each rank. It includes eight students, two from each of the four class years. The Council also includes a variety of persons from relevant areas of law and government outside the University, such as the Vice-President of the Supreme Court, the Deputy Minister of Justice, and the Deputy Procurator General. The total Council membership is approximately fifty. The types of persons from outside the university who serve on a Law Section Council vary, depending on the section's field of concentration. In Leipzig and Halle (where the economics curriculum is followed) the Councils include persons from the contract courts, state-owned enterprises, and combines, but they do not include representatives from the Ministry of Justice.

Apparently there is no such thing in the GDR law sections as a "faculty meeting" in the sense that this phrase is used in American law schools. That is, there is little or no occasion on which all teachers in the law section meet together unto themselves. Section council meetings, which take place three or four times a year, are perhaps the nearest approach to a faculty meeting.

One of the council's most important tasks involves the filling of vacancies for the positions of Professor and Docent. When a vacancy occurs, the council proposes three persons to the Minister for Higher Education. Theoretically the council applies standards in selecting the three nominees similar to those that an American law faculty would use in recruiting a new professor. These factors include scholarship, teaching experience, and other relevant professional experience. Given the context in which the council functions and the premises of the official and philosophical system, it is almost certain that the council would not propose a person who was not perceived to be solid on Marxist-Leninist theory.

In addition to the section council there are—at least in the Humboldt Law Section—two other groups involved in the section's administration. One group consists of the director, the two associate directors, a representative from the trade union organization in the University, and a student representative from the Free German Youth. That group meets every week. The other group consists of all those persons plus the nine professors who head the departments. That group meets once every six weeks.

The director is the administrative head of each law section. He is the counterpart of the dean of an American law school or the head of a department in a college of arts and sciences.

He is appointed by the Minister for Higher Education from among the professors in the section. He holds office for a term of four years, but he can be reappointed for an additional term. The two associate directors in each section are appointed by the rector of the university from among the faculty members of the section, based on the recommendation of the director.

Although no firm statistics are available, it is likely that a large percentage—more than half—of the professors and docents are members of the SED. Members typically wear the SED pin in their lapels, and numerous such pins can be seen among the teachers in the law sections. Directors and associate directors all seem to be SED members.

Apparently it is considered an appropriate part of the teacher's function to issue statements on political matters. In the fall of 1983 the dominant official subject in the GDR was the deployment of American missiles in Europe. On bulletin boards in the Humboldt corridors, statements from several law teachers were posted, all sharply critical of American and Western European foreign policy. Nowhere on these bulletin boards at any time did I find a statement adverse to any policies of the Soviet Union or of the GDR.

Law teachers in the GDR travel outside the country more than one might imagine. Their travel, however, is largely confined to other Communist and Third World countries. They attend conferences and lecture at universities in the Soviet Union and in Eastern Europe. They also serve as visiting teachers in developing countries. The most popular teaching sites seem to be Angola, Mozambique, and Ethiopia. Several law teachers have spent substantial time in these countries. One Professor, for example, in the fall of 1983, was returning to Ethiopia for the third consecutive year. Another had lived and taught for three years in Mozambique. GDR law teachers have visited Angola regularly, usually teaching for one semester. Professors from other countries in Eastern Europe visit the GDR, and they present lectures from time to time in the law sections. Halle has a special relationship with the University of Ufa in the Ural Mountains, and one of its professors visits the Halle Law Section every year.

Some law teachers do make trips to non-Communist countries. One with whom I talked had recently lectured in Japan on the GDR Criminal Code. Another had attended a conference on procedural law held in West Germany. An international law professor had attended a conference in Manila and had been to the United Nations in New York more than once. However, most GDR law teachers have never been to any part of the Western world.

The life of a law teacher in the GDR universities is—like that of law teachers almost everywhere—taken up with a combination of teaching, research, writing, and talking with and supervising students. The lectures are in the hands of Professors and Docents. However, those persons share the seminar instruction with Assistants and research students. Talking with students and supervising their work is a significant part of the teacher's job. Fourth-year students consult with their teachers in connection with the writing of their required papers. Research students must be supervised and their dissertations reviewed. Although legal research and the publication of scholarly writings form an important part of the work of the GDR law faculties, such activity is not confined to those who teach law in the universities; much of it goes on in the Academy for State and Law and the Academy of Sciences.

Legal research in the university law sections, like almost all other human activity in the GDR, is carried out pursuant to a centrally devised state plan. The research plan for each law section is formulated through the Ministry for Higher Education. Individual law teachers can make suggestions and each law section submits a proposed plan to the Ministry. The Ministry coordinates all proposed research plans and submits them for review to the Central Committee of the SED. When approved there, the plans are officially promulgated and are published in the periodical *Einheit.* Although the plan covers a five-year period, it can be modified from year to year.

A centrally promulgated plan implemented in each law section under the supervision of an associate director provides a setting for research and writing quite different from that in which American law professors function. In an American law school there is almost no direction or supervision over legal research. Each law professor devotes his thoughts and energies to the subjects that appeal to him. He produces articles or books as he wants, although sometimes they are pursuant to an individually arranged contract or in connection with a project of some sort. The administration of an American law school or university, however, has virtually nothing to say about what law professors work on, although there is a measure of influence and control through the scheduling and assignment of courses. Also, research funds can be made available or withheld by the law school and university, and time can be made available through lightened teaching loads or leaves of absence. However, all of these are designed to support the professor in what he wants to do. There are, of course, limits to this, and the arranging of time or money would be influenced to some extent by the relative merits of the proposed research.

A GDR law teacher's position is quite different. He can propose subjects on which he would like to work, and these proposals may be incorporated into the research plan. If such proposals are not in the research plan, the law teacher must find time on his own to work on them. This is more difficult than an American law professor would imagine because a teacher is obliged to devote a portion of his time to implementing the section's research plan. This research is part of his normal work load. Any research outside the plan that a law teacher wishes to undertake must truly be on his own remaining time—at night or on weekends—and one has the impression that there is not much of this left. A general rule of thumb seems to be that a law teacher devotes about 30 percent of his time to research specified by the plan, with the remainder of his regular workday devoted to lecturing, seminar teaching, and talking with students.

Another difficulty confronting a law teacher who wants to do research outside the plan is the limited opportunity for publishing his work. Publications are relatively few, and book publishing is limited by constraints of paper shortages, funding, and demands from many quarters for more publishing outlets. In short, there is insufficient book publishing capacity in the GDR. Thus even if a law teacher does research and writing on his own time, it may be impossible to have his manuscript published.

In large part the research plan aims to have law teachers devote their energies to legal problems that are of practical concern in running the justice system and the economy, all directed toward the further "realization of socialism." In Berlin and in Jena the research plan focuses on problems concerning the courts and the procurators' offices. In Leipzig and Halle research is focused on legal problems in the economics sphere. As the economy has developed and become more sophisticated, legal problems have grown. These problems have arisen from the multitudinous relationships among the many state-owned enterprises. The emergence of combines or conglomerates as new economic organizations has also raised many legal questions. While there are these differences in research efforts because of the specialization of the law sections, the Leipzig and Halle Sections nevertheless do some research on civil and criminal law problems.

A substantial amount of research is carried out by the research students—those young, recent law graduates who are working toward the degree of *Dr. jur.* Other research is conducted by fourth-year students in the course of writing their papers, usually based on their practical work experiences during the summer between the third and fourth years. It is doubtful, however, that many of them make substantial contributions to serious scholarship.

The research and writing efforts of numerous GDR law teachers are devoted to preparation of the officially authorized textbooks. (For the 20 currently in print, see Appendix D.) Each textbook (there is one in every major subject) is written by a team or collective of authors assembled by the Ministry for Higher Education. These authors are experts in the field. Their names are listed at the beginning of the book. The collective is sometimes as small as three or four and sometimes as large as six or eight, with one member selected as leader. He serves as overall editor and directs the writing of the book, assigning chapters for initial drafting among the members of the team. The writing sometimes takes several years. When the manuscript is finally assembled it is reviewed by an editorial committee convened by the Ministry for Higher Education. The manuscript must be defended orally by the authors before that committee, a proceeding that may take several hours or longer. If the editorial committee gives final approval, the book is published through the *Staatsverlag,* one of the official state publishing houses under contract with the Ministry. This process thus produces a comprehensive text covering a field of law—a text that has an authoritative imprimatur. This kind of officially created and approved legal treatise has no counterpart in the Anglo-American legal world.

A major center in the GDR for legal scholarship is the Academy for State and Law. In its present form the Academy came into being in the early 1950s. It evolved out of three earlier enterprises, two of which originated from the need, as perceived in 1945 by the Soviet forces and some of the East Germans themselves, to provide quickly a modicum of legal training for the "man in the street," to fill the void in the legal system caused by the removal of judges and lawyers having Nazi connections or sympathies. A "judges' school" was established for this purpose. A similar need existed to train administrators for the towns and villages, and an "administrative academy" was established for that purpose. In both of these schools, courses lasted only a few weeks or months. A third enterprise set up shortly after the war was an Institute for the Theory of State and Law. All three of these were merged to form the present Academy.

The Academy today is a highly prestigious organization functioning directly under the Council of Ministers. It occupies premises in Babelsberg, a suburb of Potsdam, only a short distance from the western border of West Berlin. If it were not for the sealed border, a person at Humboldt University on Unter den Linden, wanting to go to the Academy for State and Law, could pass through the Brandenburg Gate and drive, with only a few turns, straight through the city to the Academy—a distance of about fifteen miles. As it is, to go to the Academy today, one must make either a three-hour train trip around West Berlin to the opposite side or drive in an automobile for two or three hours. Perhaps in no other setting in the GDR is the inconvenience and physical dislocation of the German division more vividly felt. Nevertheless, numerous persons appear to shuttle frequently back and forth between the Academy and East Berlin.

The Academy has a permanent staff of over two-hundred persons. They are organized into various institutes and sections devoted to international law, administrative and economic law, civil and criminal law, agricultural law, foreign and comparative law, as well as other subjects. Most of the professionals in the Academy are engaged in research and writing for publication in periodicals dealing with legal and economic subjects. In addition, book-length manuscripts are also produced. The Academy itself publishes a major legal periodical, a monthly entitled *Staat und Recht* (State and Law). It contains articles written by members of the Academy staff and also by university law teachers.

In addition to its research functions the Academy continues to run two educational programs. One is designed to train persons to work in the foreign and diplomatic service. This is a four-year program enrolling perhaps one-hundred students annually. Graduates of this program are awarded the *Diplom rer. pol.* They take positions in the Ministry of Foreign Affairs and in the international departments of numerous other state organs and agencies. Most of the GDR diplomats who go abroad have been trained here. The other program, also for four years, trains persons to work as administrators in regional and local governmental agencies. This is essentially a program in public administration and leads to the award of the *Diplom Staatswissenschaft.* Programs of graduate study are also offered by the Academy. Two doctoral degrees can be earned there: *Dr. jur.* and *Dr. rer. pol.*

Another institution, the Academy of Sciences in East Berlin, undertakes legal research through its Institute for the Theory of State and Law. The Academy of Sciences is an old German institution dating back to 1700. It is, of course, now an organization that is committed to the objectives of the SED. The word *science* in the title is misleading to Americans. It is the usual translation from the German word *Wissenschaft.* It is not confined to subjects technical in nature, as Americans tend to think, such as physics, biology, and even the social sciences. Rather, the word refers to any subject of intellectual pursuit, an academic field of study. Thus law is a "science" (*Rechtswissenschaft*) and law professors and legal scholars are "scientists."

The Academy's Institute for the Theory of State and Law, established in the mid-1970s, has approximately twenty-five legal scholars on its staff. Because space at the Institute is limited, these scholars, like university law teachers, work mainly at home or in libraries. They pursue research and writing of a rather theoretical nature on the subjects of state and law. They serve in some of the authors' collectives engaged in writing textbooks and they participate in symposia.

The university law sections themselves do not produce any publications, although their teachers may contribute to general university publications. Each university publishes an academic periodical entitled *Wissenschaftliche Zeitschrift,* and these publications occasionally contain articles by law teachers. Otherwise, writing done by law teachers must be published, if it is published at all, in periodicals that are under other sponsorship or through the state-owned book publishing houses. Of the periodicals in which law teachers and legal scholars publish articles and short pieces, the two having the most general, unspecialized readership are *Neue Justiz* and *Staat und Recht. Neue Justiz* is viewed as a practitioner's publication. *Staat und Recht* is a more scholarly journal. In physical appearance *Staat und Recht* resembles a small-scale American law review. *Neue Justiz* is more like a flimsy magazine.

Neue Justiz appears monthly, and each issue runs to forty or forty-five pages. At the beginning of each issue are several articles dealing with a variety of GDR legal and administrative problems. An examination of the issues published during 1982 and 1983 reveals that there are usually one or more articles on international subjects, such as disarmament or U.N. activities, and on some aspect of Marxist theory relating to law or the state. Each issue also contains several special sections that appear as regular monthly features. One of these special sections is "From Other Socialist Countries." Most of the material here concerns the Soviet legal system, but treatment is also accorded to other Eastern European legal problems and to law in countries such as Mongolia. Another regular feature is "State and Law in Imperialism." Most of the material here is devoted to the FRG and deals with crime, juveniles, tenants, former Nazis, and workers—always in an adverse light. Occasional pieces deal with the United States and "bourgeois" and "capitalist" problems in general. Other special sections that appear almost every month in *Neue Justiz* have the following titles: For Discussion; Reports; Questions and Answers; Jurisdiction in Labor, Family, Civil, and Criminal Matters; Practical Experiences; New Legal Provisions; People's Representative Bodies and Legality; and General Supervision of Legality by the Procurator.

Occasionally *Neue Justiz* prints a topical interview. Three of these were published in 1983. One was with the President of the Supreme Court, Dr. Heinrich Toeplitz, on the India-GDR seminar on problems of law and justice. Another interview was with Sergio Insunza, former Minister of Justice in "anti-fascist Chile." Another published interview was with the Minister of Justice and Procurator General of Afghanistan.

Staat und Recht, published by the Academy in Babelsberg, a more scholarly and theoretical publication, is not read as much by practitioners as is *Neue Justiz*. It is viewed, however, as an important medium for scholarly thinking on fundamental questions about law and government. Its articles, notes, and book reviews are on subjects that Americans would consider to be in the fields of political science, public administration, international relations, and law. Each monthly issue runs from 80 to 100 pages. From time to time an issue is devoted to a special theme. In November 1982 the theme was "On the 65th Anniversary of the Great October Socialist Revolution and on the 60th Anniversary of the Founding of the USSR." In the issues for February and April 1983 the theme was "On the 100th Anniversary of the Death and the 165th Birthday of Karl Marx." The theme of the June 1983 issue was "On the 400th Birthday of Hugo Grotius." The theme of the November 1983 issue was "On the 500th Birthday of Martin Luther." In each of these issues several articles dealt with political or legal aspects of the subject.

Most of the writing in *Staat und Recht* concerns GDR administrative and legal subjects. However, a significant amount of space is devoted to other Eastern European countries, the Soviet Union, and the developing countries of Africa and Asia. The "bourgeois countries" get occasional treatment, especially the FRG and the United States. For example, the November 1983 issue contained an article entitled, "Political, Economic and Legal Aspects of the United States' Attitude in the Sphere of the Transfer of Technology." The December 1983 issue ran a book review entitled, "Ghettos and Prisons—Racism and Human Rights in the USA."

One of the most important of the specialized legal publications is *Wirtschaftsrecht*. It is the principal medium for the publication of research and ideas on law and the economy. *Aussen Wirtschaft* is a weekly publication devoted to economics internationally; several times a year it carries a supplement on law in foreign trade, written in the Academy for State and Law.

In addition to research, writing, and teaching, some law teachers in the top rank of the academic establishment play an important role countrywide in academic law. They do this as members of the Council for Legal Education, an advisory body maintained by the Ministry for Higher Education. This Council is the major link between the Ministry and the four university law sections. It is one of numerous advisory councils authorized by statute for the various academic fields over which the Ministry has jurisdiction. Although statutes limit council membership to thirty-five, the Council for Legal Education is larger. It currently includes thirty law professors from the four law sections (out of a total of approximately sixty-five law professors in the country), several academicians who teach law courses in other institutions, the head of *Staatsverlag* (the publisher of law books), and representatives from the state organs concerned with legal education—the Ministry of Justice, the Office of the Procurator General, and the State Contract Court. The Directors of the four law sections are also Council members. Currently the Chairman is Professor Erich Bucholz, a member of the Humboldt Law Faculty, a former Director of that Section, and a leading GDR authority on criminal law. Members hold office for four years. Apparently members have been reappointed routinely to successive terms, but there is currently a move to reevaluate the participation of each member with a view toward reappointing only those who have actively participated in the three annual Council meetings and intervening committee work. Within the Council there are several working groups, a small executive committee, and committees concerned with subjects such as legal research and the development of law teaching materials. One or two members of the Ministry staff attend each Council meeting.

One of the Council's important tasks is a continuing evaluation and review of the law curriculum, with a view toward proposing revisions in the *Study Plan.* Another important task is identifying areas in which new law textbooks are needed and commissioning groups of authors to develop manuscripts for such textbooks. This process for producing textbooks was described earlier in this chapter.

There is no precise counterpart in the United States of a council such as this. One can imagine an analagous group if a large American state—one having several law schools—were to establish a council of law professors and government officials to advise the state's Department of Education concerning the law curriculum and teaching materials. Such a body, however, would probably be perceived as a threat to the autonomy of the individual law schools of a sort not posed by accrediting agencies such as the American Bar Association and the Association of American Law Schools. In the GDR, of course, there are no such independent accrediting agencies.

Apart from the Council for Legal Education, there is a Council for Research that functions under the aegis of the Academy for State and Law. The role of this Council is not clear, as ultimate authority over the national legal research plan (as one part of the Social Science Research Plan) is vested in the Ministry for Higher Education. There is an overlapping membership in these two councils, as some law professors are members of both. Councils such as these are considered to be part of the country's "democracy," enabling those in the trenches, such as law professors, to be directly involved at the top in formulating the national policy under which they function.

Considering the GDR law teachers' research and published writings, classroom teaching, and work with students, one can say that their professional lives are similar in some respects to those of law teachers in the western world. But there are also marked differences. The departmental organization, the limited office and work space on the university premises, the officially fixed nature of the curriculum, and the Marxist-Leninist underpinnings from which there can be no deviation combine to create an atmosphere unlike that in American law schools.

It is difficult, however, to disentangle characteristics that are traditionally German or European from those that are unique to the GDR. For example, it is characteristic of German universities and European styles in general that there are more formalities and rigidities than in the United States. In Europe one does not simply pop unannounced into a professor's office, expecting to find him there available for a chat, in the way that one would do along the corridors of an American law school. That is equally true in the GDR. University legal education in Europe tends to be more authoritative in character than it is in the Anglo-American world, and the GDR lectures and seminars are not different in that respect. Moreover, in European universities generally one also finds GDR-type departmental structures and sometimes lack of adequate individual working space. All German universities have for a very long time been under government control in a way that would be novel to Americans. That tradition continues in West Germany today, in that universities are publicly operated and financed and every professor is appointed by a government ministry, based on faculty recommendations. In those respects they are no different from the GDR universities. Thus, in the end, the feature that sets the GDR law faculties apart from those in Europe, and the Western world generally, is the Marxist-Leninist ideology that permeates the officially prescribed curriculum and all teaching and writing, giving a strongly political orientation to the educational enterprise in the GDR.

6
Law Students

As has already been made clear, in the GDR all higher education is directed toward a specific purpose under an overall national plan. The purpose of legal education is to train the appropriate number of persons to man the legal machinery of the country—persons schooled in the doctrines of Marxism-Leninism. The system is also designed to produce persons who are loyally committed to existing authority and who will actively advance the development of socialism. We look now at the procedures for admitting students to law study, some aspects of law student life in the universities, and the placement of students at the conclusion of their legal studies.

The admissions process is one of the few areas of legal education that is not centrally controlled. Each university runs its own admissions process and makes its own admissions decisions. The universities are bound, however, by central directives specifying the number of full-time law students to be admitted at each university annually. As earlier stated, currently these numbers are: Berlin, 170; Leipzig, 100; Halle, 100; and Jena, 60. The figures fixed in the country's five-year plan are arrived at through an analysis of the projected number of persons needed to staff the various aspects of the legal system and law-related activities. The aim is to produce yearly the amount of manpower needed for this purpose—but no more than is needed—in relation to all other manpower requirements of the country. In determining these numbers the Ministry for Higher Education receives information and advice from the law sections' "practice partners," mentioned previously: for Berlin, the Ministry of Justice; for Jena, the Procurator General; and for Leipzig and Halle, the State Contract Court. A comparison of the number of places allocated for law study in the universities, in relation to other fields of higher education, is shown in table 7 (at the end of this chapter).

Under the decentralized admissions system, the application is sent directly to the university law section of the student's choice. The application is not sent by the student himself but by his school, his employer, or the military service, depending on where he is at the time of applying. A committee in each law section receives the applications, reviews and evaluates them, and decides which should be accepted. The committee's action is only a recommendation to the central university administration where the final decision is made; however, the committee's recommendations seem to be followed in almost all cases. In striking contrast to American practice, multiple concurrent applications to different law sections are not permitted. Although a student may apply to only one law section each year, if he is denied admission there, he may then apply to another law section in the following year.

The admissions committee in each law section consists of the Associate Director for Education and Training, one or more faculty members in the section, a member of the Free German Youth already enrolled for the study of law and a representative from the section's practice partner. Estimates are that each year approximately twice as many applications are received as there are places available for the study of law. Thus the committee has the task of selecting for admission approximately one out of every two applicants.

The basic requisite for admission is possession of the *Abitur*. To earn this educational certificate a student must complete twelve years of schooling—two years more than the ten years required for all children. This advanced schooling bears some resemblance to that afforded by the *Gymnasium*, a type of academic institution that long existed in Germany before the Second World War. The name has been dropped, but the general concept of a superior academic program to qualify students for university study is retained. It is possible for a person to obtain an *Abitur* through part-time study and extension courses, a program designed to take care of members of "the working class" who took jobs in industry before completing the necessary additional schooling. Inasmuch as law is an undergraduate discipline—as it is in Europe generally—no university or college prelaw courses are required; the *Abitur* is the only academic prerequisite.

The only other specific prerequisite for admission to law study is the work requirement. As mentioned previously, emphasis is placed on combining the academic and the practical in all GDR education, and this admission requirement reflects that emphasis. The theory is that persons destined for careers in the legal system need to understand the people with whom and for whom they will be working in later life. The work requirement, however, varies among law sections and disciplines. In the Leipzig Law Section there appears to be no preadmission work requirement, while in Berlin, there is a strict rule that every person, man or woman, must work for two years after the *Abitur* before being admitted to law study. For men, this requirement can be satisfied by military service which, in any event, is compulsory. Every male is inducted into the armed services at the age of 18 for a period of 18 months. Women may join certain branches of the armed forces, but service is not compulsory. Women may satisfy the work requirement by taking jobs in trades and industry. In Halle, at least for women, there appears to be no work requirement; many of them enter the university immediately after receiving the *Abitur*. Where the preadmission work requirement is enforced, most students are approximately twenty years old when they enter the universities; otherwise, they enroll at age eighteen.

The application process may begin while a student is still in school, before he has received the *Abitur*. Students considering the study of law are encouraged to talk with persons in the legal system, such as a judge on the county court in the student's home area, a Justice Ministry official, or a law teacher. Such conversations can assist the student in understanding the legal system and in deciding whether to pursue a legal career. They also provide a basis on which the official can evaluate the student and advise the admissions committee.

An admissions committee's explanation concerning its criteria for admission sounds superficially like the explanation one would get from an admissions committee in an American law school. It is said, for example, that the most important factor of all is the quality of the student's performance in school, that is, in the academic work leading to the *Abitur*. No special admissions test is administered to applicants. The committee considers evaluations and recommendations submitted to it by teachers in the schools, by supervisors in factories where applicants have worked, by military personnel, and by others who have been associated with the applicants. Evidence of character and personality is important. However, these traits are not looked at in the way that an American law school admissions committee would likely look at them. What seems to be important is the student's commitment to the system. It seems doubtful that a political maverick would be admitted. Here the student member of the Free German Youth who sits on the admissions committee probably plays an important role. It is plausible to believe that he would be interested in evaluating the applicant's activity—or lack of it—in relation to the FDJ and the development of socialism and collective life. A working-class background is said to be less important today than it was some years ago; in theory such a background confers an important advantage on the applicant, but in practice class lines are becoming more difficult to draw.

Once admitted, a student is supported entirely by the state, the purpose being to make it possible for the children of workers' and farmers' families to attend a university. Every student receives at least 200 marks per month. Out of this the student is expected to pay all his expenses. Lodging in university student housing costs approximately 10 marks per month. Meals in student dining halls are quite inexpensive. No tuition is charged. Apparently 200 marks per month is considered by the authorities to be adequate to cover lodging, food, clothing, books, and incidentals. However, many students appear to receive additional money from home. One section director said that he does not know any law student who thinks that the monthly stipend is sufficient. Supplemental monthly stipends are awarded on the basis of superior academic performance. There are three gradations of additional monthly payments: 40 marks, 100 marks, and 140 marks. The highest payments of all go to those few students designated as Karl Marx Scholars; they get a total of 500 marks per month.

This state-provided financial support explains in part why many law students marry before graduation. In Humboldt it is estimated that more than half of the law students are married by the end of the second year. In Halle it is estimated that 80 percent of the law students are married by the time of graduation. Another explanation for a high percentage of student marriages is the assurance of employment after graduation.

Women currently comprise about 50 percent of the law students in the country. This is lower than it was some years ago, when it was above 60 percent. The proportion of women varies considerably among the law sections. In Berlin it is approximately 35 percent (down from 60 percent a few years ago). At Jena there is a similar downward trend in female enrollment. In Halle, however, women comprise approximately 60 percent of the enrollment, although they accounted for 80 percent of the law students there a few years ago.

University student housing typically consists of high-rise concrete apartment buildings of the sort erected throughout the GDR since the Second World War. These buildings are often grouped in clusters, some distance from the academic buildings. Students usually travel by trolley or bus to lectures, seminars, and libraries.

The only student organization in each university is the Free German Youth (FDJ). As pointed out earlier, this is a countrywide organization for persons from fourteen to twenty-five years of age; it is not limited to students. Like all organizations, it is under the control of the SED. Each university has a local unit or chapter. Probably over 90 percent of all GDR law students belong to the FDJ while they are in the universities. In Leipzig, membership is reported to be 100 percent. Within each university the organization has subunits, sometimes organized on the basis of the seminar groups within the law sections. These small subgroups hold meetings and discussions.

One of the responsibilities of the FDJ is to carry out a function considered crucial in all aspects of life in the GDR, namely, to educate persons politically—meaning to reinforce adherence to Marxist-Leninist tenets and the political positions of the SED. As to international matters, the education is designed to convey and reinforce the positions taken by the USSR and the GDR, which have always been the same. The FDJ also provides some social life for students, and social activities may provide a major incentive for students to maintain membership in the organization. Its importance in the university was symbolized during the weeks before the national holiday, on October 7, by the presence of a huge blue banner bearing the letters "FDJ" hanging alongside GDR and red banners on the front of the main Humboldt University building. The FDJ's special role in legal education is manifested in at least the three ways previously mentioned: an FDJ member sits on the admissions committee of the law section, an FDJ member sits on the council of the section, and an FDJ member can be present during the oral examination of any student and can comment on the examination to the teachers. More than one law teacher said that no important decisions are made in the administration of a law section without the involvement of FDJ representatives.

Another feature of GDR university life is the university newspaper. Each institution publishes a newspaper every week or two. The law sections themselves have no newspaper or other publications. The newspaper in each university has a similar format and content. A subheadline on the top of the front page states that the paper is an organ of the SED. The extent to which students write for these papers is not clear. In general appearance these newspapers superficially resemble American college papers. The tone, however, seems much more political and propagandistic. Each issue contains articles about assorted SED party activities within the university. The party secretary and the FDJ officers write regular columns. The themes of "peace" and of socialism as its main protector are pervasive. Articles frequently criticize "imperialism" and Western policies. Pieces about student activities often include articles about military training and summer work projects with students from other communist countries. There are exhortations to achievement and productivity. Members of the teaching staff are often the subjects of special features, usually lauding them as "communist fighters." Amidst these politically oriented encomiums and exhortations there are some factual news items concerning work in the various sections, such as experiments in physics, biology, agriculture, and medicine. Almost every issue carries items concerning the works of Marx, Engels, and Lenin. There are frequent references to friendship with the USSR and other communist countries.

In addition to the newspaper, an important source of information for students in each law section is the bulletin board in the corridor along the section offices. Here are posted the weekly lecture and seminar schedules as well as items of general information. In Halle, in the fall of 1983, the bulletin board included a section publicizing trips to the Soviet Union. At Humboldt, as pointed out earlier, law professors' anti-NATO statements were posted. The SED and the FDJ have special sections of the board for their notices.

The academic year is organized into two semesters much like that in American universities. Each semester lasts for approximately fifteen weeks. Students arrive and lectures and seminars begin for the fall semester in mid-September. There is a two-week Christmas recess and a four-week break between semesters. The second semester begins in late February and ends in

July. However, there are several variations and interruptions in this normal pattern.

During the first year of law study in Berlin all students in the class suspend academic work entirely for a two-week period in the fall. During that time they perform janitorial services throughout the main university buildings. The university employs no janitorial staff, relying instead on its students for this service. Each academic section takes its turn at performing janitorial duties, with this responsibility rotating from section to section throughout the year. The law section assigns this chore to the first-year students for this two-week period in the fall. This is the only time during the four years of law study that the law students must serve as janitors. They sweep floors, empty trash cans, and clean restrooms during these two weeks. Another interruption in the normal academic year, already mentioned, is the civil defense training. This takes all second-year students away from the university and into training camps for one month.

Another assignment away from the university is the four-week practical training at the end of the second year. Although the *Study Plan* specifies four weeks for this training, in some of the law sections it is said to be six weeks. During this time students take jobs in local government organs throughout the GDR. At the end of the third year, the law students are again assigned to jobs in various parts of the country, this time for twelve weeks; these work assignments are in the places where the students are destined to be employed upon graduation a year later.

Because of this latter arrangement, the placement process begins during the spring of the third year. In each law section the process is keyed to the sectors of the legal systems for which that section is training its students. Each section works with its practice partner in placing its third-year students in training positions, and every student is in fact placed somewhere. As will be discussed more fully later, in Berlin all placement activity is tied to the Ministry of Justice, under whose aegis come the personnel of the courts, the notaries, and the practicing lawyers; in Jena all placement activity is tied to the Office of the Procurator General; in Leipzig and Halle placement activity is linked with the State Contract Court, the agency that resolves legal disputes among state-owned enterprises.

Every student admitted to university law study knows that upon graduation he or she will have a position within the field for which the particular law section supplies graduates, although the student does not know precisely what or where the position will be. The nearest analogy that comes to mind in the United States is in the service academies of the armed forces. When a person is admitted at West Point, for example, he is guaranteed employment in the army upon graduation. However, he does not know until graduation nears the branch of service or the location to which he will be assigned. The assignment is determined by the authorities considering the individual's preferences and the needs of the service. And so it is in the GDR law sections.

The placement process in each law section is handled through a committee of its teachers which works closely with the section's practice partner. The nature and location of vacancies are made known by the practice partner to the law section committee. This information is posted or otherwise communicated to the students. The process thereafter involves a mixture of discussion and negotiation between the student and the committee. A student in Berlin, for example, may say that he wants to go to work in the courts with a view toward becoming a judge. He would like to live and work in Dresden. However, there is no vacancy on the court there; there are court vacancies in Cottbus and Rostock, and a position for a lawyer in Dresden. The student must then decide which is more important—the line of work or the location. This process is not unlike that undergone by many American law students in considering opportunities as graduation nears. However, in the GDR the available opportunities are much more structured and limited.

As part of their training for later work in educating the public in reinforcement of the political system, law students are expected to participate actively during their student days in informing citizens about the law. These efforts are promoted and directed by the FDJ. Such public educational activities include working with youth groups and speaking to workers in collectives and enterprises.

Available data are confusing as to the exact number of full-time law students in the GDR. Under the admissions quotas set by the Ministry for Higher Education, the four law sections should be accepting a total of 430 applicants annually. If there were no attrition at all, this should mean that the total full-time university law enrollment in the GDR is 1,720 annually. However, according to *The Statistical Yearbook,* in 1981 there were 2,061 full-time law students in the universities. This is 341 more than the admissions figures suggest, and there is no apparent explanation for the discrepancy. *The Statistical Yearbook* also shows 1,312 part-time students studying law in the universities in 1981. This makes a total of 3,373 law students in the GDR for the year.

As these figures show, part-time students account for more than one third of all GDR law students. All part-time law study is administered under the Law Section in Humboldt, although all four university law sections participate in providing instruction for these students. This five-year program is designed to make legal education available to persons working in industry whose employers approve such study and make arrangements for it. The study plan specifies the details of this curriculum, as it does for the full-time program. Although the part-time program is not examined here, the subject matter of the two is essentially the same.

The allocation of the country's manpower to the legal systems, as compared to all other fields of professional and technical work, is revealed by table 7, which shows the number of students in 1981 enrolled in all disciplines in the universities and higher technical schools.

It is not clear whether the figures on law enrollment include foreign students. These students are selected and sent by their

TABLE 7. ENROLLMENT BY FIELDS IN GDR UNIVERSITIES AND HIGHER TECHNICAL INSTITUTIONS

Technical sciences	38,865
Teacher training	27,007
Economic sciences	17,707
Medicine	13,577
Mathematics/Natural Science	8,145
Agricultural sciences	8,117
Philosophy, History and Political Science	5,171
Law	3,373
Arts	3,056
Sports Education	2,874
Literature and Language	2,271
Theology	453
Total	130,616

governments. Not all of them remain enrolled for the entire four-year program, although some do. In any event, these enrollment figures suggest that in popularity and importance, law in the GDR ranks relatively low, a position quite different from that which it occupies in the United States and other western countries. It is noteworthy, for example, that enrollment in medicine is nearly four times greater than in law, and that law enrollment is barely larger than that in "arts."

A new five-year plan will be promulgated in 1986 and it will fix the size of the annual entering class for each law section for the ensuing five years. By 1994 it is anticipated that the number of university-age persons in the GDR will have decreased by one third. However, in discussions about the new five-year plan, there seems to be no disposition (although the idea is under consideration) to decrease the number of entering law students. This suggests that there is a perceived need for a relative increase in the legal manpower of the country.

As is evident from earlier discussion, university law study has an intensely practical objective—to prepare students for work in the various aspects of the country's legal systems. The organs and activities that make up these systems are described in the following chapters, along with the placement and career patterns of law graduates in each field.

Part 3

Legal Systems and Legal Careers

7
The State Courts and Judicial Careers

Service as a judge on the GDR state courts is a professional career similar in some respects to judicial careers in Western Europe. Persons who currently become judges in the GDR are all graduates of the Law Section in Humboldt University. This chapter describes the state court system and the process of selecting and promoting judges. It should be borne in mind that these are the courts involved in "the administration of justice," and that they constitute one of two court systems; the other, called the State Contract Court, is concerned with "economic law" and will be described in a later chapter.

The three-tiered GDR court system resembles an American state court system more than it resembles the German judiciary of old or the judiciary in the FRG today. The present judicial structure was created in 1952. The objective of the reorganization was to simplify the system and to conform it to the new governmental organization under which the country had been divided into fourteen administrative-territorial regions, plus the city of East Berlin. The GDR has abandoned the multiple "jurisdictions" (there are five in West Germany, each with its own Supreme Court) and the old four-tiered German structure. It has established in their place a single system, having three levels (apart from the State Contract Court). Table 8 shows the traditional German four-tiered system in the "ordinary jurisdiction" of the FRG (one of its five jurisdictions) and the three-tiered system in the GDR.

In the GDR the district court (*Kreisgericht*) combines functions performed by the two trial courts under the old system (*Amtsgericht* and *Landgericht*). The county court (*Bezirksgericht*) has the appellate functions performed by the *Oberlandesgericht* as well as some of the trial jurisdiction exercised by the *Landgericht*. In other words, there is no perfect match between the old and the new; the system has simply been redesigned and streamlined into three tiers instead of four. A common feature, however,

TABLE 8. FRG AND GDR COURT STRUCTURES

FRG	GDR
Bundesgerichtshof (Federal Supreme Court)	Oberstesgericht (Supreme Court)
Oberlandesgericht (19 regional appellate courts)	Bezirksgericht (15 county courts)
Landgericht (93 courts)	Kreisgericht (234 district courts)
Amtsgericht (557 courts)	

is that the courts in the middle tiers of both systems have mixed appellate and trial functions.

Like the traditional German court system, the GDR courts have exclusive jurisdiction over all criminal cases. However, in civil litigation the jurisdiction of the GDR courts is different from that found traditionally in the "ordinary" German jurisdiction. The GDR jurisdiction is narrower in that all legal disputes among the state-owned enterprises have been placed in a separate set of tribunals known as the State Contract Court. The Civil Code of the GDR does not embrace those matters. That Code has also been narrowed by removing provisions thought inappropriate for a society in which the means of production are all publicly owned, personal autonomy is deemphasized, and collective activity stressed. In addition to jurisdiction under the Criminal Code, and the narrowed Civil Code, the GDR courts also have jurisdiction over family and labor cases, each of which is the subject of a separate code.

In at least three respects the GDR courts have carried forward features of the traditional German judiciary. First, the GDR courts, at least at the appellate levels, are organized internally on a subject-matter basis. That is, judges are assigned to work on specified types of cases or groups of cases and not the whole docket indiscriminately, as is the custom in many American courts. Second, the system uses lay judges in combination with professional judges. Third, the professional judges enter judicial office at an early stage after completion of university law study and an apprentice period, and make a lifelong career in the judiciary. These features of the system will be described more fully hereafter.

There are 234 district courts forming the first tier of the system, although the number of districts totals 252. Apparently in some places the districts are combined for purposes of court administration. These are courts of original trial jurisdiction. Although they hear appeals from the Social Courts (lay forums which form a sub-tier to the district courts, explained in chapter 8), such cases are dealt with essentially as de novo proceedings. The district courts also hear appeals from notaries (officials explained in chapter 9). On each of these 234 district courts there are typically two to four professional judges, although in some of the larger districts there are more. They are organized into "chambers," or divisions. Lay judges sit with a professional judge in every case, as will be explained in the next chapter. The territorial dimensions of each district vary considerably. Large cities contain two or more districts. In a rural setting, a district may embrace a wide expanse of territory, including numerous towns and villages.

The district courts are organized under the jurisdiction of the county court in each of the fourteen counties and the city of East Berlin. Table 9 shows the number of district courts in each county and the total number of district judges in the county.

The procedure in the district courts resembles in some respects traditional German legal procedure, as well as Continental procedure generally. There are differences, however. The GDR judge is said to have much more responsibility than the traditional German judge to develop the "objective truth" in the case. He is to exercise an affirmative role in developing the evidence; he is not to rely solely on facts presented by the opposing parties or by the lawyers. This, of course, has long been characteristic of Continental legal procedure in general as distinguished from the Anglo-American adversary style. The real difference may be that a major objective of a GDR court proceeding is the education of the parties and the public; the objective is not merely to settle a particular dispute. The judge is to be unbiased, they say, as between the parties to the particular case, but he is not to be disinterested in the result. He is to be partial in the sense that he must see that a "right result" is reached, a result based on "objective truth" that will serve the ends of the socialist state in accordance with socialist principles. One observer has said that whereas the Anglo-American

TABLE 9. GDR DISTRICT COURTS AND JUDGES

County	District Courts	District Judges
Berlin	9	100
Cottbus	15	48
Dresden	20	92
Erfurt	16	60
Frankfurt/O.	11	44
Gera	13	37
Halle	23	106
Karl-Marx-Stadt	25	97
Leipzig	19	80
Magdeburg	23	74
Neubrandenburg	14	37
Potsdam	16	71
Rostock	11	52
Schwerin	11	38
Suhl	8	29
Total	234	965

symbol of justice is a blindfolded woman holding a pair of scales, the Marxist-Leninist symbol of justice would be an unblindfolded woman holding no scales, with eyes wide open and arm outstretched pointing the way toward further socialist development.[1]

How all of this translates into actual decisions is not clear. In most of the run-of-the-mill civil and criminal cases the proceedings would probably not vary radically from those in Western European courts. But the ever-present concern with insuring that Marxist-Leninist principles are observed raises the possibility of a judge's assuming an affirmative and ideological role that American lawyers would find inconsistent with their view of the judge as a neutral decider of controversies under law. The mission of courts and law to help achieve social control may also restrict possibilities for American-style settlements negotiated between the parties.

Another procedure novel to Americans is that of allowing persons and groups who are not parties to the case to participate in the litigation. This procedure was also unknown in former German practice. Although such appearances can occur in civil

[1]Inga Markovits, "Socialist vs. Bourgeois Rights—An East-West German Comparison," 45 U. Chi. L. Rev. 612, 626 (1978).

cases, they most often occur in criminal cases. Typically such groups come from the defendant's place of work or neighborhood. They may appear in support of the prosecution or in support of the defendant. For example, in a case in which a woman is charged with stealing money, her co-workers may appear as "social defenders" to tell the court that she has long been a good worker in the plant (or has long supported the Party or done other good works) and that she has recently fallen on hard times—for example, her husband has left her, her children have been sick, and so on. They can urge that she not be sent to prison. On the other hand, groups like this can appear in support of the prosecution to say just the opposite, that the defendant has been a bad man, that he has not cooperated in the development of socialism, that he has not supported his family, and so on. Some information of this sort might be offered in an American court at the sentencing stage by way of a sentencing report. But in the GDR it is believed that the most effective way to present matters of this sort is by the direct statements of persons with first-hand information, or at least with strongly held views about the defendant. Moreover, the participation of such groups in the judicial proceeding furthers the educational objective of heightening the collective consciousness about proper social behavior.

The number of criminal cases in which such third parties appear is substantial, running to over 40,000 annually. The 1981 *Statistical Yearbook* divides these persons into three categories and shows the percentage of criminal cases in which they appeared: representatives of social collectives, 74.9 percent; social complainants, 11.8 percent; social defenders, 2.8 percent.

There is said to be a principle that a criminal case should be concluded by a district court within four weeks after presentation of indictment, and an appeal should be disposed of by a county court within another four weeks. If a case is not concluded within this time, the court must state in writing the reason for the delay.

Family law cases occupy a considerable portion of the district courts' time. Divorce forms the bulk of this business. The GDR divorce rate is among the highest in the world. A two-stage procedure is employed in these cases. In the first stage, the court holds a hearing to attempt to determine whether the marriage can be salvaged. If the judges conclude that the couple can be reconciled, the proceeding is suspended for a year, during which the couple's reconciliation is assisted by a district agency that includes psychologists on its staff. When reconciliation is not feasible, the second stage of the litigation ensues. This involves an additional hearing at a later date to resolve questions about division of property, custody of children, and the maintenance to be paid. As the country has grown gradually more affluent, married couples have more property and money to be divided, and these questions now occur more often and are more difficult.

The civil cases coming before the district courts generally involve disputes arising out of the purchase and sale of goods, disputes between occupants of housing and the housing management, questions of inheritance, and, occasionally, questions arising out of automobile mishaps. Most of the latter disputes are resolved through the state-run insurance scheme and do not get to court. It is estimated that normally three-quarters of all civil cases are concluded by the district courts within three months. Ten to 15 percent require six months and the remainder even longer. About 10 percent of the civil cases are appealed, and this process usually consumes another six months.

The labor cases usually involve disputes between a worker and the enterprise for which he works, concerning such matters as pay, bonuses, and the legality of a discharge from employment. These cases, however, are within the exclusive first instance jurisdiction of the social courts and come to the district courts only be way of appeal (as explained in chapter 8).

Precise judicial statistics in the GDR are difficult to obtain. There is little doubt that statistics are kept concerning the volume and type of cases as well as other features of the judicial system. But they are published only in part and in a generalized and unrevealing form. The figures shown below concerning the business of these 234 district courts have been gleaned from *The Statistical Yearbook* for 1981. These statistics treat civil and family cases as "Applications for Commencement." Labor cases, however, are shown as "filed." The following figures must be read with that in mind: Civil, 48,119; Family, 87,781; Labor, 12,677; these total 148,577.

The statistics do not show the number of criminal prosecutions commenced; they show only the number of criminal defendants convicted. This figure is 71,288. Estimates are that pleas of guilty are entered in about 85 percent of the criminal convictions. The statistics do not show how many defendants, if any, were tried jointly in one proceeding; moreover the number of persons acquitted is not shown. However, the figure given can be taken to be at least a rough approximation of the number of criminal cases annually in the district courts. One lawyer estimated that 7 to 10 percent of all criminal prosecutions could be described as "political" and that of these about half involve charges of attempting to leave the country illegally. He also estimated that probation is given in about 90 percent of all criminal cases. Combining the criminal cases with the noncriminal cases shown above produces a total annual caseload of 219,865 for the 234 district courts during the year 1981.

The volume of district court criminal business should have been decreasing in recent times as the result of a move to decriminalize certain petty offenses. Such offenses have been channeled into an administrative process where fines can be imposed. Normally those fines are limited to 50 marks, but in some cases they can go up to 500 marks and in extraordinary instances up to 1,000 marks.

All judgments entered in these district courts can be appealed to the next higher court, the county court. It is estimated that fewer than 10 percent of all district court decisions are appealed. From an American perspective, this county court resembles an intermediate appellate court in a three-tiered judicial system. It may review and either affirm, reverse, or remand any decisions made by the trial courts within its county. At the same time, this court also has some original jurisdiction. Prosecution of some of the more serious crimes must be commenced in the county court; these include treason and crimes against peace and humanity. The procurator has authority to bring any criminal case to the county court for trial; such action would normally be taken where the crime is considered serious or sensitive (estimates are that 5 percent of all offenders in the GDR receive prison terms of two years or more, a rough measurement of the seriousness of an offense). Also, noncriminal cases initiated in the district courts can be transferred to the county courts by the procurator's office or the county court itself. This noncriminal trial business is not heavy. For example, in one recent year the Halle county court had no first-instance civil, family, or labor cases.

One of these middle tier courts is located in each of the counties—the fifteen major administrative regions (including East Berlin). The court is located in the city that is the seat of the county administration, the city whose name the county bears. The court goes by the name of its county. For example, the county court sitting in Magdeburg would be called the *Bezirksgericht Magdeburg.* In Berlin, however, this court is called the *Stadtgericht.*

One characteristic of the county courts shared with German appellate courts throughout history is the large number of judges on each (large at least in comparison with American appellate courts). The county court in Halle, for example, has thirty judges. The court in Berlin has upward of forty. Legal chaos is avoided, however, by the organization of each of these courts into several divisions, with judicial business assigned to the various divisions by categories or subject matter of the cases. This is the traditional German style of appellate subject-matter organization, and it is continued also today in the FRG.

In the GDR this internal organization is based on the four codes that define the courts' business—Criminal, Civil, Family, and Labor. The number of divisions in each court varies. In the county court in Halle, for example, there are four criminal divisions, one civil division, one family division, and one labor division. The court in Berlin, with a slightly larger number of judges, has three criminal divisions (one of which sits in the first instance), one division for civil cases, one for family cases, and one for labor cases. Each division is headed by a senior judge designated as chairman. The Leipzig county court is unique among the GDR county courts in that it has exclusive, first-instance jurisdiction over all patent, copyright, and trademark cases, thus continuing the long-standing German tradition, still found also in the FRG, of concentrating litigation on these subjects in a single trial forum.

A division hearing appeals in criminal, civil, and family cases always consists of three professional judges. Labor appeals are heard by a division consisting of one professional judge and two lay judges. Normally, lay judges are used only in the first instance; but in labor appeals, lay judges are thought necessary because matters concerning work and employment are closely tied to the interests of the people and the working class. Lay judges are used in the county courts in one other situation, namely, when those courts sit in first instance. Because first-instance cases and labor appeals constitute a minority of the docket, most of the county courts' work is done through panels of three professional judges.

Here again precise statistics about the volume of court business are difficult to obtain. But oral estimates given by judges on two county courts indicate the size of their annual dockets. These estimates for the county court in Halle for appeals coming up from the district courts are as follows: 200–250 criminal; 350–400 civil; 500 family; 100 labor. For the court in Berlin the estimate for appeals annually is as follows: 800 criminal; 1,200 civil; 1,200 family; 280 labor. Thus the total annual appellate caseload is approximately 3,480 in Berlin. The rate of appeal in criminal cases varies from one place to another. In Halle it is estimated to be 10 percent of the district court convictions, while in Berlin the estimate is 30 percent. Criminal cases tried in the first instance in the county court are estimated to be approximately 40 annually in Halle and fewer than 100 annually in Berlin.

The county courts have developed internal procedures for the handling of criminal appeals—procedures that resemble those adopted by some American appellate courts. These procedures are designed to facilitate disposing of large volumes of criminal cases in circumstances where a sizeable percentage present no issues of substantial merit. The judges undertake a preliminary screening of the cases on the basis of the papers filed with the appellate court. After reviewing these papers, including such record of the trial court proceedings as is kept, the three judges on the appeals court may dispose of the case without an oral hearing, if they believe that the proper result is clear. Estimates are that in Halle approximately 35 percent to 40 percent of criminal appeals are disposed of in this fashion. In the other cases the court holds an oral hearing.

Like the English Court of Appeal and the appellate courts in West Germany, the GDR county courts have authority to take additional evidence on appeal. This authority apparently is exercised sparingly and only if there is a special reason for receiving evidence not offered in the lower court. In theory, these courts, like the district courts, should pursue objective truth and are entitled to go beyond points made by the parties and their counsel. Thus a criminal appeal may be decided on a ground not mentioned at all by the defendant, and evidence may be called for and received even though not tendered by the parties. GDR law allows the defendant himself to appear at the hearing. In the main, however, the cases are decided on the basis of the record made in the lower court proceedings.

Each of the fifteen county courts is headed by a director, who is the presiding judge of the court. There are two deputy directors. One of these typically is responsible for all criminal matters, and the other is responsible for all other cases (civil, family, labor). The deputy directors and the chairmen of the divisions are appointed by the Minister of Justice from among the judges on the court; the director is elected by the county assembly. Each court has a *Presidium* consisting of the director, the two deputy directors, and the chairmen of the divisions. This body sets rules and regulations for the court, and it can issue policy directives to govern the district courts under its jurisdiction. The county court, acting through its *Presidium,* is responsible for the administration of justice in all district courts throughout the county.

The *Presidium* acts as an advisory body to the director of the court concerning its internal organization. However, the director has final authority in assigning judges and cases to the various divisions. These assignments are embodied in a written document called the "work distribution plan." Every appellate court in West Germany also has a plan of this type, which is printed annually and made available to lawyers and the public. In the GDR, however, this document is apparently considered confidential and is not made available. One can assume, however, that lawyers and other persons knowledgeable about the court's business learn from practice which judges sit on what divisions and what categories of cases are assigned to each division.

Above these fifteen county courts, at the apex of the judicial pyramid in the GDR, is the Supreme Court (*Oberstes Gericht*). This court currently consists of forty-seven judges. It is headed by a president, who is roughly analogous to an American state chief justice. He is not only the head of the Supreme Court, but he is also the head of the entire GDR state court system. Under him there are two vice presidents.

The President of the Supreme Court is currently Dr. Heinrich Toeplitz. The son of a lawyer, he was born in Berlin in 1914 and studied law in the universities at Leipzig and Breslau during the 1930s. He is one of a very few GDR judges (possibly the only one) still in active service who studied law before the Second World War. His activities for several years, beginning in the late 1930s, are not publicly explained, but he apparently left Germany and was confined in a work camp in France and Holland during the last year of the war. He returned to legal work in Berlin and became a member of the Christian Democratic Union (CDU). In 1950 he was appointed state secretary in the GDR Ministry of Justice and served in that position until he became President of the Supreme Court in 1960. While in the Ministry of Justice, Toeplitz was responsible for the 1952 reorganization of the court system. For many years he has been President of the Lawyers' Association. He is clearly the leading figure in the GDR legal order.

The Supreme Court is housed in East Berlin in a large, multistoried building stretching along Littenstrasse, a block south of Alexanderplatz. The building was constructed in the early twentieth century to house the civil divisions of the old *Landgericht*—then the major trial court for the entire city of Berlin. (The criminal divisions of that court were located in what is now West Berlin.) The building has several entrances and houses other entities, including two of the East Berlin trial courts, the Lawyers' Association, and the procurator for East Berlin. The entrance lobby is flanked by curving stairways rising several stories—an architectural feature not uncommon in German court buildings of that era. Locating the GDR Supreme Court at the seat of government marks a break with German tradition. As mentioned earlier, the Imperial Supreme Court established for the Reich after 1871 was located at Leipzig. In the FRG the Constitutional Court and the Supreme Court for the ordinary jurisdiction are at Karlsruhe, not Bonn. It is not difficult to understand why the GDR authorities would find unappealing the symbolism in such a separation. To pretend that the judiciary somehow is independent of the will of the ruling class, they say, is to hide reality. Moreover, having one top state organ at such a distance from all other top state organs might have been seen as inconsistent with the concept of centralism. Thus, although the old *Reichsgericht* building in Leipzig survived the war and could have been magnificently adapted to house the GDR's Supreme Court, the authorities chose instead to place the court in the less impressive quarters of the old *Landgericht* in the heart of East Berlin, only a few blocks from the highest state and party organs.

Like the fifteen county courts below it, and like all German appellate courts traditionally, the Supreme Court is organized into numerous divisions, among which cases are assigned on a subject-matter basis. These divisions are grouped under three departments. One department embraces all criminal cases;

another has civil, family, and labor cases; the third is limited to military cases. (The lower military courts function under regulations issued by the National Defense Council and are not part of the state court system, although their decisions are reviewable in the Supreme Court's military department, whose judges are military officers trained in the law.) In the criminal department the dockets of the divisions are based on the groupings of substantive offenses in the Criminal Code.

In GDR court organization there is a principle that no case should go through more than "two instances." Thus, if a case originates in a district court, it will go on appeal to the county court, and that review will conclude the matter. On the other hand, if the case originates in a county court, it will then go on appeal to the Supreme Court. The Supreme Court's direct appellate jurisdiction, in other words, is limited to reviewing decisions in those cases that are decided in the first instance in the county courts.

In addition to this direct appellate jurisdiction the Supreme Court has authority to review lower court judgments by cassation. The cassation procedure was introduced in the GDR after 1949. It is viewed there as a salutary innovation in German practice and as the Supreme Court's most important work. Under this procedure the Supreme Court is vested with authority to review and quash the judgment of any court in the country within one year after its rendition.

No person has a "right" to cassation. The only way a case can come before the Supreme Court through this procedure is by application of either the President of the Court or of the Procurator General. Thus the first step toward getting review of a case on cassation is to persuade one of these two officials to petition the Court. Even then, apparently, the Court may not grant the petition. However, one suspects that if one of these two officials does petition for cassation, the Court is likely to review the matter. Only a small percentage of all requests made to these two officials lead to cassation. In practice, the President refers cassation requests to the appropriate divisions of the Court for recommendations before he decides whether formally to petition the Court. Cases can come to the Court on cassation in all four fields of lower court jurisdiction. Thus the various divisions of the Supreme Court perform two functions: reviewing judgments from the county courts on direct appeal and acting on petitions for cassation involving cases that were decided in the district courts as well as in the county courts. Most cassation proceedings involve criminal cases and relate to the imposition of punishment. The county courts themselves have a power of cassation over district court judgments in their respective counties.

As in other instances we have no precise official figures on cassation petitions. An approximation from knowledgeable sources, however, indicates that the President of the Supreme Court receives approximately three thousand requests annually to petition the court for cassation. The Procurator General receives a somewhat smaller number. During 1982 the Supreme Court exercised its power of cassation in 84 criminal cases and in 109 civil, family, and labor cases. Direct appeals to the Supreme Court from the county courts during that same period numbered 261. Of these, 26 were civil, family, and labor cases; the remaining 235 were criminal. As these figures suggest, the county courts act as courts of first instance more often in criminal than in other types of cases. Considering both cassation proceedings and appeals, one can see that the Supreme Court's work is heavily weighted toward the criminal side.

The cassation procedure gives the Supreme Court significant authority to superintend the administration of justice throughout the country. Its ability to take up any case from any court, at least within one year of judgment, gives this tribunal a wide-ranging authority to correct what it sees to be misapplications of the law, actions of the lower courts inconsistent with the fundamental premises of the system, and miscarriages of justice. By this means, the Supreme Court can in fact review district court decisions, even though it has no jurisdiction over such decisions on direct appeal.

The Supreme Court's decisions in the various fields of law within its jurisdiction are published in separate sets of books. The quantity of published opinions is not large. For example, the reported civil cases from the creation of the court to 1983—a thirty-year period—are contained in seventeen volumes. County court decisions are not published.

In overseeing the administration of law in the courts throughout the country, the Supreme Court also issues regulations and directives from time to time, usually one or two every year. This is an idea borrowed from the USSR, where the Supreme

Court has a similar power. This power enables the GDR Supreme Court to lay down rules of law that have a prospective operation. Some of these rules are substantive in character, and they are not made in the course of deciding cases. This quasi-legislative function is alien to courts in Anglo-American systems. For example, in 1983 the court was considering issuing a ruling to clarify the law concerning property distribution and spousal maintenance after a divorce. An uncertainty that could be clarified by such a ruling is whether special supplements to a basic salary, under the state-prescribed wage scheme, are to be taken into account in computing the amount of maintenance to be paid by one spouse to the other. Supreme Court directives of this type have been issued in the past on the subjects of arrest warrants, procedure for obtaining expert psychiatric opinion, and procedure for taking evidence.[2]

In issuing rulings of this sort and in carrying out a variety of administrative functions, the Supreme Court acts through its *Plenum*. The *Plenum* consists of the President, the Vice-Presidents, all the judges of the Supreme Court, the directors of the fifteen county courts, and the heads of the three lower military courts. It is thus a body of some sixty-five judges. The Procurator General, the Minister of Justice, and a representative from the Free German Trade Unions, although not members of this body, may participate in its proceedings. The *Plenum* meets three times a year. Reports are made to it by the chairmen of the Supreme Court's divisions and the directors of the county courts.

Another administrative body within the Supreme Court is the *Presidium*. It functions in effect as an executive committee for the Court. It consists of the President, the Vice-Presidents, and the chairmen of the divisions of the Court. The Minister of Justice and the Procurator General are entitled to take part in its proceedings. Among other duties the *Presidium* prepares the agenda for the meetings of the *Plenum*. Another important function of the *Presidium* is to advise the President as to the contents of the Court's "work distribution plan." In this plan the President assigns the judges to the various divisions and assigns categories of cases to the divisions. As in the county courts, the plan is not available publicly.

[2]English translations of these directives are in *Law and Legislation in the German Democratic Republic*, 1/71, p. 42; 1-1/80, pp. 131–40.

No judge in the GDR wears a robe. The judges wear ordinary business suits when sitting to hear cases. Here one is reminded of the American reaction against judicial robes beginning in the Jacksonian era in the nineteenth century. A similarity can be detected between the American populist view of robes and the view in the GDR that robes are part of the mumbo jumbo of bourgeois law designed to conceal the fact that law is the will of the ruling class and not a detached force in human life administered by objective and neutral judges. This is one of several examples of American-style populism that can be detected in GDR life.

A superficial hint of populism can be detected also in the selection of judges. It is a basic premise in the GDR that all judges should be "elected," that they all should be subject to recall at any time, and that they should hold office only for short terms, subject to reelection. In form, judicial selection below the Supreme Court seems quite different from that in Germany historically and in the FRG today. However, close examination shows that there are considerable similarities. To say merely that GDR judges are elected is to obscure much of what really goes on in the selection process. The reality is that in the two levels of courts below the Supreme Court, the judiciary is a professional career much as it has always been in Germany, and the Minister of Justice plays an important part in the selection process.

To begin with, a person aspiring to be a state court judge must study law at Humboldt University in Berlin. Although it is possible to enter the judiciary through the study of law in Leipzig, Jena, and Halle, such a career pattern is rare, and it is not in accordance with the way things are supposed to work. Under the specialized allocation of functions among the university law sections, Humboldt is the law section designated to educate persons to be judges.

The key official in launching a person on a career in the judiciary is the Minister of Justice. He and the Ministry staff work closely with the Humboldt Law Section to place its graduates in apprenticeships with the courts on a track leading to judgeships. As described earlier, the placement process involves the assigning of law students at the end of the third year for practical training in district courts where they can enter full-time service upon graduation. These assignments are made to district courts where there is an existing or anticipated vacancy in a judgeship. On graduation from Humboldt the student begins the year of apprentice training in that district court under a work contract with the Ministry of Justice. At the end of the year the apprentice must submit a paper and undergo an oral examination by the director of the district court. It is possible that the apprenticeship can be extended for a second year if the apprentice is deemed not quite ready to assume a judgeship.

If at the end of that period of training the judges of the court and the Minister of Justice deem the person suitable for a district court judgeship, he will be proposed for election to that position. This is not a popular election but is an election in the people's representative assembly for the district where the court is located. The assembly is composed of delegates "elected" by the people in the same way that delegates to the People's Chamber are elected; that is, by an uncontested election through a ballot on which only one candidate is listed for each delegate position. Elections for members of the district assembly are held every five years. The newly elected assembly proceeds to elect the district court judges for five-year terms running concurrently with those of the assembly delegates.

Before a person is finally proposed to the assembly for election he must appear before public meetings. At these meetings the potential candidate explains his background and says anything he deems appropriate about his fitness to become a judge. One who is just completing an apprenticeship will have had no experience as a judge, so he cannot talk about his past performance, as a judge seeking reelection might do. However, the apprentice will have been cleared by the judges of his court as suitable for a judgeship before appearing at these meetings.

In deciding whether to propose the apprentice to the assembly, the Minister of Justice takes into account reactions at these public meetings. The Minister is informed of these reactions by persons present at the meetings. Reactions from members of the SED may be especially important. In theory, the major function of the Minister's review is to assure that the candidate has the requisite professional background and training and that he has no character flaws. The Minister's role is important because the candidate may not be a native of the locality in which he is standing for a judgeship. If he has been reared in a distant part of the country, no one in the locality where he is to be elected will know his background. The Minister is in a position to ascertain this, and he has access to the candidate's record at Humboldt University. Although no one can be elected a judge by the assembly unless he is certified by the Minister of Justice, anyone who is so certified will be elected. Thus the system involves a screening and selection by the Minister of Justice in a way similar to that in traditional German practice, but in addition it involves a public screening through open meetings of a sort unknown previously in Germany.

The GDR style of democracy can be seen in this judicial selection process. It is a consultative style of democracy. The assumption is that a sufficient degree of adverse reaction in the public meetings could prevent a person's becoming a judge, although no votes are taken in those meetings. Of course the basis for the adverse reaction is important, and one must bear in mind the premises of the system. It is difficult to imagine, for example, a person's being blocked from a judgeship because someone at a public meeting says that the candidate is insufficiently committed to freedom of speech and to the right to criticize the government. One can imagine that a candidate might be blocked by an assertion that he is insufficiently committed to the interests of the working class or that he does not subscribe adequately to the principles of Marxism-Leninism. However, the only formal criteria for selection are set forth in the GDR Constitution and Court Organization Act. The wording is the same: "Only persons loyally devoted to the people and their Socialist state and endowed with a high measure of knowledge and experience, human maturity and character may be judges." Persons are usually about twenty-five years old when they are initially elected to district court judgeships. Once elected, a judge is typically reelected every five years.

County court judges are elected by the representative assembly for the county at the conclusion of a similar process of public-meeting exposure and certification by the Minister of Justice. This assembly is composed of delegates from throughout the county, elected for five-year terms in the usual uncontested, one-name-on-the-ballot election. When a new assembly convenes, it elects the county court judges for five-year terms to run concurrently with the terms of the assembly delegates. These county elections do not coincide with the district elections; rather, they are over two years apart. Thus, elections of district judges occur midway during the terms of county judges and vice versa.

Candidates for county court judgeships are normally selected from among the district judges in the county. On the county courts in Berlin and Halle, for example, every judge has previously served on a district court. Before election by the county assembly, potential candidates appear at public meetings in the same way that potential district judges do. Because each candidate has had district court experience, he can discuss his work on that court as well as his views about law and social problems. The reactions at these public meetings are taken into account by the Minister of Justice in deciding whether to certify the candidate to the county assembly. If the certification is made, the candidate will be elected. Once elected to a county court judgeship, a person is typically reelected every five years.

The question remains as to how a candidate is initially picked from among the district judges. The key figures in this process seem to be the judges on the county court. They themselves have served on the district courts, and they review those courts' decisions. They are likely to know the district judges and to have an opinion as to which of them would be best suited for the higher court. Their views are communicated to the Minister of Justice. In selecting these candidates, the county court judges and the Minister take into account the performance of the judges on the district courts, including the number of times they have been reversed on appeal and the number of times their judgments have been quashed on cassation. Normally a judge serves two terms on the district court before being considered for election to the county court. Once candidates are tentatively selected, they must survive scrutiny at the public meetings.

Thus in the filling of judgeships on both the district and county courts there is an element of public discussion combined with the formality of election by the assembly. However, what the GDR has, in effect, is a career management and promotion system for judges which is similar to that found in traditional German practice and which obtains in most states of the FRG today. The major difference is that in those FRG states—as in traditional German practice—the Minister of Justice makes the decision in the initial selection of a trial judge and in the promotion of a judge from a trial to an appellate court without having popular discussion, and the appointment is made without limit of time. These are, of course, important differences, but the similarity is striking, namely, that service on the judiciary in the GDR is a career that from the beginning is under the management and control of the Minister of Justice.

The present Minister of Justice is Hans-Joachim Heusinger. He was born into a working-class family in Leipzig in 1925. He underwent training as an electrician from 1939 to 1942, but the publicly available information does not indicate what he did for the remainder of the war. For several years after the war he worked as an electrician. In 1947 he joined the Liberal Party (LDPD). During the ensuing years he held various positions in that party and in local government organs in Leipzig and Cottbus. He did not undertake the study of law until the age of thirty, when he enrolled as a part-time extension student in the Academy for State and Law, where he received the degree of *Diplom jurist* in 1960. He seems to have been involved in little significant legal work before he became Minister of Justice in 1972. In his present post he is, of course, a member of the Council of Ministers.

The judicial career and promotional pattern continues into the Supreme Court, although with two significant differences: the Minister of Justice has no part in the selection process, and there are no public meetings. Like the judges in the two judicial levels below, Supreme Court judges are elected by the representative assembly for their level—the People's Chamber—but their election is based on the recommendation of the Council of State, which in turn receives recommendations from the *Presidium* of the Supreme Court.

Almost all judges on the Supreme Court have previously been judges on the county courts. Inasmuch as all county court judges have previously been judges on the district courts, this means that, with rare exceptions, judges on the Supreme Court have already served as judges in both levels of courts below; thus they have twice been through the screening process involving the Minister of Justice and the public meeting exposure. Among the forty-seven judges currently on the Supreme Court there are presently only two exceptions to this career pattern: one judge came directly to the Supreme Court from a position on the Humboldt law faculty; the President of the Court came from a position in the Ministry of Justice.

The process through which persons are selected from among the dozens of county court judges to be candidates for the Supreme Court is not clear. An influential role appears to be played by the existing Supreme Court judges, who know something of the county court judges because they review their work. Their views are communicated through the Court's *Presidium* to the Council of State. There are, no doubt, various sources of information that serve to provide the necessary assurance that a county court judge holds the right views and is sound on the principles of the system. In any event, the Council of State recommends to the People's Chamber *the* candidate for the judgeship, and the People's Chamber then elects that candidate. The election is to a five-year term that coincides with the terms of the delegates to the People's Chamber.

The President and the two Vice-Presidents of the Supreme Court are elected to those positions by the People's Chamber. The President designates the chairmen of the various divisions within the Court. This arrangement differs from that in the county courts; there the Minister of Justice appoints the associate directors and the chairmen of the divisions, on the recommendation of the director.

In these arrangements one can see the bifurcation of responsibilities relating to the court system between the Minister of Justice and the President of the Supreme Court. In the first two levels of the court system the Minister of Justice plays the role described earlier in selecting and promoting judges and of appointing associate directors and division chairmen. In the Supreme Court, however, the President exercises a similar internal administrative function. The Minister of Justice has no role at all in the organization and administration of the Supreme Court or in the selection of its judges. However, the minister does perform an important role in relation to the entire judicial system in providing it with logistical support, including physical facilities and supplies. He also develops the budget for the court system, in cooperation with the President of the Supreme Court. In other words, the Justice Ministry is involved in administrative and financial support for the judiciary in a way similar to that seen in the Justice Ministries of West Germany and in the Lord Chancellor's office in England. In all other respects, however, the GDR state court system is under the direction of the President of the Supreme Court who, in turn, is responsible directly to the Council of State and the People's Chamber. The Minister of Justice answers to the Council of Ministers, of which he is a member.

The political party affiliation of a candidate for a judgeship is said not to be controlling in his selection for any of the three levels of courts. However, approximately 70 to 75 percent of all judges in the GDR are members of the SED. What is said to be more important than party affiliation is membership in "the working class." It is deemed essential to maintain a proportion of judges drawn from the working class that is at least equal to the percentage of that class in the country's population—estimated to be 60 to 65 percent.

More crucial perhaps than either party or class membership is the individual's sound grounding in and perceived commitment to Marxist-Leninist principles. The life of anyone growing up in the GDR will provide an abundantly documented—or documentable—basis for judging this matter; moreover, there will have been several crucial screening points along the way, making it unlikely that anyone will reach the point of being a serious candidate for a judgeship who is not seen to be solid on this ground. The task of assessing a person's views and attitudes is made easier because of the earlier checkpoints and because of the limited and integrated nature of all organizational life. The only organization for formal association not integrated into the system is the church, or more accurately, the churches. More will be said of them in a later chapter. Apart from the churches, all organizations and activities in the GDR are knit together at the top, tied into the SED and subordinated to its policies.

To begin with, there is the Young Pioneers, the organization to which elementary school age children belong. Next there is the Free German Youth, beginning at age fourteen and continuing all the way through university age. A major checkpoint on the road to the bench is at the application stage for admission to the study of law in the university. Given the programmatic commitment to Marxism-Leninism that controls the university law curriculum, it is unlikely that a student will be admitted unless the admissions committee is satisfied about his commitment to those ends. Although membership in the Free German Youth is said not to be essential to admission, active participation in that organization would clearly be an affirmative factor in the application. Nonmembership, if combined with some other indications of lack of sufficiently vigorous attachment to the system, could be disqualifying. Moreover, in the case of male applicants, the required military service can provide a basis for assessment by commanding officers and colleagues.

The four years in the university law section provide another basis for assessing the desired qualities in the student. Performances on examinations such as those in State and Law and in the various aspects of Marxism-Leninism can provide useful data on which the faculty members can assess the individual's attitudes. The next major screening point comes when the Minister of Justice places students in positions with the courts, with an eye to their becoming judges at the close of the apprenticeship period. Finally, there is the apprenticeship period itself under the tutelage and eye of judges sitting on the district court. If the student survives all of these steps it seems unlikely that he will be found wanting on the question of commitment to the premises and goals of the system.

Once a person becomes a judge, there are periodic checkpoints along the way. There is the reelection process every five years, with the judge appearing before public meetings and discussing his record, his work, and his ideas. There is also the screening done by the Minister of Justice. When the time comes to consider the person for a place on the county court, there is added screening provided by those judges who have sat over him for a period of years.

In sum, judicial selection appears to be based on a combination of ability, philosophical views, commitment to the system, class identification, and party affiliation. The weight accorded each of these factors is unknown; it probably varies from case to case.

Altogether the GDR state court system is manned by 1,297 judges, as follows: 965 district court judges, 285 county court judges, and 47 Supreme Court judges. The annual vacancy rate in the district court judgeships can be roughly guessed from the figures concerning placement of the Humboldt University law graduates. Between 140 and 150 students are graduated there each year. Of that number, approximately 50 to 60 enter service with the courts. These are the persons who become trial judges after one or two years of apprentice training. Because of emphasis on central planning concerning the allocation of manpower, one may assume that this is also approximately the number of vacant judgeships annually on the district courts. In other words, the vacancy rate at this entry level for judicial careers is about 6 percent annually.

Women occupy approximately 55 percent of all GDR state court judgeships. This percentage, however, varies considerably from one court or place to another. In the city of Berlin, for example, women occupy approximately two-thirds of all judgeships, while on the Halle county court only eight of the thirty judges are women. Several persons in various positions commented on difficulties associated with this large number of women judges. The problem has nothing to do with the competence and the abilities of the women judges, but rather derives from the fact that they are often absent for protracted periods in connection with children. Under GDR law, a woman is entitled to a paid leave of six months following the birth of her first child; and a leave of one year after the birth of a second child. Because judges come on the bench at a relatively young age, many of the women judges go through their prime childbearing years after they are judges. Thus there are frequent and protracted absences, and this causes difficulties in the conduct of judicial business. Some women, after the birth of two or more children, decide to give up a career on the bench in favor of some other kind of legal work. Because female enrollment in the Humboldt Law Section has diminished to approximately 35 percent and the Humboldt Section is the training ground for new judges, it is predictable that the percentage of women judges will decline over the next decade.

In some of the states in West Germany university law graduates pursue a mixed public service career, alternating between work as a prosecutor and as a judge, and sometimes serving in the Ministry of Justice. Although this is not unknown in the GDR, it seldom occurs. A career as a judge is a distinct and fixed career, separate from that of a prosecutor or other kind of legal functionary. It is rare in the GDR today for anyone to enter the judiciary other than from the bottom, following completion of law study in Humboldt University. A person who becomes a judge normally stays in that work until retirement or death.

The pay of judges is based on a centrally prescribed schedule which, like most official information, is difficult to obtain in precise detail. The basic scale is approximately as follows: district court judges, 1,100 to 1,200 marks per month; county court judges, 1,600 to 1,700 marks per month; supreme court judges, 2,700 marks per month. These basic salaries are supplemented in some locales, apparently on the theory that judges incur higher than usual living expenses in those places. Judicial compensation is similar to academic compensation, as can be seen from the pay scale described earlier for law teachers. A district judge earns somewhat more than a young assistant in a law faculty. A Supreme Court judge makes slightly more than a law professor. But these differences are not radical.

The judges described in this chapter work exclusively in cases arising under the Criminal, Civil, Family, and Labor Codes. In this work—at least in a large part of it—they are joined by citizens who have no formal legal training. Thus, to round out this picture of the state court system, the role played by these citizens is explained in the next chapter.

8 Citizen Roles in Dispute Resolution

Citizens without formal legal training are involved in the resolution of disputes in the GDR in two important ways: they serve as lay judges in the state court system, sitting alongside the professional judges discussed in the last chapter, and they also man the entire system of social courts. Although these persons are not products of the university law sections, they play a large part in the administration of justice. Many of them work closely with university law graduates, and no account of the GDR legal world would be complete without reference to these lay participants. Hence the two forms of citizen involvement are briefly described here.

Lay judges—known as *Schöffen*—have long been on the German judicial scene. Traditionally they have served only in criminal cases at the trial level, but in the GDR their role has been considerably expanded. Today lay judges participate not only in criminal cases but also in civil, family, and labor cases in the first instance; moreover, they also sit on labor cases in the county courts and in the Supreme Court, where they perform a review function.

When hearing a case at first instance, a GDR court always consists of one professional judge and two lay judges. Thus a district court is always constituted in that manner. A county court also acts through one professional judge and two lay judges when it is sitting as a court of first instance. The professional judge presides, and he is responsible for seeing that the proceedings move along in proper form; he is the expert, the trained lawyer. But the concept also obtains that each judge has the same responsibility for participating in the proceedings and in deciding the case. The views of the professional judge are accorded no greater weight, at least in theory, than those of the lay judges. As a practical matter, however, it is likely that in many situations lay judges defer to the professional judge. On the other hand, the two lay judges sometimes decide the case contrary to the views of the professional judge. In short, these citizens are full judicial participants; they are not merely jurors in the Anglo-American sense.

Each lay judge must devote two weeks each year to sitting with the court. Having a specific two-week segment of full-time sitting is viewed as an improvement over the traditional German system of having each lay judge come in for a day or two at different times of the year. Under the GDR system a citizen who is a lay judge can have a voice in choosing the time of year he or she wishes to sit; the choice can be made in light of job and family responsibilities. A lay judge makes arrangements at his place of employment to be excused for that specific two-week period. Regular pay at the place of employment continues while the employee is absent to serve on the court.

Each lay judge is obligated to participate regularly in an educational program involving attendance at lectures approximately six times a year. A one-day program is offered about every two months. At these sessions lectures are given by judges and lawyers on topics of current legal interest, particularly new statutes that may be involved in litigation. There is no special training in court procedure. The main purpose of these periodic educational sessions is to keep the lay judges abreast of developments in the law likely to be pertinent to litigated cases.

The number of lay judges needed to staff the district courts can be arrived at by simple arithmetic because each district court judge has two lay judges sitting with him at all times, each for a two-week period. Thus each district judge requires 52 lay judges. If, for example, in a particular district there are five trial judges, a total of 260 lay judges will be needed. Most of the lay judges are involved in the first tier of the system, that is, in the district courts. However, there are also lay judges at each of the two higher levels. In the county courts lay judges are needed to sit on appeals in the labor law cases and in the trials of criminal and, occasionally, other cases being heard there in the first instance. The number of lay judges needed on a particular county court thus depends on the makeup of its docket and cannot be ascertained by an arithmetical formula. Figures from the Halle county court are illustrative: with 30 professional judges, that court has 60 lay judges for labor cases and 80 lay judges for criminal cases. When lay judges participate in a county court case, 2 of them sit with one professional judge, as in the district courts. In the Supreme Court lay judges serve only on labor law cases.

Lay judges are elected at the same time and in the same manner as professional judges. Thus at the district level the local representative assembly elects the lay judges. The terms are likewise for five years. The assembly elects those citizens who are put forward as the single candidate for each position, following discussion of those persons at public meetings conducted in the same way as the public discussions of the professional judges. The persons proposed for these lay judgeships are put forward by the various political parties and mass organizations that make up the National Front. Exactly how a person is selected within the National Front is not clear. One way or another a single person is agreed upon within these groups and exactly the right number are put before the assembly.

Within a particular district the lay judges come out of the various residential areas or other geographical subdivisions. The difficulty is not that there are too many persons proposed for these positions; rather, the difficulty is in getting enough good people to fill these lay judgeships as well as all of the other citizen positions necessary to run the system. Large numbers of citizens are needed to assist the police, to oversee various retail establishments, and to assist generally with party and administrative functions. Widespread citizen involvement is said to give the system its "democratic" character.

Lay judges for the county courts are elected by the county assemblies. The process is similar to that at the district level. It parallels the selection process for the professional judges on the county courts. The lay judges on the Supreme Court (who are involved only in labor cases) are elected by the People's Chamber. To be elected a lay judge on any of the courts, a person need not be a member of the SED. However, given the premises of the system and the overall authority of the SED, it seems unlikely that anyone would be made a lay judge of the court system unless he is acceptable to the Party.

The values ascribed to the use of lay judges in the GDR are similar to those usually assigned to the use of juries in Anglo-American law. First, there is thought to be value in having the general commonsense and real-life experience of citizens brought to bear in the resolution of controversies coming before the courts–criminal, civil, family, and labor. Second, service as lay judges is thought to provide a valuable education for citizens in the workings of the law and the court system and to promote understanding and support of the system among others with whom the lay judges communicate. If this educational theory works in practice, the impact could be substantial because there are approximately 56,000 lay judges in the entire country. Most of these serve on the 234 district courts spread across the GDR. The others serve on the 15 geographically dispersed county courts; a few serve on the Supreme Court.

Citizens are brought into the dispute-resolution business on an even more massive scale through the Social Courts. These are informal tribunals forming a broad base below the district courts. A Social Court exists in every residential area or community, every enterprise, and virtually every agricultural cooperative. In 1982 a total of 292,111 persons, all of them nonlawyers, served on the Social Courts of the country.[3] These bodies are of two types: dispute commissions and conflict commissions. The two were created separately, but in 1968 they were brought together under the generic label "Social Courts." The dispute commissions exist in residential areas, villages, and agricultural cooperatives. The conflict commissions exist in the state-owned enterprises. A person may be within the jurisdiction of a Social Court both at his work place and also in his residential area.

According to one set of statistics, in 1982 the conflict commissions made a total of 68,741 decisions, the bulk of which were labor law cases initiated by enterprise managers against their workers. The dispute commissions made a total of 19,237 decisions, the bulk of which involved petty disputes and insults

[3]This figure along with other information concerning the Social Courts is drawn from an unpublished paper entitled "Pursuing One's Rights Under Socialism" (February 1985), by Professor Inga Markovits of the University of Texas Law School. The author is indebted to her for permission to use this information.

between neighbors. These figures include both civil and criminal matters. The criminal cases involve relatively minor offenses that would generally be considered misdemeanors in the Anglo-American legal world. These cases go to the Social Courts either by direction of the procurator, or the investigating agency, or by reference from a district court. In 1981, according to the *Statistical Yearbook,* 20,719 persons (under criminal charges) were referred by the district courts to the Social Courts. It is estimated that the latter handle one out of every four offenders.

With one exception all of the commissions handle the same kinds of business. The one exception concerns disputes arising out of employment. In such disputes the conflict commission in the enterprise has exclusive original jurisdiction; the matter must be brought before that commission, and it cannot be brought before a dispute commission in the residential area or initially in a district court.

Although there is a right of appeal to a district court from a decision by a Social Court, appeals are taken in relatively few cases. It is estimated that 90 percent of the labor cases terminate in the Social Courts.

Proceedings in the Social Courts are informal and not legalistic. No rigid rules of evidence or procedure are enforced, and lawyers are not permitted to appear. The purpose is to get at the facts and underlying cause of the dispute and to resolve the immediate problem in a way that will remove the cause and leave the parties better educated as to their responsibilities to socialist society.

The Social Courts superficially resemble some of the so-called alternative dispute-resolution procedures much discussed in the United States since the late 1970s. The American litigation explosion, accompanied by escalating costs and delay in the courts, has spurred growing nationwide interest in devising informal and inexpensive means of resolving controversies where court attention is not thought essential. Alternatives developed thus far in the United States include neighborhood justice centers, arbitration and mediation programs, and other dispute-settling processes not necessarily in the hands of judges or lawyers. However, nowhere in the United States is there a comprehensive set of forums, blanketing an entire state or other sizable territorial jurisdiction. That is what the Social Courts provide in the GDR through a countrywide network embracing all citizens, either in their residential areas or in their work places.

In function, however, the Social Courts differ from these American entities in that they also have a major educational role. This educational task may explain why the 292,111 Social Court members decided a total of only 87,978 cases in 1982. Such citizen-manned bodies, designed to strengthen public support for the system, are a standard part of the regime in every communist country. The distinctive feature of the Social Courts in the GDR is that they are considered part of the state court system. They form a massive underpinning for the district courts. They are linked to those courts through a right of appeal and they are subject to the authority of the Supreme Court. Although technically part of the state court system, they are not really courts in the Anglo-American sense because their main task is to enforce socialist standards of behavior through education; it is not their primary purpose to settle disputes through an adversarial process.

Persons are selected to serve on the Social Courts in two ways. For the conflict commissions, workers in the enterprise are chosen by the trade union organization and are then "elected" (usually ratified without contest) by their fellow workers. For the dispute commissions, persons are nominated by the National Front in their residential areas and are then elected by the local parliamentary body in the usual unanimous way.

Citizens serving on the Social Courts form a pool from which lay judges for the district courts can be selected. Service on a Social Court provides an opportunity for one to gain experience in hearing and resolving disputes. Such work can be observed and evaluated by others, thereby providing a basis for a judgment as to how a person might function as a lay judge. Many lay judges apparently have had previous service on Social Courts.

Adding together the number of persons serving as lay judges and the number serving on Social Courts produces a total of over 348,000 (about 50 percent of whom are women). When compared with the 1,250 professional judges, this figure points up the extensive involvement of nonlawyers in the administration of justice. In all of their other aspects, however, the country's legal systems are in the hands of university law graduates. We return now to consider the various legal positions, other than the state court judgeships, into which the law graduates are fed.

9

Lawyers and Notaries

Practicing lawyers and state notaries, like judges, receive their legal education in the Law Section of Humboldt University in Berlin. They also come under the jurisdiction of the Minister of Justice. These two lines of legal work, and the processes through which Humboldt graduates enter them, are described here.

The term *practicing lawyer* is used here to mean a lawyer who devotes his time to counseling or representing a variety of clients and who is not employed by any state organ or enterprise. The clients are mainly individual citizens, although they may also be enterprises or other entities. The work is similar to that of an American lawyer engaged in general practice. The most striking fact about the practicing lawyers in the GDR, from an American perspective, is the smallness of their number: a total of 600 in the entire country (according to informal estimates of officials). Of these, 550 are members of a collegium; 50 practice independently. Approximately half the lawyers in Berlin are women, but the percentage is somewhat smaller nationwide.

The figure of 600 understates the lawyering services available to the citizens of the country. Many enterprises and institutions have lawyers employed full time on their staffs—persons whom Americans would call house counsel. In the GDR such a person is called *Justitiar*. It is estimated that there are perhaps 3,000 such lawyers in the GDR, most of whom probably studied law at the Universities in Leipzig and Halle. Those lawyers not only do legal work for their employers, but they are also available to offer legal assistance to the employees. Most of these lawyers are probably in the state-owned enterprises, but they are in other places too. Each university, for example, has at least one lawyer, and he is available to offer legal assistance to the University's staff, faculty, and employees. Thus it is more realistic to say that the country's 16.7 million citizens are served by approximately 3,600 lawyers. Moreover, district courts are required to provide legal advice to citizens, thereby augmenting still further the available legal services. We are interested here, however, only in the 600 who are not employed by any entity but who engage full-time in the representation of clients, and who are what Americans would think of as practicing lawyers and not as house counsel.

That 550 out of the 600 lawyers are in a collegium reflects the reality that practice through a collegium has become the normal and preferred way of engaging in law practice. One practitioner said that most of the fifty nonaffiliated practitioners (of whom fifteen are in East Berlin) are older lawyers, some of whom are left over from the pre-1949 period. A new, independent practitioner is admitted only about once every three years. Increasingly, as a practical matter, if one wishes to pursue law practice he must do so through a collegium.

There is a collegium in each of the fifteen counties. Each collegium is composed of the practicing lawyers admitted to it in that county. They constitute the "members' assembly" which in turn elects an executive committee and an auditing committee. Each collegium governs its own admissions and enforces disciplinary rules among its members. Although these bodies date back some thirty years, they all function now under a new statute adopted in 1981. The chairmen of the fifteen county collegia constitute the Council of Chairmen. Its function is to coordinate the work of the collegia and to submit proposals to the Minister of Justice, who has supervisory authority over the collegia. Although the collegia have a measure of autonomy, they do not have the independence enjoyed by American bar associations.

A Humboldt law graduate is admitted to membership in a collegium through a process that, in its first phase, is like that involved in the placement of Humboldt law graduates in the courts. The Minister ascertains from the collegia throughout the country the number of positions available for the upcoming year; this information is conveyed to the law section and, in turn, to the students. Those students who are interested can then discuss the available possibilities. Through these discussions interested students are assigned by the Minister of Justice to the positions available for that year in the collegia throughout the country.

The number of lawyers in the collegia is fixed centrally, as is almost everything else in the GDR. This figure is part of the overall national plan that allocates all manpower in the country. The number of 550 for the collegia has been set for some time. There is presently discussion as to whether 600 lawyers are sufficient for the country. Some think that perhaps 100 more are needed, but others think the present number is sufficient. The Minister of Justice is rumored to favor adding 50 lawyers. It seems unlikely that a significant increase will be made soon, probably because of more pressing manpower needs in other fields of work. Some lawyers also say that because of the building shortage, office space for additional lawyers is not available.

The ceiling on collegia membership means that an opportunity to become a practicing lawyer in a collegium arises only when one of its lawyers dies or retires. The annual turnover is not large. In Berlin, which has one of the largest collegia in the country, there are sixty lawyers, and only two or three vacancies for new lawyers occur each year. In the Rostock Collegium (serving the GDR's major seaport and shipbuilding center) there are only twenty-one lawyers, and one can imagine that there are years when there is no vacancy. In the entire country there are only some twenty positions available annually for new lawyers. (In 1983 between twenty and twenty-five Humboldt graduates became practitioners.) Thus it is likely that some, and perhaps many, law students will be frustrated, simply because there are more students in a particular year aspiring to become practitioners than there are places for practitioners.

Even if a graduating law student is selected by the Minister of Justice for a vacancy in a collegium, the student is not guaranteed the position. Here the Minister's selection is only a recommendation; the final decision is left with the collegium. Its members may reject the student for reasons best known to themselves. If the law graduate survives this two-step selection process, he then pursues a year-long period of apprentice training in the collegium. At the end of that year, the person is accepted into full membership in the collegium if its members deem him to be qualified. He is then entitled to engage in the practice of law in all respects. This last step is analogous to admission to the bar in the United States.

Within a collegium, lawyers are usually associated in small groups for the purpose of sharing offices. Some of these groups have as few as two or three lawyers; others have upward of a dozen. These law offices are located near the centers of cities and towns. They are on street level, often next to retail shops. On the front of each appears "Collegium of Advocates," followed by the name of the county and the names of the lawyers who have offices there. Each lawyer has a room to himself where he can consult in confidence with clients. Each group of lawyers has secretarial help and a modest library. One GDR lawyer commented that these offices operate on a relatively small budget and cannot be compared to better-equipped, more luxuriously furnished American law offices.

Each lawyer practices individually and earns his own fees. The group is not viewed as a partnership. One lawyer in an office can, for example, represent a party in a case where another lawyer in the same office is on the opposite side. In some respects these offices resemble barristers' chambers in England in that barristers share rooms but practice individually and not in partnerships.

Each lawyer charges his own fees. Apparently there is a fee schedule that is generally followed. The fees are paid directly to the collegium, not to the lawyers or to the law offices. Each collegium has a central administrative office in the county. The collegium office takes 40 percent of the fees, which it uses to pay expenses for all the lawyers in the county collegium, including office rent, secretarial help, stationery, telephone, and all other operating expenses. The lawyers themselves and the various law offices do not pay any of these expenses; they are all handled centrally out of the county collegium office. After taking 40 percent of the fee, the collegium office pays the remaining 60 percent to the lawyer who earned it. The lawyer must then pay 20 percent of this amount as a tax to the state. The remainder is the lawyer's net income.

The pattern of lawyers' incomes is unlike the general pattern of incomes in the GDR in two respects. One is that lawyer incomes span a wider range from lowest to highest than do incomes in the GDR generally. Another is that top incomes among lawyers are higher than the top incomes in almost all other fields of work. The gross fees earned by lawyers are estimated to range from approximately 1,000 marks per month, for a young, beginning practitioner, up to approximately 10,000 marks per month for the best and most-experienced lawyers. After the adjustments for administrative expenses and taxes, the top-earning lawyers in the country are left with a net income of 4,000 or more marks per month. That is substantially more than the incomes of university law professors and Supreme Court judges. The only persons in the GDR who earn as much or more are Politburo members and combine directors.

Most lawyers are generalists, practicing in the four fields that lie within the jurisdiction of the state courts—civil, family, labor, and criminal law. For many lawyers, work is distributed as follows: one-third criminal, one-third family, and one-third civil and labor. On the other hand, some lawyers do concentrate in one field. Family law is one area of specialization. Some lawyers say that it is the most lucrative. Other specialities focus on inheritance and on criminal matters. But apparently only a minority really specialize.

Lawyers practicing independently, outside of a collegium, apparently have a similar distribution of work and a similar pattern of income. One big difference is that an independent lawyer must pay all of his expenses out of his fees. In theory, a law student unable to obtain a place in a collegium could enter practice independently, either by himself or in association with a lawyer already engaged in independent practice. This does not seem to have occurred much, however, at least in recent years. There seems to be an official frowning upon it; the collegium is favored, and there may be a hope that the independent practitioners will gradually disappear from the scene. Their presence is somewhat inconsistent with the fundamental notion that all economic and human activity is integrated into the system and is knit together at the top into the SED. But there is no real inconsistency here because the independent lawyers are under the ultimate control of the Minister of Justice. They can be called to account by the Ministry for their activities. This means that these fifty lawyers are not independent in the sense that American practitioners are. It is unlikely that they have significantly more independence than the lawyers in the collegia.

It is said that all lawyers have an obligation to provide legal advice or information without charge to citizens seeking such. At least some law offices designate certain hours during which the lawyers are available for this purpose. Although some consultation seems to be done on a fee-paying basis, much of it seems to be offered without charge to citizens who drop in with questions. In an initial conversation the lawyer can identify the problem, advise the citizen where to go to take care of it, or take it in hand himself for a fee. One estimate is that in the collegium in Berlin the number of matters handled by the lawyers annually is approximately 10,000 on a fee-paying basis and approximately the same number on a non-fee-paying basis. The volume of fee-paying matters has not been increasing. Several years ago when there were forty-five lawyers in Berlin, there were 10,000 fee-paying matters handled annually, the same as today when there are sixty lawyers. Some persons in the GDR rely on this fact to show that the country is adequately staffed with lawyers.

The extent to which criminal defendants are represented in court by lawyers can only be approximated. The 1982 statistics show that 70,365 persons were convicted of crimes during that year. To provide each of them with representation would have required each of the 600 lawyers to handle 117 criminal cases during the year. But no one asserts that every defendant has counsel; one estimate is that one-fifth of the defendants are represented. If this estimate is accurate, it means that approximately 14,060 convicted defendants had counsel, an average of 24 cases per lawyer during 1982. These figures may underestimate lawyer involvement because they represent only persons convicted; they do not include criminal proceedings commenced or pending that did not result in convictions during 1982.

A criminal defendant in the GDR is no longer compelled to be represented by counsel. Some GDR lawyers praise this change as a liberating step, enabling persons to speak for themselves and not forcing them to speak through what was perceived as an "elite" group, namely the lawyers, who before the war belonged to other than the working class. "Our citizens readily understand the law and are quite able to speak for themselves in most situations," remarked one lawyer, who added that many defendants do not desire counsel. However, the law does specify certain situations in which counsel must be provided for a defendant, whether or not he wants representation. These include cases where the defendant is a minor, where he is incapacitated or incompetent, and where he does not speak German. Also, defendants charged with offenses carrying a prison term of two or more years must be provided counsel. A penalty of two years imprisonment seems to be the line in the GDR between what Americans call misdemeanors and felonies. In these circumstances counsel is provided by the state without expense to the defendant. Apparently the defendant, at least in theory, is entitled to choose his counsel in these circumstances from anywhere in the country, if that counsel is available.

Some lawyers and legal scholars in the GDR say that generally the work of an advocate there is quite similar to that in Western Europe and in the United States in most run-of-the-mill cases, criminal and otherwise. They enunciate some of the same concepts concerning the obligation of an attorney to a client, the necessity of confidentiality, and the obligation of the attorney to do all that he legally and ethically can in behalf of the client. Those are the abstract concepts that are articulated. How they are applied in specific cases is beyond the scope of this inquiry.

It appears from what is said in the GDR that if a citizen wishes to consult a lawyer he will be able to find a lawyer to consult, either among the practitioners, or among the lawyers in his enterprise, or at the district court. However, GDR citizens do not appear to want or to need to consult lawyers with any frequency. Although in East Berlin there are upward of 1.2 million people, 20,000 matters a year are dealt with by the sixty lawyers in the city. This means that on the average each lawyer is handling 333 matters annually. Many of these are probably no more than brief conversations in which a rather simple piece of advice is given. The country appears not to be one heavily dependent on lawyers. Instead of looking to lawyers for help the population is supposed to rely for the protection of its interests on the Party, mass organizations, collectives, and other social and state organs.

In addition to becoming practicing lawyers and state court judges, Humboldt law graduates also enter careers as notaries. The office of notary has long been established in Germany as well as in the rest of Europe. The office bears little resemblance to that of notary public in the United States. In the GDR today, as in traditional German law, the notary is an important state functionary with a variety of tasks. These include authenticating documents, administering estates, and handling guardianships. Much of this work is like American-style probate work.

The function of authenticating certain kinds of documents and transactions has a superficial resemblance to the work of notaries in the United States. A sale of land in the GDR, for example, must be authenticated by a notary. Certain other transactions are not legally valid unless so authenticated. Transfers of the ownership of chattels do not require such notarial involvement. A notary's "authentication" often involves much more than merely attesting signatures. The notary can draft deeds, contracts, and other documents for the parties, acting as a neutral third person.

An important and growing role of the notary relates to inheritance matters. As the GDR becomes more prosperous and people there acquire more material possessions and money, there are increasing problems concerning disposition of these assets at death. The whole subject is one that is exclusively within the jurisdiction of the notaries. A GDR citizen can make a will with a notary and leave it on file with that official. A person can also make a will and keep it in his own possession; in that event, at the testator's death, the will must be taken to a notary and placed on file for the administration of the estate. In either event, the notary is responsible for notifying all legatees and heirs, and ultimately for distributing all assets. Apparently some of this work gets complicated where children of large families are scattered in foreign countries. The notary often works through foreign governments in notifying such heirs. Some of these estate administrations can take many months and even years. When there is a contested question concerning the administration of an estate or the distribution of assets, the notary holds hearings and resolves those disputes. A person can be represented by a lawyer in dealings with the notary, but this is not necessary.

The Minister of Justice exercises "guidance and control" over all notaries. He not only provides logistical support for their offices, he also sees to it that socialist legality is observed in their work. The district courts play a limited role in reviewing actions by the notaries; these courts can act on complaints against notaries' rulings when the complaints are certified to the court by a notary's office.

The placement process in the Humboldt Law Section for future notaries works in essentially the same way it does for judgeships in the district court. Only a certain number of positions are available to be filled each year, and the Minister of Justice and the Humboldt law faculty work together to identify students for those openings. Although the process is collaborative, in the end the Minister of Justice must approve the selection of students to become notaries.

A person who becomes a notary normally does not shift into any other line of work. However, the position is apparently one into which a person can be moved from somewhere else. For example, if a Humboldt law graduate who goes with a district court initially, intending to become a judge, does not prove to be suitable, he could be offered a position as a notary. The latter involves certain talents and personality traits that are different from those required in the position of district court judge.

In the entire GDR there are approximately five hundred notaries. Between thirty and forty Humboldt law graduates were placed as notaries in 1983, suggesting an annual turnover of about 6 to 7 percent. There is at least one notary office in each district. In Berlin there are approximately thirty notaries. According to some officials, there is a shortage of notaries in the GDR.

The legal positions discussed thus far—those of judge, lawyer, and notary—are all filled by graduates of the Humboldt Law Section. The procurators' offices form another important segment of "the system for the administration of justice," and law students are trained for that work in the University Law Section at Jena. The next chapter describes the work of the procurators.

10
Procurators

In the GDR the office of procurator has replaced the traditional German office of public prosecutor. This development represents a significant rearrangement of governmental power. Under the traditional German system—and in the FRG today—a Minister of Justice is responsible for all personnel in the legal system: judges, prosecutors, practicing lawyers, notaries, and lawyers in government organs. In the GDR, however, the prosecuting attorneys have been removed from the Ministry of Justice and placed in a separate state organization headed by the Procurator General, who has considerably more authority than the public prosecutor had. This separation is emphasized by assigning to the University Law Section at Jena the exclusive responsibility for educating future procurators. Under this arrangement the Procurator General is viewed as a far more important official than the Minister of Justice. He is chosen for office in the same way that the President of the Supreme Court is chosen, namely, by election in the People's Chamber on the recommendation of the Council of State. He is responsible directly to those two bodies and may be removed by them at any time.

Although the term *procurator*—not prosecutor—is the English translation used in the GDR, the German title for this officer—*Staatsanwalt*—remains unchanged. It is an office that goes far back in German history and still exists today in the FRG, where the English translation continues to be "prosecutor." The switch to "procurator" results from the influence of the Soviet legal system—the source of this title. This shift in translation reflects a shift in function, for the *Staatsanwalt* in the GDR today has duties and responsibilities that go far beyond the prosecution of criminal offenses in the courts. This official's authority is essentially the same as that of the procurator in the Soviet Union.

The flavor of the Procurator General's broad authority is reflected in the language of the statute that charges this official with the responsibility for "implementing the decisions of the party of the working class on the basis of the constitution, the laws, and other legal provisions of the German Democratic Republic." The statute also provides that "the procurator's office watches over the strict observance of socialist law."

There are approximately 1,000 procurators in the GDR, all under the authority of the Procurator General. The bottom tier of the structure is at the district level. There is a procurator's office in each district (whether or not there is a district court located there); thus there are 252 district procurators' offices. The number of lawyers and other personnel in each district office varies considerably, depending on the population and volume of business in the district. The smallest have approximately three or four lawyers plus an assistant that resembles a paralegal in American law practice, as well as one or two secretarial/clerical persons and perhaps a driver. In the larger districts the procurator's office may be several times that size.

At the middle level of the system—the county—there is a procurator's office located in the city where the county court is also located. Each of these fifteen county procurator's offices is larger than most of the district offices. The smallest of the county offices has about fifteen lawyers; the largest has about fifty. There are some forty lawyers in the Berlin procurator's office. Every lawyer in these offices has previously worked as a procurator in a district office. A county office is responsible for overseeing the work of the district offices within its jurisdiction.

The lawyers in a county office are usually organized into departments. A typical district office is not divided into departments. Every lawyer there is involved in all aspects of the office's work. In other words, there is a measure of specialization at the county level that is not found at the district level.

At the top of the structure is the Office of the Procurator General in Berlin. It has approximately one hundred lawyers on its staff. They are organized into several departments. One deals with offenses against the economy and socialist property, one deals with general criminal business, and one is responsible for supervising legality. Another is responsible for working with the public, still another is responsible for research on crime and delinquent behavior in cooperation with other research activities, and the two remaining departments are concerned with budget and finance and with statistics, information, and analysis.

The Procurator General, operating through this three-tiered, countrywide structure, is clothed with substantial powers. He and the procurators under him have all of the powers that prosecuting attorneys traditionally have had in Germany; they are the officials vested with the authority to initiate and conduct criminal prosecutions at all levels. In addition, the procurators are vested with authority to oversee all investigations carried on by any agency, including those conducted by the police, the Ministry of the Interior, and the customs officials. Pursuant to this authority, the Procurator General issues regulations governing the conduct of investigations; he oversees such official activity and sometimes gives instructions as to when and how particular investigations should be carried out.

Procurators are authorized to participate in any civil, family, or labor case "for the sake of a correct application of the law and safeguarding the uniformity of jurisdiction." In Anglo-American litigation such official intervention into what are regarded as private disputes is rare, if not altogether unknown. Procurators also have the authority to appeal any district court decision to the county court. A decision to take such an appeal is apparently made in the district procurator's office, but it is made in consultation with the county procurator's office because the lawyers there will handle the case in the county court.

Beyond these powers, however, is perhaps the most pervasive one of all, namely, the power to oversee the legality of the activities of all state organs and enterprises. In theory the

Procurator General is charged with the responsibility of seeing that the country functions in accordance with the principles of socialist legality. This authority goes considerably beyond the authority to prosecute for crime. It empowers the Procurator General to take a variety of actions to identify and correct illegalities. The concept of such authority is copied from the Soviet Union and represents a significant departure from the role of the prosecutor in traditional German law.

The Procurator General is also vested with authority to recommend to the Supreme Court that it review a case through its cassation procedure. Only the Procurator General and the President of the Supreme Court have this power, and the Supreme Court can only consider a case on cassation if requested to do so by one or the other of those two officials. The Procurator General is authorized to attend sessions of the *Plenum* of the Supreme Court and to participate in its discussions and deliberations, although he has no vote. He may likewise attend and participate in meetings of the Council of Ministers, similarly without a vote.

The present Procurator General is Josef Streit, who has held this office since 1962. He is a member of the SED. Although no biographical information about him seems to be officially available, it appears from other sources that he was born in Czechoslovakia, became active in the Communist movement there, and was imprisoned in a concentration camp from 1938 to 1945. His only formal legal education consisted of one of the short courses immediately after the war to train "people's judges."

The training ground for lawyers who become procurators is the Law Section in the University at Jena. With rare exceptions the graduates of that law section all go into the service of the Procurator General. That official has a relationship with the Law Section in Jena similar to that of the Minister of Justice with the Law Section in Berlin. In other words, the Procurator General's office is the "practice partner" for the Jena Law Section, collaborating with it on curriculum matters and in the placement of its graduates. The students studying law at Jena do their practical work at the end of the second and third years under the aegis of the Procurator General. At the end of the third year they all work in procurators' offices throughout the country.

Usually a student begins work immediately upon graduation in a district procurator's office. Inasmuch as those offices are relatively small and their work unspecialized, they are thought to be the best training grounds for young apprentice procurators. The apprentice goes through a one-year probationary training period under a work contract with the Procurator General. If performance is satisfactory he is appointed a procurator at the end of the year and is assigned to an office other than the one in which he has trained. A common career pattern involves service in a district procurator's office for several years followed by assignment to a county procurator's office. Some move eventually into the Office of the Procurator General in Berlin.

All procurators are appointed by the Procurator General and are subject to removal by him. The Procurator General also specifies the office to which each procurator is assigned. Here again is a highly centralized organization with total countrywide control vested in the official at the top. Although the Procurator General can remove anyone in his service from the position of procurator, he must adhere to the general principle in the GDR that an employee cannot simply be fired outright unless he commits a criminal offense; some work must be found for the person, either somewhere in the Procurator General's organization or in another agency.

It is possible for a person who has studied law at Berlin, Leipzig, or Halle to become a procurator, although this is relatively rare. Moreover, it is also possible for one who has served as a procurator to become a judge or to enter some other line of legal work, but this is likewise unusual. Normally, a person remains in the service that he initially enters. Here we see the significance of a student's choice of university for his future legal career. A decision to enroll in the Law Section at Jena is, for all practical purposes, a decision to make a career as a procurator. Correspondingly, enrollment in the Law Section in Berlin, Leipzig, or Halle realistically forecloses the possibility of a career as a procurator.

The interchanging of judges, prosecutors, and Justice Ministry officials which occurs in some West German states and which sometimes occurred in the old Germany is much less feasible in the GDR because of the division of authority between the Minister of Justice and the Procurator General. The former has no authority over procurators, and the latter has no authority over judges. Functionally, judges and procurators in the GDR should be interchangeable, because their university education is essentially the same; both Jena and Berlin follow the "justice curriculum" prescribed in the *Study Plan*. But the future judges and procurators do not get to know one another as students. The future procurators are segregated at Jena, 130 miles southwest of Berlin. One can only speculate as to the effect on procurators of their lack of association with students bound for other legal careers and their isolation in the small city of Jena. The refusal of the Ministry for Higher Education to arrange for my visit to the Jena Law Section prevented an examination of the educational program there.

11 Lawyers and Judges for the Economy

The judges, lawyers, notaries, and procurators who have been discussed thus far are all involved in the "system for the administration of justice." As just described, they are trained for that work in the University Law Sections at Berlin and Jena. They are products of the "justice curriculum." However, the "system for the administration of justice" is concerned only with those areas of the law covered by the criminal, civil, family, and labor codes. Apart from those codes, and outside the state court system, there is, in effect, a separate legal system and a separate body of law concerned with the economic activities of the country. The lawyers and judges who staff that system are trained in the University Law Sections at Leipzig and Halle, where they pursue the "economics curriculum." They are involved as lawyers with state-owned enterprises, as functionaries in various state organs dealing with the economy, and as judges in disputes arising out of economic activity.

The key organ in this second legal system is the State Contract Court. Among other tasks it is charged with adjudicating one of the most important categories of legal disputes in the GDR—those arising between two or more state-owned enterprises. This business of the State Contract Court is, in a sense, at the opposite end of the spectrum from that of the Social Courts. In the latter the matters are relatively small and simple. In the State Contract Court, however, the bulk of the business consists of cases that are large in terms of monetary value and impact on the economy. These cases tend to be more complex than matters handled either in the Social Courts or in the state courts—the other dispute-resolution mechanisms. In addition to its adjudicative work, the State Contract Court plays a substantial role administratively in the management of the GDR economy. It functions directly under the Council of Ministers.

To understand the work of the State Contract Court, one must realize that all means of production in the GDR are publicly owned. Private ownership of businesses has diminished over the years, and what is left is limited to small-scale activities, such as one-man retail outlets. Only 2 percent of the entire labor force is employed in the private sector. Among shops and service establishments, perhaps 10 percent are privately owned. Thus virtually all manufacturing, mining, transportation, processing, and merchandising are carried out through state-owned enterprises. These state businesses are typically identified by the letters "VEB" appearing before their names, meaning "People's Owned Enterprise." A relatively new state-operated entity on the GDR economic scene is the *Kombinat*. This is a combine, a conglomerate of related state-owned enterprises, all contributing to the production of a product. Automobile manufacturing is a good example; enterprises producing tires, engines, and seats, all contribute to the final product.

The various state enterprises and combines enter into contracts and carry on a variety of monetary transactions. These transactions resemble those among corporations and other private businesses in the United States. An enterprise making clothing, for example, must acquire its cloth from one enterprise, its thread from another, its buttons from another, and so on. If it is to build an addition to the plant, it must deal with a construction enterprise. The possible array of commercial and other economic relationships is nearly endless. Out of this array of relationships, transactions, and contracts arise disputes that superficially resemble disputes arising in a private enterprise setting, a major difference being that all the parties have a common owner—the state. These disputes form the business of the State Contract Court.

Although it is called a "Court," this is really a system of courts, organized into two levels—regional and central. There is a contract court in each of the fourteen counties and in East Berlin. Above these county contract courts is the Central Contract Court, sitting in Berlin. This system functions under the authority of the Council of Ministers. It plays an important role in managing the GDR economy.

The State Contract Court is headed by a president. He is appointed by the Council of Ministers and is removable by the Council at any time. The president appoints all the judges of the Central Contract Court. The president also appoints the director (presiding judge) of each of the fifteen county contract courts. All of these persons who are appointed by the president are also removable by him. The director of each county contract court appoints the judges of that court, and he can remove them at any time. In short, unlike the judges of the state courts, the judges of the contract courts have no fixed terms of office and they are not responsible to any representative assemblies. They are responsible only to their directors and the Council of Ministers. The Ministry of Justice plays no part in the selection of contract judges or in the administration and operation of these courts.

The reason that the State Contract Court is responsible to the Council of Ministers as a whole, and not to any one ministry, is that the court is concerned with the entire economy of the country. It is involved in disputes arising among enterprises in all areas of economic activity. Thus there is no one ministry whose jurisdiction would be coextensive with the concerns of this court. Its business cuts across almost all of the ministries. The reason that contract judges are not selected by assemblies, as state court judges are, can probably be traced to the centrally and tightly managed economy of the GDR. It would probably be viewed as discordant and disruptive to allow any assemblies or other localized entities to have a role in picking the persons who are to play such an important part in the management of that centrally planned economy.

The State Contract Court—or, more precisely, the Central Contract Court—is the "practice partner" for the Law Sections at Leipzig and Halle. It cooperates with those sections in discussions of curriculum and other academic policies, in arranging the practical training for their students, and in the placement of their graduates. The Central Contract Court makes known to these law sections the openings for lawyers in enterprises throughout the country, in the county contract courts, and in other government agencies. The court collaborates with the two sections and coordinates the assignment of their graduates to the vacancies in the enterprises and in the county contract courts.

A law graduate from Leipzig or Halle can become a judge on a county contract court in two ways. One is that he may go directly from the university to work in one of these courts. If he is found suitable and otherwise qualified after a period of perhaps one to three years, he can then be made a contract judge on that court. The other way is for the law graduate to join the legal staff of an enterprise. After a few years in that position he can be made a judge on a county contract court. However, on the county contract courts not all of the judges are lawyers. Estimates are that approximately 80 to 90 percent are university law trained. The others have been educated in economics. Some who have studied economics later pursue the study of law through the part-time program.

Although the director of the county contract court can remove a person from a judgeship, he cannot, under GDR law generally, discharge the person from all employment except for cause as specified in the law, chiefly the commission of a criminal offense. Thus, if the director does remove him from his position as judge, the director must provide other employment on the court or arrange for the person to be placed elsewhere in suitable work.

The judges on the Central Contract Court are drawn mainly from among those persons who have served as judges on the county contract courts. They are selected for the central court by the president and they hold office at his pleasure. The Central Contract Court is organized into several departments. These include a department concerned with developing new legislation governing the economy, a department of statistics and information, and an administrative department. Thus there are numerous staff positions and opportunities for work other than work as a judge.

The State Contract Court has functions beyond that of adjudicating disputes between enterprises. It monitors the implementation of the five-year economic plan. It proposes modifications in the plan from time to time, and it participates in the formulation of new plans. To an American lawyer this governmental entity would probably appear more like an administrative agency than a court, in that it combines adjudicative, executive, and legislative functions relating to the country's economy.

That the court goes beyond the kind of adjudicative functions to which Anglo-American courts are confined can be seen in several ways. For example, when one enterprise files a complaint against another seeking some sort of relief, either an order requiring the other enterprise to comply with a contract or an award of damages, the contract court can alter the existing contract. Although the contract court is bound by the national five-year plan, it is not bound by contracts entered into by enterprises. If the court deems it necessary to achieve the goals of that plan, it can alter a contract to achieve that end. Moreover, the contract court can hold a case in abeyance while it seeks a modification of the national plan from the appropriate central authorities. The court might recommend a modification in light of difficulties revealed by the case before it. The plan can then be altered by other authorities, and if it is modified, the court can proceed to dispose of the case under the changed plan. On the other hand, if the plan is not modified, the court proceeds to dispose of the matter under the plan as it is. Still other evidence of its administrative character is the court's self-starting power. It need not await the filing of a complaint before taking hold of a matter, but may on its own motion reach out and bring before it a case or problem for consideration.

When the court is sitting to adjudicate a dispute, it functions much in the style of an ordinary judicial tribunal. It hears witnesses, receives documentary evidence, resolves disputed factual questions, applies the law and the terms of the contract, and ultimately renders a decision resolving the matter. The law applied is the GDR economic law; the court is not concerned with the criminal, civil, family, and labor codes. In hearing cases the judges sometimes sit alone, but at other times they sit with two other persons analogous to lay judges in the state courts. The court can give two forms of judicial relief: an award of money as compensation for harm caused or an order requiring an enterprise to do or not to do certain things.

Ordinarily a complaint by an enterprise is filed initially in a county contract court. However, the Central Contract Court has authority to take a matter up in the first instance. It does this where it considers the subject matter to be of special national importance. Apparently it can either do this on a case-by-case basis, or it can adopt a policy that certain types of cases must be initiated in the central court. For example, cases arising in the shipping industry were at one time dealt with directly by the Central Contract Court. But unless this body is sitting as a forum of first instance, it acts as a reviewing forum for decisions made in the county contract courts. Apparently any decision rendered by a county contract court can be appealed to the central court.

Decisions of the Central Contract Court and the county contract courts are published annually in a single volume of approximately two hundred pages. Many of the reported decisions are quite brief, occupying less than a page.

Data concerning the internal organization of the contract courts and the exact number of their personnel are even more difficult to obtain than data concerning the state courts. Estimates are that on the 15 county contract courts there are approximately 150 judges. The number ranges from 5 to 10 on the smaller courts and from 20 to 30 on the larger courts, depending on factors such as volume of economic activity and population. The busiest, and perhaps the most important, of the county contract courts is in Berlin because many major enterprises are based there. On the Central Contract Court there are approximately 30 to 40 judges. Judges on all of these courts are organized along subject-matter lines, in the traditional German style, relating to the economic activities that generate their business.

Some measure of the amount of legal manpower involved in the entire contract court system can be derived from the number of law graduates annually going to work in that system. Estimates are that approximately 20 graduates from the Leipzig and Halle Law Sections (10 from each) are assigned each year to the county contract courts. This is only about 10 percent of the graduates from those sections. Another 10 percent take positions in various state organs concerned with the economy. The remaining 80 percent, a total of 160 annually, go to legal positions in the state-owned enterprises, where there are approximately 3,000 lawyers. As mentioned before, the annual manpower needs of the entire economic law system are supplied by the Law Sections at Leipzig and Halle.

Proceedings of all types in the fifteen county contract courts total 20,000 to 30,000 annually. In the exercise of its review function over these county cases, the Central Contract Court handles an estimated 1,000 matters annually. The State Contract Court is concerned only with disputes arising among enterprises inside the GDR, that is, only with domestic transactions. The court has no jurisdiction over disputes that arise out of dealings between enterprises in the GDR and persons or enterprises in other countries. Such disputes are governed by a different body of law and lie within the jurisdiction of another forum, the name of which is generally translated into English as the "Arbitrage Commission."

The Arbitrage Commission has been in existence in the GDR for approximately thirty years. It is based in East Berlin, in quarters near the Pergamon Museum, not far from the University. The Commission is made up of forty persons, each of whom serves on a part-time basis to adjudicate disputes arising out of transnational economic activities. Its staff consists of a permanent secretary and a few clerical personnel. The forty members are all engaged full-time in other work. They are scattered throughout East Berlin and the GDR. Most of them are law-trained persons, although some are economists. Even the law-trained members, however, often have a degree in economics as well. All of them are engaged in one way or another in work relating to law, economics, and international transactions. They work as either teachers or researchers in universities or other institutions and as officials in various government organizations. The Chairman works in the Academy for State and Law in Babelsberg. The members come to the Commission's quarters in Berlin only to hear cases.

Approximately 75 percent of the Commission's work involves disputes between enterprises in the GDR and enterprises in other Eastern European countries. Under the multinational agreement known in the West as Comecon, and in the GDR as CMEA (Council for Mutual Economic Assistance), disputes between enterprises in two or more of the signatory countries must be resolved by the GDR Arbitrage Commission or by a similar commission in one of the other countries. Because of the substantial volume of such cases, members of the GDR Commission become quite expert in the relevant law and hence can usually dispose of these cases expeditiously.

Where the dispute is between an enterprise in the GDR and an enterprise in a country outside this communist trade group, the matter is more difficult. In the first place, the Commission does not automatically have jurisdiction, as it does under Comecon. Jurisdiction depends upon the terms of the particular contract. Parties may agree that their disputes will be taken to the GDR Commission, or they may specify some other entity such as the International Chamber of Commerce in Paris or the American Arbitration Association. Enterprises in the GDR tend to insist upon having a clause inserted giving jurisdiction to the GDR Commission, but enterprises in other countries often resist that. In any event, approximately a quarter of the Arbitrage Commission's business is derived from disputes arising out of transactions with parties in noncommunist nations. These take more time and are more difficult for Commission members because they are less familiar with the applicable law.

The Commission normally decides cases through panels of three members. The complaining party picks one member and the opposing party picks another; those two then pick a third member. The procedures permit a single member of the Commission to hear and decide a case, if all parties agree. The single-member procedure is often used for disputes of smaller magnitude and less complexity. If all parties can agree on a single member's resolving the case, but they cannot agree on who that person should be, the Chairman of the Commission can designate a member. Usually, though, when the disputants want to have a single member resolve the matter, they mutually select that person.

The forty-member Commission is composed of experts in the various fields out of which disputes can arise. For example, if there is a question involving banking practices, the parties can designate one or more members of the Commission who have substantial experience in that field. Virtually every area of the economy has its expert on the Commission. Thus, according to one member, enterprises have considerable confidence in the Commission's work; they know that expertise is being brought to bear on the disputes and that reasonable solutions will be reached.

The Secretary of the Commission performs a screening function. He advises claimants and potential claimants as to how they should prepare their cases. He also discourages the filing of complaints where he believes there is little likelihood of success. Apparently numerous potential cases are resolved as the result of the Secretary's suggestions to the parties as to a reasonable compromise. Of the claims that are filed, approximately 90 percent are settled before any hearing takes place.

Cases not settled are set for hearing before a Commission panel—either three members or one member. The proceedings resemble those of a court. The evidence offered usually consists of affidavits and documents involved in the transaction. Apparently it is not common for witnesses to testify in person. However, representatives of the parties do appear and make arguments. The lawyers appearing for the GDR enterprises are often those employed in the enterprises, but sometimes practicing lawyers are engaged by the enterprises to represent them in the Commission hearing.

The Commission panel usually renders a decision promptly. Most cases turn on one or two fairly well understood issues. Sometimes, for example, there is a single issue of fact, such as whether certain goods crossed an international boundary on a certain date, or whether the goods specified in the bill of lading were in fact the goods delivered. Such factual issues—or mixed fact-law questions—can normally be resolved readily by the three Commissioners. A small percentage of the cases are more complex and difficult, requiring extended study and deliberation.

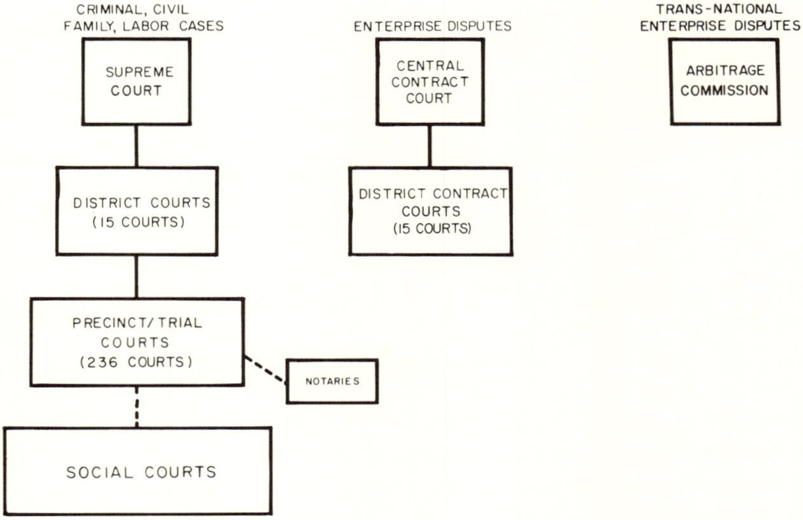

Fig. 5. The machinery for the resolution of disputes in the GDR.

In 1984 the Arbitrage Commission celebrated its thirtieth anniversary. It is estimated that by that anniversary year the Commission had handled approximately seven thousand cases since its creation. Cases are currently coming to the Commission at the rate of several hundred annually. The general perception is that there is no substantial backlog; the Commission disposes of matters expeditiously once they are ripe for decision.

To sum up, the State Contract Court and the Arbitrage Commission together hear and decide a large array of important legal disputes arising out of the GDR's state-run economy. These disputes—governed by the economic law and regulations—involve collectively more substantial monetary amounts and have a greater economic impact than those that come before the state court system under the civil, family, and labor codes. Moreover, they are certainly more important economically than the large number of cases that come before the Social Courts. As this chapter should make clear, if one looks only at the state court system, as an American tends to do, he gets a truncated view of the GDR legal order. One must consider together the Social Courts, the three-tiered state court system, the State Contract Court, and the Arbitrage Commission in order to have in view the entire legal apparatus and dispute-resolving machinery in the GDR. This system is portrayed in figure 5.

12
The Lawyers' Association

The lawyers' association is the one organization in the GDR that embraces all types of law-trained persons in both the justice and economic fields. It has approximately six thousand members. Its President is Dr. Heinrich Toeplitz, the President of the Supreme Court. Its full-time Secretary General heads a staff of six, three of whom are lawyers. The staff offices and the Association's headquarters are on Littenstrasse in the center of East Berlin in the building that also houses the Supreme Court.

Membership in the Association is open to anyone in the GDR who is a *Jurist*. This broad title includes anyone who has the degree of *Diplom jurist* or who studied law through the short postwar courses previously described. There is no word in American or English usage that is as all-encompassing. One is a *Jurist* in Germany (in the FRG as well as the GDR) if he has a university legal education, whether he is a judge, prosecutor, practicing lawyer, notary, enterprise counsel, or government lawyer. All of these types of legal work are represented in the membership of the GDR Lawyers' Association. Officials in the Association say that there is no exact count of the total number of such persons in the GDR. However, they estimate that the 6,000 members in the Association constitute about 90 to 95 percent of such persons. This estimate seems plausible when one considers that the country has approximately 600 practicing lawyers, 3,000 enterprise lawyers, 1,250 state court judges, 1,000 procurators, 190 contract judges, 250 or more law teachers, and an unknown number of lawyers in various government agencies.

Lawyers also belong to the trade union at their places of work. Some lawyers belong to an industrial union, some to an office workers' union, and others to the state administrative workers' union. In other words, in relation to trade union membership, lawyers are viewed the same as all other workers. But the Lawyers' Association provides them with a separate organization of their own.

According to the Association staff, the organization is supported entirely by membership dues. Monthly dues range from 2 to 10 marks, depending on the income of the member. No figures are available on the total income of the Association from this source. However, assuming that monthly dues average 5 marks per member, a membership of 6,000 would produce an annual income of 360,000 marks. This is roughly 11 times the annual salary of a Supreme Court Judge in the GDR. An organizational income of this magnitude, or indeed somewhat less, seems adequate to sustain a staff of six and some educational and publishing activities.

The Association was founded in 1949 by thirty to forty jurists in East Germany. It came into being against a backdrop of a decimated legal profession. According to GDR estimates—as mentioned in an earlier chapter—when the war ended in 1945, 80 to 85 percent of the judges and prosecutors then in office had been members of the Nazi party. The proportion of university law teachers and practicing lawyers with Nazi affiliations is also put at a high figure. It was deemed imperative to remove all such persons from the administration of justice. The resulting void was made even larger by the movement westward of numerous law-trained persons who were genuinely antifascist but who were also genuinely democratic and found it increasingly difficult to remain as the Marxist-Leninist vise tightened. This severe shortage of legal manpower led to the creation of the crash programs described earlier through which persons "off the street," many with no previous university education of any kind, were given law courses lasting only a few weeks or months and then put into service. The Lawyers' Association was established to provide a means to bring these people together, to provide a forum for the sharing of views, and to further their educational development.

The organization's purposes today are at least superficially similar to those one would find in bar associations in the United States, namely, to provide a means for disseminating information about new developments in the law, for exchanging views about professional and legal problems, and for providing continuing education. It is also the vehicle through which the lawyers of the GDR communicate with lawyers and legal organizations elsewhere in the world, especially those in other Marxist-Leninist countries.

The Association is a voluntary organization in the sense that no *Jurist* is officially compelled to join. Whether failure to join the Association is harmful to one's professional career is not clear. The Association is not independent and nonpolitical in the way that bar associations are considered to be in the United States. Like all other organizations in the GDR, it is tied to the SED. This political connection is explicitly enunciated in the opening paragraphs of the Association's charter. The following is an excerpt:

> The Association of Lawyers of the GDR works, under the leadership of the Party of the working class, for the strengthening of the socialist state and legal system. It supports the sovereign rights and interests of the German Democratic Republic, cooperates in further developing the socialist democracy and champions socialist

> legality and the conscientious application of the law in all spheres of society. It promotes and spreads the Marxist-Leninist political and legal science and contributes toward consolidating the socialist and civic and legal consciousness of the citizens of the German Democratic Republic.

The Association is structured in line with the administrative organization of the country. In each of the fourteen counties (and in Berlin) and in each of the districts, there is a branch of the Association. These branches elect delegates who meet in a national conference every five years. At this conference the delegates elect the central board of 100 members which is the governing body of the Association. The delegates' conference also elects an 11-member executive committee of the central board. The membership of the Association as a whole never convenes in a national meeting.

In addition to branch meetings there are also periodic meetings of the sections of the Association. There are sections on civil law, family law, criminal law, economic law, administrative law, and international law. Each of these from time to time presents an educational program of special interest to its members. These programs are part of the continuing legal education function of the Association. The section meetings are the only occasions on which members from throughout the country come together.

The only publication produced by the Association regularly for its entire membership is an information bulletin that appears four times a year. However, the Association does sporadically publish special items. For example, when a new law is promulgated, information about it may be mailed to the membership.

The Lawyers' Association is affiliated with the International Association of Democratic Lawyers. This is a worldwide confederation of legal organizations. Most of its affiliated groups are in communist countries, although numerous noncommunist countries are also represented. Three organizations in the United States are affiliated: the National Lawyers' Guild and the National Conference of Black Lawyers, both based in New York City, and La Raza of Houston. The GDR Lawyers' Association seems to play a relatively active role in the IADL, by contributing articles to its publications and otherwise.

Another international involvement of the Lawyers' Association concerns foreign visitors to the GDR. The Association acts as semiofficial host for foreign lawyers; it is the point of contact between such visitors and the GDR legal organs. It provides information to foreign visitors and arranges meetings between them and GDR lawyers, judges, and officials. In arranging such meetings, the Association was helpful to me in carrying out this study.

The most substantial international involvement of the Lawyers' Association is its publication of the English language periodical entitled *Law and Legislation in the German Democratic Republic.* Publication of this periodical began in 1952. Originally a French edition was also published, but it was discontinued in 1973. This publication appears two or three times a year; each issue contains between 60 and 150 pages. Its editor holds a full-time staff position in the Association's offices in Berlin. Today *Law and Legislation* is the only legal publication produced in the GDR that is in any language other than German. There is no legal publication in the Russian language. The purpose of this periodical is to inform the English-speaking world about law and legal developments as seen from inside the GDR. Three-thousand copies of each issue are printed. Copies are mailed to every English-speaking country and to a total of ninety countries throughout the world. Copies are sent to many institutions and individuals on an exchange or complimentary basis; others are sold on a subscription basis. The main value of *Law and Legislation* is in its English translations of important GDR statutes dealing with the legal system. The significant statutes concerning the state courts, the administration of justice, and criminal, civil, family, and labor law have all been translated into English and printed in this periodical. A list of some of these translations is contained in Appendix M.

In addition to publishing translations of statutes, *Law and Legislation* also contains articles written by law professors, judges, and others. These deal with various aspects of GDR law and often treat jurisprudential themes from the Marxist-Leninist perspective. To an American reader these articles have several common characteristics. First, they are verbose and awkwardly worded. Whether this results from the relative verbosity of much German writing or from translation problems is unclear. Many GDR translators use wordy and cumbersome phraseology, stating matters in ways that Americans find awkward. There is, in addition, a use of multisyllabic and abstract words that tend to obscure meaning or, rather, to convey little or no meaning. Much of this writing seems propangandistic to Americans, replete with the repeated usage of words such as *socialism, working class,* and *imperialism* and lacking concrete examples and specific facts. An American reader is likely to think that he learns nothing about what is really going on or how the law really functions. One is not likely to find here the empirical or analytical type of writing appearing in American law reviews. Nevertheless, one can get a flavor of the legal thinking in the GDR.

Because of their commitment to Marxism-Leninism, jurists in the GDR are different from those in the Federal Republic and from their predecessors in an earlier Germany. However, their relative roles and status in the society are similar to those of jurists in prewar Germany. German judges and lawyers have never had the status, influence, and power that such persons have in the United States. Their position has been analogous to that of middle- to upper-level bureaucrats. They have been important functionaries in the running of the system, but they seldom have occupied top positions in the government. This is true today in the GDR (although jurists in the FRG seem to play more important roles than has been traditional, e.g., in Parliament and on the Constitutional Court). In the GDR, for example, no member of the Council of State is a lawyer. On the Politburo only one candidate member is a lawyer. Among the 32 members of the Council of Ministers, only the Minister of Justice is a lawyer. According to a 1982 directory of the People's Chamber, only 14 of the 500 members of that body have a legal education. These include the President of the Supreme Court and 3 law professors.

Another way of gauging the relative importance of the legal profession is to compare the ratio of lawyers to population in the GDR with that in other countries. Such a comparison is difficult because the exact number of law-trained persons in the GDR is unknown. However, if the 6,000 members of the Lawyers' Association constitute at least 90 percent of all jurists, as is estimated, the total would be approximately 6,700. Using that figure, Table 10 presents a comparison of the GDR with selected other countries in terms of ratio of lawyers to population, based on statistics for recent years from various sources.

Among other things, these figures reflect the well-known facts that common law countries have more lawyers than civil law countries and that the United States has far more lawyers

TABLE 10. LAWYERS PER CAPITA IN SELECTED COUNTRIES

Country	Lawyers (Per 100,000 Population)
USA	286
United Kingdom	95
FRG	85
GDR	40
Japan	12

than any other nation. The table also reveals the widely known fact that Japan has far fewer lawyers than any other industrialized nation. By that standard, the GDR seems well stocked with lawyers, having over three times as many per capita as Japan. Because of various ways of counting lawyers (i.e., whether to include judges, corporate counsel, etc.) there may be inaccuracies in these figures, but they are at least suggestive of differing national patterns.

In relation to the impact of Marxism-Leninism on the role of law and lawyers, the most significant comparison is between the GDR and the FRG, because the historical, cultural, and legal backgrounds of these two societies are the same. The differences have come about since the East-West division of 1945. As this table shows, the FRG has more than twice as many lawyers per capita as the GDR, a fact consistent with the view that law plays a lesser—or at least different—role in a Marxist-Leninist society than it does in a western-style parliamentary democracy.

The next chapter offers some impressions of that role and some comparative observations about legal education and law in the GDR.

Part 4

Concluding Observations

13
On Law and Legal Education

In the previous chapters I have undertaken to set out information gathered in East Germany about that country's legal education and legal systems. Here I offer some summarizing observations and personal impressions on those subjects.

In each of the two German states now existing in portions of the territory of the former German Reich, the task of creating a new government and society since the Second World War has been formidable. The political, legal, and economic lines of development in East and West Germany have, of course, been radically different.

In the larger of the two states—the Federal Republic of Germany—there is a greater sense of continuity with the past despite some American influences. Although efforts were made from the beginning to eliminate the undesirable elements of that past, in law and government most of the historical structure was preserved. The major nineteenth-century codes were essentially carried forward with modifications. The decentralized state structure was preserved, with some redrawn boundaries, in a new federal government. The long-existing four-tiered court structure was continued, with the *Bundesgerichthof* in Karlsruhe replacing the *Reichgericht* in Leipzig. Many of these courts occupied the same buildings they had occupied since the turn of the century and earlier. The custom of having a law faculty in each university was continued, and the plan for legal education remained essentially the same. The Minister of Justice in each state remained in overall control of all legal careers and professions, including those of judges, prosecutors, practitioners, and government lawyers. After 1949 all of this functioned in the context of a parliamentary democracy with multiple competing political parties, under a newly written "Basic Law," with a constitutional court to interpret it.

In contrast, the founders of the German Democratic Republic aimed to make a clean break with the past. This aim was not realized immediately, and for some years after the war the preexisting court structure and system for legal education continued, although denuded of the university-educated personnel that had been manning these institutions. Within the preexisting framework, however, the authorities began moving toward the establishment of a Marxist-Leninist system. This movement was hampered in the early years by the lack of legally trained persons and appropriate laws and legal texts. Once the GDR was established in 1949, there was no longer any doubt that the society, including educational and legal institutions, would be reshaped along Marxist-Leninist lines. There was little sense of maintaining continuity with the past. The break was evidenced in part by the abolition of the old political subdivisions, by the discarding of the former court structure, by the changes in university organization and curriculum, by the introduction of a completely new government and party structure, and by the rewriting of laws. By thus undertaking to build a new state and scrapping so much of what existed, the GDR faced a considerably more difficult task than the FRG, even had it not been for its more serious economic and political difficulties. The objective was to create a socialist state based on Marxism-Leninism that would gradually evolve into communism.

Progress in the GDR in that direction was uneven. In law and legal education one has the sense that it was not until the 1970s that the comprehensive building of a new system was substantially accomplished. During that unusually active decade in the legal sphere, most of the substantive and procedural law administered through the state court system was rewritten in a way that divested it of remaining traces of the "bourgeois system" and infused it with the principles of Marxism-Leninism. By that time the GDR's means of production had been brought almost entirely under state ownership, and its economic law became well developed as a separate legal system governing the state-owned economic enterprises and the centrally planned economy. By the 1980s the various organs and institutions making up the two legal systems seemed firmly grounded and integrated. The GDR had a mature and well-established system of socialist law and legal education.

Today all legal institutions in the GDR are manned increasingly by persons who have known no other system. The year 1985 marks the fortieth anniversary of the German surrender and the onset of Soviet occupation in the East. In 1984 the country celebrated its thirty-fifth anniversary as a separate, independent German state. Thus two generations have been reared under Marxism-Leninism. Jurists educated before the Second World War and in the turbulent postwar years are passing from the scene. The President of the Supreme Court, Dr. Heinrich Toeplitz, may be the only remaining active jurist who had no Marxist-Leninist university experience. Persons who were put through the short cram courses to fill the void in the legal system in 1945 and 1946 were at or approaching retirement age by the 1980s and are now becoming rarities.

The legal organs today are largely in the hands of persons who have received their training since 1949 in the four GDR university law sections or in the Academy for State and Law. The typical male *Jurist* in the 1980s, if he is less than fifty years old, is likely almost to a point of certainty to have the following combination of experiences: he will have been a member of the Young Pioneers and later of the Free German Youth (FDJ); he will have served on active duty in the military service for at least eighteen months; he will have studied law at either Berlin, Jena, Leipzig, or Halle. Throughout all of this he will have been schooled in Marxism-Leninism. There is about a 75 percent chance that he is a member of the SED. Among the 50 percent of jurists who are women, the only significant difference in career pattern is likely to be the lack of service in the armed forces. The totality of these experiences means that the typical *Jurist* is a tested and reliable citizen of the GDR, supportive of the system, whether or not he or she enthusiastically believes in it. There are, of course, a few mavericks. There are several among the fifty independent practicing lawyers in the country. Those among the university law-trained persons who found the system intolerable before 1961 left, but those who have found it so since that time have not had that option.

An American observer must remind himself, however, that in the GDR law rests on different premises and is designed to serve different ends from law in the Anglo-American world. In the GDR law is designed to promote, preserve, and perfect a collectivist society. It looks constantly to the "further development of socialism" (a commonly heard phrase) leading ultimately to communism. Law is not designed to protect individuals *from* the exercise of state power; the interests of individuals and the state are the same under Marxist-Leninist theory, and hence there can be no conflict. There can, of course, be "enemies of the working class" and hence of the workers' party and the state. Whatever their precise conduct, such persons are variously labeled capitalists, imperalists, individualists, or parasites. The Criminal Code enables the system to deal with them, but much of the law is aimed at educating, cajoling, managing, and directing the masses toward the collective ends fixed by the Politburo and Central Committee of the SED. In other words, law is simply part of the apparatus through which the working class and its ruling party manifest their will. One might fairly say that the GDR is in considerable measure a government by law or through law but not a government under law in the Anglo-American sense. Law, in short, is a means of control.

As mentioned before, according to Marxist-Leninist theory, law will "wither away" in a state of pure communism, but law in the GDR shows no signs of doing so. Rather, it flourishes in the new codes, the four university law sections, and the two legal systems. At times citizens show great interest in the law. The Civil Code, promulgated in 1975 after seventeen years of work, became a best-seller. Some two million copies were sold through bookstores in a population of 16.7 million. More than twice as many students apply for admission to the university law sections as can be admitted. Yet, for all of this, Professor Inga Markovits makes an impressive case that law and legal process are not really meaningful to GDR citizens; they seek legal redress through the courts to a relatively small extent. When they do assert individual grievances, they tend to do so through an administrative complaint procedure which gives them no "rights." According to this analysis law is primarily a means of social control rather than a means for effectuating individual rights and autonomy.[4]

Law apparently is seen as involving duties as often as it involves rights. Here the United States might learn a useful lesson. The GDR concept that citizenship involves a duty to pursue an education to the limit of one's abilities, a duty to work, and a duty to support one's country is not something to be dismissed lightly. In the United States we speak of such things loosely as among the "duties of good citizenship," but they are often not taken seriously. In any event, Americans do not consider such duties to be part of the Constitution.

Sometimes Westerners say, in a disparaging tone, that many disputes in the GDR are handled outside "the regular court

[4]*Ibid.*

system." That statement is virtually meaningless. It is true that many matters that would be handled by courts in the United States are handled through Social Courts, the State Contract Court, and the Arbitrage Commission, and not in the state court system (the three-tiered judicial structure headed by the Supreme Court). But that is simply a matter of organization and form. In function and reality it makes little difference whether one says that matters are in the latter court system or in other forums. There is no set of forums in the GDR manned by the kinds of "independent" judges known to the Anglo-American world. The selection processes, limited terms, and lack of any tenure security combine to insure that GDR adjudicators will be at all times in tune with the policies of the ruling party. In the United States the statement that something is "outside the regular courts" may be meaningful because our conception of a "court" carries with it notions about judicial independence, separation of powers, and government under law that are not present in the GDR. In the GDR the entire machinery for the resolution of disputes—whatever the particular forum—is functionally designed to do a job, namely, to settle disputes, to educate the people, and to steer matters toward the common end of developing a better socialist system under the policies of the SED.

The American doctrine of separation of powers is viewed by GDR jurists as a myth or an illusion. A law professor explained that there can be no such thing as a separation of power because all power is ultimately in the hands of the ruling class, whatever that class may be. In the GDR it is the working class, while in the United States, he said, it is the capitalists. What Americans have, he explained, is a division of functions and competencies in their government because no one agency or body can do everything; one body can be assigned to draft laws, other bodies can be designated to resolve disputes, and so on. But this separation of tasks is not a separation of power because no ruling class will relinquish its power or share it with others.

When one considers that all aspects of GDR life are centrally planned and controlled by the state, it is perhaps not surprising to find that such total management of human activity requires a plethora of institutions and written prescriptions. Also perhaps one can see here the German tendency toward bureaucratic structures with their peculiar vertical and horizontal relationships. These complex organizational relationships can be seen in the GDR's legal education and legal systems. The university law sections are directly under the authority of the Ministry for Higher Education. At the same time, however, each section is subordinate to its central university administration and is officially tied to another state entity—its "practice partner"that works with it on academic policy and controls the placement of its graduates. These practice partners—the Ministry of Justice (for Humboldt), the Procurator General (for Jena), and the State Contract Court (for Leipzig and Halle)—are in turn tied to different sources of authority and to different controls. The Ministry of Justice and the State Contract Court are under the Council of Ministers, while the Procurator General is directly under the People's Chamber and the Council of State. The judges on the two lower court levels are subject to the Supreme Court's control, but the Minister of Justice plays a significant role in selecting and promoting them and in providing their administrative support. Whatever the criss-crossing lines of authority, however, all of these entities ultimately come together at the top under the control of the Politburo and Central Committee of the SED.

The concept of centrally planning and controlling all human activity has been taken to a high degree in the GDR. In legal education this concept underlies the centrally prescribed curriculum and the centrally directed writing and publishing of legal textbooks. The thoroughness with which the law curriculum has been centrally designed and the teaching books commissioned and produced is impressive. This curriculum and teaching material, as well as the legal research plan, are developed through the Council for Legal Education functioning under the Ministry for Higher Education. Inasmuch as the Council is made up of representatives from all four university law sections, as well as from various state organs, it embodies a kind of "participatory democracy" in the development of the central legal education plan. Here we see the concept of "democratic centralism" on which much emphasis is placed. However, as mentioned before, despite the participation of a representative number of law teachers in the planning process, individual law teachers have little or no room left to design courses, to develop their own teaching material, and to pursue their own research. In effect, the law teachers are persons commissioned to implement the official curriculum and to convey its message.

Perhaps an American can best grasp the flavor of GDR university legal education not by thinking of it as he would think of academic activity in an American university but by thinking of it instead as a training program for soldiers. Indeed, much of the language in the *Study Plan* and elsewhere has a military flavor. Law students are taught to be "militant" and "committed" fighters for socialism and the interests of the working class. They are to be taught "to defend" socialism against arguments made by bourgeois lawyers or by others in the imperialist and capitalist countries. Law students are to be instilled with the importance of political action to further the development of socialism and to educate the people in socialist legality. A law student's experience is a four-year, tightly structured and programmed indoctrination in Marxism-Leninism, designed to develop him into a firm supporter of the regime. A reading of the *Study Plan* in Appendix A conveys the flavor of the law sections' mission. The textbooks have the same flavor. Marxist-Leninist ideology is not simply one of many subjects or merely an initial or peripheral concern; it is the heart and soul of the whole enterprise.

American law schools, in striking contrast, announce no special mission. A survey of the catalogues published annually by law schools across the United States shows that many of them state no purpose or objective at all. Many catalogues do no more than give a brief history of the institution, tersely describe the courses offered, and provide administrative information. Even those law schools that do undertake to state objectives do so only in brief and unrevealing terms, indicating that their academic programs are designed to equip persons to pursue the practice of law effectively or to pursue a career in the law with skill and understanding. Other law schools go a bit further and explain that they aim to inculcate in their students an understanding of the social forces that shape the law and to provide them with an academic experience that will equip them to become leaders in society. In none of these American law school statements, however, is there an enunciation of a political or philosophical framework such as appears in the GDR *Study Plan*. The nearest approximation to such program statements in American law schools is found in the catalogues of some church-related institutions which explicitly assert that the study of law is premised on the existence of divine authority and on Christian principles.

This dearth of articulated purposes and objectives in American law school catalogues is more than simply an editorial omission. It reflects a general lack of consensus as to purpose among American law faculties; a lack that is also evidenced by the disarray of the curriculum. In most American law schools the curriculum is almost entirely elective after the first year, and in many schools even some of the first-year work is elective. Many of the electives are offered because they are subjects of special interest to individual faculty members, not because they relate to a defined overall objective of legal education. The common core of law students' three-year experience has shrunk to a third or less of the subject matter studied. In short, American law schools, unlike the GDR law sections, have no specific "program."

This same contrast can be seen in the governments of the two countries. The GDR as a nation, unlike the United States, has a specific program. Consider the preamble to its Constitution:

> In continuation of the revolutionary traditions of the German working class and in consequence of the liberation from fascism, the people of the German Democratic Republic has, in accordance with the processes of historical development in our time, realized its right to socio-economic, political and national self-determination and is building an advanced socialist society.
>
> Imbued with the will freely to decide its own affairs and to continue unswervingly along the road of socialism and communism, peace, democracy and international friendship, the people of the German Democratic Republic has given itself this socialist Constitution.

Consider also the following provisions in the first few articles in the GDR Constitution:

> The German Democratic Republic is a socialist state of workers and farmers. It is the political organization of the working people in town and countryside led by the working class and its Marxist-Leninist party. (Article 1)

> The inviolable foundations of socialist society are provided by the firm alliance of the working class with the class of co-operative farmers, the intelligentsia, and other sections of the population, by the Socialist ownership of the means of production and management and planning of social development in accordance with the most advanced scientific knowledge. (Article 2)

> The German Democratic Republic is forever and irrevocably allied with the Union of Soviet Socialist Republics. (Article 6)

No comparable political program can be found in the United States Constitution.

An insight into the difference of view between the GDR and the United States concerning the relationship of man and government is provided by the textbook on the *Constitutional Law of Bourgeois States*. In the chapter on the United States Constitution there is a section headed "Basic Rights" (set out in Appendix K). That section presents statistics showing that in America there is considerable crime, poverty, unemployment, and inadequate housing. This evidence is presented to show that "basic rights" do not exist under the United States Constitution. The point is made—quite correctly—that the American Constitution does not even purport to guarantee rights to employment, housing, education, and medical care. In the GDR, on the other hand, these are considered to be *the* basic rights, and they are guaranteed explictly in the GDR Constitution. But these "rights" are not enforceable by individual citizens—through the courts or otherwise. Their fulfillment depends upon the efficacy of the collectivist society.

The United States Constitution, unlike that of the GDR, says that the American program is whatever the people, speaking through freely contested elections, want it to be at any given time. The people's choice is limited only by the strictures that speech, press, and religion must be left free of government control and that government cannot move against persons unless it does so in a circumscribed way, consistent with certain principles that ultimately the courts can enforce, even against government itself.

Yet despite the fundamentally different premises, one can sit and have conversations with GDR law professors that are intelligent, rational, and interesting. I had several such discussions that did not differ significantly from those among American law professors. For example, a civil procedure professor explained his view that in teaching the subject it was important to convey to the students an understanding of basic procedural concepts, rather than a lot of detail and the mechanics of procedure. A criminal law professor discussed ideas concerning decriminalization of various kinds of conduct and the importance of retaining persons in the community as functioning workers rather than sending them to prison. Many of the law professors are obviously intelligent and scholarly types of persons. An American academician cannot help wondering how they can function comfortably in a situation where the scholarly freedom to pursue ideas and to write candidly and critically about existing law and institutions is so circumscribed.

Given the programmed nature of the whole academic enterprise, one also wonders about the objectivity of the scholarship. An analogy here may be that of an advocate's writing a brief as distinguished from a scholar's writing a text. The advocate's job is to marshall all of the arguments and data in support of a given result; in contrast, the scholar's task is to marshall all available data and to bring to bear upon it his critical faculties to develop new insights and understandings. Those engaged in scholarship in the GDR—for example, those writing the textbooks—begin with a given premise and conclusion. They must write pursuant to the Marxist-Leninist theory, and they must explain how that theory sustains the existing legal and governmental system.

Apart from problems of objectivity, there is reason to doubt the quality of the scholarship. The explanation of the United States Constitution, set out in Appendix K, taken from the textbook on *Constitutional Law of Bourgeois States*, can hardly be called good professional work. Even if one wants to describe the American Constitution and government from a Marxist-Leninist perspective, he could surely assemble data and information from sources better than the *Daily Worker* and Gus Hall. Moreover, some significant aspects of the American system are not mentioned at all. This writing has the flavor of a political leaflet rather than that of a scholarly treatise.

In the Ministry for Higher Education there is apparently some discontent with the current law textbooks. This discontent, however, does not stem from the tenor and substance of their contents. Rather, there is concern about the length of these books and their usefulness for law students. A Ministry official explained that they are proud of the existing textbooks, but these books are too voluminous. Currently they weigh a total of about seventy pounds; the official said (with a straight face) that the Ministry would prefer to have a series of books that weigh no more than forty-five pounds. Apparently the Ministry is beginning to plan now for a new series of textbooks that would be somewhat shorter and simpler. The official stressed, however, that the Ministry does not mean to diminish the academic demands on the students. The objective is to produce books more useful as teaching books than as reference books.

At least one professor with whom I spoke apparently agrees with this view of the textbooks and assigns the summary instead, explaining that the latter publication is more helpful to students than the textbook.

GDR law professors sometimes talk like American legal realists. They stress that law is not a set of principles, rules, or norms that can be applied in a detached, objective fashion and from which judges can arrive at decisions free of political ideology. Rather, they say that law is a political instrument to be used to serve specific human ends. Those who make, administer, and apply the law are all political actors serving specific political objectives. In the GDR these objectives are the development of socialism and the protection of the interests of the working class as articulated by the controlling Marxist-Leninist party. There are, of course, important differences between those views and the views of American legal realists, but there is at least a discernible similarity. Also discernible are resemblances to American populism in GDR views about the people's control over judges, as pointed out earlier in the discussion on the state court system. Still another similarity can be seen between Marxist-Leninist views of law in Western countries and the views of some Americans involved in so-called critical legal studies, in that the latter, like the former, assert that law works to preserve a power structure and perpetuates injustices.

In a curious way one can also see in GDR legal education the implementation of some ideas that have long been advocated in American legal education. One of these is clinical education. American law schools have been urged to bring law students directly into contact with real legal problems involving live people. GDR education in general stresses the blending of the practical and the theoretical at every stage. The clinical component for GDR law students is provided by the four weeks of practical training at the end of the second year and the twelve weeks of work at the end of the third year; the latter is the basis for the fourth-year paper. Although many American law students work in law offices during one or more summers of their law school experience, such work is not structured into the curriculum or planned and organized in the way that this work is in the GDR law sections.

Since the Second World War, American law schools have been pressed to give increased attention to the study of comparative, foreign, and international law. Although attention to such subjects has grown, and in some of the larger or more affluent law schools there are several offerings in these fields today, no American law school devotes as large a share of its curriculum to instruction in these subjects as do the GDR law sections. Moreover, such courses are almost never mandatory in American law schools, as they all are in the GDR. The significant amount of instruction in these fields in the GDR may be attributed to the international character of communist ideology. Much stress is placed on the brotherhood of all workers and the community of socialist nations throughout the world. A basic tenet is that the ultimate course of history will bring the union of all mankind under a communist society.

The constitution and laws of the Soviet Union are studied because that country is viewed ideologically as the leading light of the world and, in effect, the GDR's founding parent. The legal systems of other socialist countries are studied because they are considered comrades in ideology and the global struggle. The constitutions and laws of developing countries are studied because they are seen as the wave of the future; friendships with these emerging nations are to be developed, and it is for that reason that GDR law professors go there to teach, and students from these countries come to study law in the GDR. The constitutions of bourgeois states are studied because it is believed to be necessary to know the enemy and to appreciate the threat to "democracy" and to human rights posed by imperialistic capitalism. It is also considered important for GDR law students to understand, as taught in Marxist-Leninist doctrine, how human rights are denied in those countries and how their claims of freedom are fraudulent. Thus the study of foreign law, like the study of all other subjects, is heavily infused with a Marxist-Leninist political orientation. While from a Western standpoint GDR law students appear to have a distorted and peculiar view of law and government in other countries, at least they do have a substantial exposure to the rest of the world that exceeds that of American law students. They know far more about American government—distorted though much of their knowledge may be—than American law students know about GDR government or indeed the government of any other country. International law is approached from the same perspective.

Legal and constitutional history likewise is studied to a much greater extent by GDR law students than by American law students. Two substantial courses are History of the Theory of State and Law and History of the Perceptions of State and Law. These courses trace the sweep of history from the Middle Ages to the present. Students also get substantial segments of history in the courses on the Constitutional Law of the USSR and the Constitutional Law of Bourgeois States.

One of the senior law teachers remarked that in the late 1940s it was necessary to rewrite completely the history of Germany because the only available books dealt with the subject from a bourgeois perspective. This rewriting task occupied the time and efforts of numerous law teachers and other people for several years. Lectures were revised, and textbooks were rewritten, to portray German history in a way that Western scholars would consider novel. This portrayal can be seen by visitors in pictures and texts in the Museum of German History, located just a block from Humboldt University in the old Armory on Unter den Linden. According to this exhibit, the central and dominant theme of German history has been the workers' movement, culminating in the establishment of the German Communist Party in 1919 and ultimately in the creation of the GDR. The heroes and leading actors are communists who otherwise have been accorded little space in the history books.

Although in some respects the subject matter required of GDR law students is broader than that required of American law students, the GDR law students are closed off from many of the ideas and much of the literature and history that students in the United States and a large part of the world take for granted. Although bookstores are not uncommon in the GDR (several are located in the vicinity of each university), and some are quite large, their stock has significant subject-matter limitations. Typically the major book display near the entrance features the "classics of Marxism-Leninism." Here one can find numerous works by and about Marx, Lenin, and Engels. The bookstores contain the usual categories that one finds in bookstores anywhere, under such labels as history, philosophy, mathematics, physics, and so on. My perusal of the stocks of several bookstores in the vicinity of the universities in Berlin, Leipzig, and Halle failed to turn up a single book by or about the philosophers usually studied in the Western world. There was a total absence of writings by or about Plato, Aristotle, and Kant, to name only a few (although Hegel was well represented). Also I found no book on the history of England, the

United States, France, or any other Western country, other than works dealing with them as imperialistic, capitalistic threats to people's democracies. There were works of history on Czechoslovakia, the Soviet Union, other Eastern European countries, and on various African nations.

Newspapers published in the West are apparently not available to students in the University libraries without special permission. The one Western newspaper readily available was the *Morning Star*, the English Communist Party paper. One compensating factor is that students do have access to television from West Germany, and from that source they get news as well as films and plays of various sorts, although not always those that display the Western world at its best. "Dallas," for example, runs regularly on West German television, and it is seen and known in the GDR.

Perhaps this electronic intrusion of Western views and ideas is responsible in part for what seems to be an ideological overkill in the GDR universities. Not only is a sizable portion of the law curriculum devoted to Marxism-Leninism, but in each of the universities substantial attention is also given to that subject through special, separate academic sections. Every university has a Section on Marxism-Leninism. In addition, at Jena there is a Section of Marxist-Leninist Philosophy, and at Leipzig there is a Section of Marxist-Leninist Philosophy and Scientific Communism. Humboldt has two additional groups devoted to the subject: a Section of Marxist-Leninist Philosophy and an Institute of Marxist-Leninist Sociology. Apparently in the GDR view it is impossible to have too much of a good thing.

Because of this ideological setting, Americans might find few GDR ideas and institutions that could inspire improvements in the American legal system. Nevertheless, one GDR institution—the Social Courts—has a feature that might hold some promise for the American dispute-resolution movement. In the United States, since the mid-1970s, growing attention has been devoted to developing more effective means for the resolution of minor disputes through "alternative dispute resolution" procedures. The objective is to provide means that are more informal and less expensive and time-consuming than traditional court adjudication. That is in effect what the Social Courts provide in the GDR.

The distinctive feature of the Social Courts that provides food for American thought is their territorially comprehensive nature.

These bodies constitute a nationwide network of forums covering every inhabitant, either in his work place or at his residence or both. Thus any controversy of the sort embraced by this minor dispute-resolution system can find a readily available local forum. No American jurisdiction has yet attempted such a comprehensive network of this sort. However, there is no reason why a state legislature could not authorize a statewide system, with an informal dispute-resolving body of citizens available in every urban neighborhood and in every town or rural area. Such a network of lay tribunals for relatively small-scale matters would also be in line with venerable practice in England, where some 20,000 lay magistrates currently handle approximately 96 percent of all criminal business.

As intimated earlier, some other aspects of the GDR legal scene may have at least a superficial attraction for many Americans. For example, the concept of a citizen's duty to his society, if taken more seriously in the United States, could improve the quality of American life, although few would advocate that stringent legal measures be taken to enforce such duty in all of its dimensions. American legal education would be improved, in the opinion of many law teachers, if all law students studied more foreign, comparative, and international law, as well as legal history; although virtually none would suggest that those subjects be taught in American law schools with the kind of specific political content that they have in the GDR. Likewise, many American legal educators believe that the law school curriculum would be improved if it had a more coherent structure and more clearly defined objectives, but few, if any, would urge that the curriculum be targeted at the kind of sharply defined political objectives that one finds in the GDR law curricula. Nevertheless, there is something to be said for coordinated long-range planning to assure that the law schools meet the legal manpower needs of the country but do not produce an excess of lawyers.

In the GDR and the American legal scenes we see potentially, if not actually, signs of those two ancient and contrasting threats to law—totalitarianism and anarchy. In the collective society of the GDR, where education, government, and life in general are all directed by the state apparatus toward one political program, there is relatively little leeway for human diversity, creativity, and individuality. At the other end of the spectrum, American-style diversity and individual autonomy can make for a fragmented community and individual alienation in everyday life. One does not need to embrace Marxism-Leninism or to copy precise arrangements from the GDR legal regime to endorse the idea that the American nation and the life of all within it might be improved through widespread and heightened awareness of civic duty, of a sense of purpose, and of a greater knowledge of history and the rest of the world.

In the remaining pages I move away from law and legal education to offer some concluding observations and impressions about life in the GDR and the peculiarities of this German state.

14 On the GDR

An American living for nearly three months in the GDR with time to travel about, to walk the streets, to patronize the restaurants and the theaters, to browse in the stores, to ride the public transportation, and to visit the churches—as well as to spend time in some of the universities—will unavoidably gain insights into the life of the country and form opinions about the nature of this society. In the interest of adding a modest increment to the American understanding of this unusual scene, I record here some of the enduring impressions from my visit not related directly to law and legal education.

One noticeable feature of GDR life is the way in which the authorities use to their advantage the Nazi era of German history. Hitler and the Nazi party are an enormous help to the authorities in their efforts to establish the legitimacy of the GDR and its humanitarian and democratic virtues in the eyes of their own people as well as with the rest of the world. Indeed, one can argue that in a perverse way Hitler is the greatest asset that communists could have. The Nazi regime during its twelve year rule from 1933 to 1945 was so outrageous in its aggressive warfare and inhuman measures that no one can really defend it, and no one attempts to. The East German communists have been able to say since 1945 that "we told you so from the very beginning." It is indeed a fact that the Communist party of Germany, founded in 1919, vehemently opposed the Nazi movement from its embryonic stages. The Nazis and the Communists were the bitterest of opponents. This placed the Communists in good position from 1945 onward to hold themselves out as the staunchest defenders of "democracy." They could claim with considerable foundation in fact that no other group had been so strongly antifascist. Thus the "fascists" provide the SED with an ideal opponent even though they are long gone. The SED departs from historical fact, however, when it takes a subtle next step in implying that it is the only true antifascist force and that all those who are not in league with it are fascists. This unarticulated premise is exploited with considerable diligence in much of the literature; it serves to align West Germany, the United States, and Western countries in general on the fascist side. The fact that many of these countries were seeking to overturn the Nazi regime in the Second World War is almost never mentioned. Likewise, little credit is given to the fundamental reforms in West Germany establishing a parliamentary democracy and rights under a written constitution.

"Fascism" is the leading enemy in the GDR. The word is sprinkled throughout the literature and rolls easily off the tongues of GDR officials. The word is used to describe almost everything German between the years 1933 and 1945. One hears constantly of the fascist government, the fascist professors, and so on. In the GDR one almost never hears any institutions or activities in their territory during those years referred to as "German." Those who served in the *Wehrmacht* in the Second World War speak of serving in the "fascist army." It is as though the country had been taken over by some alien force—persons other than Germans themselves. Yet the GDR citizens and officials doing the talking are the sons, brothers, grandsons, nephews, and cousins of those Germans who were alive and functioning during that twelve-year period ending in 1945. In short, it is their own country, themselves, and their relatives about whom they speak, but one would never know this because of the branding of everything in that area as "fascist," hence putting it apart as though it were a foreign regime.

The effort to disconnect the GDR from the Germany of 1933–45 is also noticeable in the lack of memorials to German soldiers who died in the Second World War. War memorials are a sensitive subject in both East and West. Although I never encountered such a memorial in the GDR, in West Germany there are memorials in some churches and villages, sometimes listing the names of the dead and sometimes bearing a religious inscription or merely "1939–1945." For example, in the village of Ratzenried, near the border between Bavaria and Baden-Wurtenberg, the centuries-old Roman Catholic Church contains memorials to the dead of both world wars. For the second war, there is a list of more than 100 names from this village of 800 inhabitants, accompanied by two inscriptions: "Whether we live or die, we are always in God's hand." "We died for you. What do you do for us?" On asking a GDR law professor about the lack of memorials to German soldiers in the GDR, I was told that the memorial on Unter den Linden was such. When I asked whether its sole inscription, "To the Victims of Fascism and Militarism," included the German soldiers who died in the German Army, he said, "Yes, of course, they were also victims of fascism and militarism."

"Militarism" is the other great enemy. Indeed the two evils are usually linked in literature and official utterances, as in the memorial on Unter den Linden. Here is one of the paradoxes and contradictions that one finds in the GDR. Although frequently denouncing militarism, the GDR seems as militaristic as any country one is likely to find. Posters and placards picturing soldiers are displayed in public places. Almost every issue of the university newspapers carries articles about military training, often showing pictures of students in uniform. Military parades are frequent. On various occasions on Karl-Marx-Allee, the major parade route in East Berlin, formations of several thousand marching soldiers, interspersed with armored vehicles, come up from the south, passing along the edge of Alexanderplatz. For years the GDR has had eighteen months of compulsory military service for all eighteen-year-old males, and in recent years paramilitary training has been introduced into the schools. The GDR army also participated in the invasion of Czechoslovakia in 1968, the only German military force to set foot on non-German soil since 1945. In addition to their own forces of some 167,000, the GDR is the base for between 380,000 and 400,000 Russian military personnel.

Besides being helped by the Nazis in their never-ending propaganda campaign, the East German communists have also been helped, again paradoxically, by the wartime destruction in their cities. Extensive damage, to the point of obliteration in some instances, enabled or compelled the East Germans to clear blocks of urban ruin and to construct new buildings from the ground up. This enabled them to create some showpieces such as Alexanderplatz in Berlin and Karl Marx Platz in Leipzig. Standing in these places where all is new and shiny, one can easily get a sense that a new order has indeed been created, that there is a clean break with the bourgeois, capitalist, imperialist, and fascist past.

It is characteristic of Marxist-Leninist societies not to leave this conclusion to the individual's own reasoning or imagination. Huge banners are strung across the tops of buildings here and there in every city, and billboards appear along the highways proclaiming the message that the population is supposed to accept. For example: "The Program of the Party is the Program of the People"; "Marx Lives in us and in our Deeds"; "For Peace and Socialism"; "We support Moscow"; "Stop NATO." Along the road from West Berlin to Potsdam there is a huge billboard with the heading "Made in U.S.A." Underneath the heading is a representation of the American flag; the stars are human skulls, and the stripes are missiles. At the entrance to every town and in the centers of cities and towns flags fly in profusion. There is always the GDR flag and a solid red flag; they never appear singly but always fly from multiple staffs.

The GDR authorities have a seemingly irresistible impulse to politicize every historical site. They seem to be unable to let the place or the event speak for itself. They make special and sometimes strained efforts to relate it positively to the workers' movement and Communist party or in an adverse way to imperialists, capitalists, and fascists. Examples can be seen in the concentration camp at Buchenwald. That site (as well as the camp at Sachsenhausen) has been carefully preserved and arranged as a prime tourist attraction—a step that is certainly justified historically—but the authorities are not willing to let the camp speak with its own grim eloquence. Exhibits and signs exalt Communist party members as the primary victims of this brutality of the fascists (never identified as "Germans"). School children by the thousands are brought to these camps in busses to be lectured on the threats to their existence by all who are not allied with the ruling authorities of the GDR, the USSR, and the other socialist states who defend "democracy" and the people. On a less ghoulish note, Goethe and Schiller cannot be left to be viewed and thought about on their own merits; in Weimar they are presented as progressive thinkers whose attitudes were essentially in tune with those of the GDR authorities today. At the massive, soaring granite monument to the Battle of Nations, on the edge of Leipzig, the literature states that at the dedication of the monument in 1913 the powers then in charge of Germany misused the occasion for their own imperialistic ends. In the museum building next to the monument the dioramas and displays on the 1813 battle are supplemented by a prominent military display on the Warsaw Pact nations. Beneath the flags of these countries a text explains the importance of this united effort of the socialist states to protect peace and democracy against aggressive imperialist forces.

A related theme is the constant and gratuitious jabbing at the United States and Western countries in general. It is especially irritating to find such expressions at historical places. For example, just off Alexanderplatz in East Berlin, in front of the building housing the Supreme Court, is the ruin of the Kloster Kirche, a medieval church. It is left there, like the Kaiser Wilhelm Memorial Church in West Berlin, as a reminder of the war. The plaque in front states that it was destroyed by Anglo-American bombing. Likewise, in Dresden there are signs reminding readers that the city was destroyed by English bombing. Similar information is conveyed in Potsdam, which was heavily damaged in the closing days of the war. All of these statements are true but nowhere does one ever read that the Red Army inflicted any damage; in fact, over one million Russian soldiers moved from the Oder into the heart of Berlin with the largest assemblage of artillery and tanks ever amassed. The destruction wrought by that force as it fought its way through cities and into the middle of Berlin was immense. In the Cecelienhof, where the 1945 Potsdam conference was held, the rooms occupied by the three powers are all preserved. In the English and Russian rooms the descriptions of the persons and activities are relatively straightforward. In the American room, however, documents and texts are displayed describing ideas suggested early in the war for the postwar administration of Germany. Some of these ideas call for the division of Germany; the Morgenthau Plan would have rendered Germany an agrarian nation. The implication is that from the outset the American intention was to divide Germany, while the Soviet Union pressed for a unified country. That none of these ideas ever found its way into official American policy is not mentioned.

The anti-Western and pro-Soviet stance sometimes results in statements that are simply untrue. For example, in a booklet about the city of Halle, printed in four languages for visitors, it is said that the city was liberated by the Soviet Union in 1945. The facts are that the American forces captured the city in April 1945 and turned it over to the Red Army some ten weeks later pursuant to the London Protocol fixing the occupation zones.

Along with the effort to project a new order of things, the GDR maintains a selective continuity with the past. The museums in Weimar honoring Goethe and Schiller are an example. The universities have salvaged many of the past academic figures. The statues still stand around Humboldt University; portraits and busts remain at the universities in Halle and Jena. To the surprise of many Western observers, Frederick the Great is now back in fashion. Statues of the Prussian generals Scharnhorst and Yorck remain in the open space near the Opera on Unter den Linden.

Yet heroes are chosen carefully and selectively. There is much editing of history. There are frequent memorials in the forms of tablets or stone markers to communists who died between 1933 and 1945 at the hands of "the fascists," but I noted only one memorial to a noncommunist. This exception is Dietrich Bonhoeffer, the Protestant pastor arrested in 1942 and put to death in the Flossenberg concentration camp in 1945. His name appears on a tablet in the rear of the main building of Humboldt University, along with the names of eight other persons who were put to death. There is also a street in East Berlin named for Bonhoeffer. He seems to be the only noncommunist of the 1933–45 period deemed worthy of commemoration.

The leading historical figure in the GDR is Karl Marx. Busts and pictures of him abound. His name is attached to streets, squares, and institutions throughout the country. Ranking next behind him is Friedrich Engels. Then comes that trio of twentieth-century German communist martyrs: Karl Liebknecht, Rosa Luxemburg, and Ernst Thälmann. No town of substantial size is without a street or school named for one or all of them. Lenin ranks close behind them.

The most interesting figure to be refurbished in recent times is Martin Luther. The 500th anniversary of his birth was observed in 1983. As might have been expected, the Protestant churches in the GDR planned extensive commemorative exercises. Surprisingly, the GDR authorities suddenly declared Luther a great German folk hero and proclaimed an official state observance of his birth. The GDR travel agency, the *Reisebüro*, organized tours of "Luther Land," primarily for Western consumption. These tours were advertised in the United States. For the first time since the Second World War, American tourists were urged to visit the GDR, and thousands of them did. It is probable that more Americans went to the GDR during 1983, primarily because of the Luther Year, than in all the years since the Second World War combined. These tours were concentrated in the places where Martin Luther lived and worked for most of his days—Wittenberg, Eisenach, and Erfurt. For the previous decade the GDR had been undertaking a substantial hotel-building program. Thus by the time of the Luther Year there were several modern (indeed first-class) hotels. Prominent among these are the Palast in East Berlin and the Merkur in Leipzig. The former was built by Swedes and the latter by Japanese. They compare favorably with first-class hotels in large American cities, a far cry from the hotels available a decade earlier in the GDR.

Among the Alice-in-Wonderland features of GDR life, the Intershops occupy a prominent place. An Intershop is a store operated by the GDR authorities in which GDR money cannot be spent. In earlier years they seemed to be located only in the Interhotels; that is, in the relatively few hotels in which foreigners were allowed to stay, and in which all rooms and meals had to be paid for in foreign currency. Foreigners must still stay in Interhotels and must pay for their rooms in foreign money. However, the Intershop system has spread now beyond these hotels. Intershops can be found in railroad stations, along the autobahns, and even occasionally on the streets, side by side with other retail shops.

All Intershops sell alcoholic beverages, candy, and miscellaneous toilet articles. The larger shops also sell phonograph records, clothing, jewelry, radios, television sets, and other consumer items. Almost all items sold in the Intershops are made outside the communist world, many of them in West Germany. The goods sold in these shops are either unavailable altogether in GDR stores or, if available, they are of lesser quality and of non-Western manufacture. The only items of GDR manufacture I discovered in an Intershop were a highly sought-after series of Christmas decorations crafted in the Erzgeberge.

These decorations, made in the southern part of the GDR, were either exported to the West or sold only through Intershops; they were not available at all in GDR stores. These shops are always crowded; indeed, one almost always must wait in line to be served. Although GDR money cannot be spent in an Intershop, the striking fact is that many of the customers seemed to be GDR citizens. It is evident that many GDR residents have access, one way or another, to West German marks.

The effect of the Intershop system would seem to be to create two classes of GDR citizens—those with access to West German marks and hence to a wide variety of desirable goods not otherwise available—and those without such access. It is difficult to imagine a government's insulting its own people by establishing a countrywide network of stores containing highly desirable goods and forbidding the people to obtain these goods with their own country's money. One wonders how the mass of citizens view these Intershops, especially those with little or no access to West German money. One would think they might consider themselves to be second-class citizens.

What the mass of people think in the GDR about anything is a perplexing question. The society is structured not to promote frank and open discussion or opposition to the existing system. One cannot imagine, for example, walking across the middle of Alexanderplatz carrying a placard saying "Erich Honecker must go" or "The Intershop system should be abolished." Yet much emphasis is placed on democracy. To Americans the Marxist-Leninist brand of democracy seems strange indeed. It is a kind of consultative democracy, but it is a one-way democracy. The discussions that take place in public meetings, for example, relating to the fitness of persons to be elected as judges, afford citizens an opportunity to stand up and speak. But it is difficult to imagine much speaking that is not consistent with the policies of the SED and of the principles of Marxism-Leninism. In any event, no votes are taken; such occasions are simply opportunities for comment. In elections, one votes for the single name on the ballot. Not to vote is difficult, and raises questions about one's attitude. There is no doubt, however, that there is a lot of meeting and talking at various levels and large numbers of people are brought into the system in this way.

This can be seen in university legal education, as previously described. For example, at the admissions stage there is involvement of a representative of the Free German Youth, the law teachers, and officials from the "practice partners." The advisory council for each section is composed of persons from different areas of the legal system, and they meet and talk. The curriculum and the textbooks are the products of the large Council for Legal Education functioning under the Ministry for Higher Education. Indeed, the system seems to aim at involving as many people as possible, although they also seem to have no decisive votes on contested issues.

The population is integrated into the system through the "mass organizations." There are three: the Federation of Free German Trade Unions, the Free German Youth, and the Democratic Women's League. Apparently almost everybody can fit into at least one of these organizations, which are sometimes referred to as "transmission belts," their purpose being to convey Party doctrine. Like all other activity, they are linked to the SED and are ultimately under the control of the Central Committee and the Politburo. There are other organizations for special interests, such as the Lawyers' Association, but they too are linked to the SED.

Another example of one of these special organizations is the Association for the Blind and Partially Sighted. This organization, too, is committed by the terms of its charter to the support of the working class. Because of my special interest in blindness, I visited its headquarters office, one block off Unter den Linden and no more than half a block from The Wall. Housed on an entire floor of an old office building are its president and a staff of some twenty-five persons. The president lost his eye-sight in 1941 while serving in "the fascist army" on the Russian front. Some twelve-thousand German soldiers were blinded in the war, three thousand of whom lived in what is now the GDR. Today there are about thirty-five-thousand blind persons in the GDR, most of whom are old-age pensioners—women over sixty, men over sixty-five. The Association publishes a variety of literature describing career opportunities for blind persons as lawyers, teachers, and so on. Rehabilitation centers for the blind are maintained at Karl Marx Stadt (formerly Chemnitz), Halle, and Neukloster, near Wismar. The library established in 1894 in Leipzig to produce braille materials for the blind throughout the German nation is still functioning and has greatly expanded its facilities to include the tape-recording of books; a service similar to that performed in the United States by a special branch of the Library of Congress.

Like officers in American organizations for the blind, the president of this Association was intensely interested in rehabilitation and training for work opportunities. He is active in several international organizations for the blind, spanning both West and East. Although like all officials and most law teachers with whom I talked he wore the SED pin and made the usual statements about the desirability of peace, he seemed more interested in problems of the blind than in political matters. He could hardly have received me more warmly; he served the customary coffee and brandy, and urged me to return for another chat, and possibly for dinner, an invitation I was unable to accept because of the shortness of my remaining time in the GDR.

It is difficult for Americans to comprehend a system in which all aspects of life are integrated. Whether one is in the workplace, in school, in the residential area, or on vacation he is in a structure and a network that is state-operated and state-controlled. Moreover, the state itself is controlled by a single party whose power is not subject to being divested by any popular election or movement. In response to my question as to whether it is possible to change this government by peaceful means, a law teacher said frankly, "No." Another law professor explained that the system is based on an historically validated scientific theory and that no one wants to put scientific theories to a popular vote. He said that when Copernicus enunciated his theory that the earth rotated around the sun, rather than vice versa, there was much opposition to it. The professor asked whether it would make any sense to submit that theory to a popular election. Most of the great scientific truths, he said, have been opposed—often violently in the beginning—but eventually have become accepted. And so it has been and will be, he said, with Marxism-Leninism, adding that "we will not submit our revolution to any popular elections." He went on to explain that the risk of elections derives from the fact that forces opposing change are nearly always stronger than those in support of change, even though the latter are right. There may come a time, he said, when there would be no risk in having popular elections in the GDR, but, in any event, in his view, elections are not really that important.

To an outsider these explanations appear to embody one of the oldest ideas known to human history; namely, that a few can and should govern the many. There is nothing new or revolutionary in that idea. They say, however, that to speak of a "few" as governing the many is to misconceive the system. The reality is, they say, that the working class governs, and that class includes a large majority of all the people. The Party is merely the voice of the working class; the will of the Party cannot be contrary to the interests of the people.

The theory of a society controlled by, for, and in the interests of "the working class" is being threatened by reality as time passes. Disparities in economic circumstances are growing among the population. Although the range from low to high economically is not nearly so great as it is in Western countries, a spectrum of the population is emerging that is significantly better off economically than the majority. One can see this in clothing, housing, and material goods. For example, one Humboldt law professor occupies an apartment in a modern high-rise building in East Berlin overlooking Alexanderplatz—accommodations that compare favorably with a good apartment in the middle of an American city. Another Humboldt law professor lives in an apartment some two miles from Alexanderplatz in a building constructed in the 1920s. The apartment is on the fourth floor—the top floor in the building—and consists of large, high-ceilinged rooms: living room, dining room, study, two or three bedrooms, kitchen, and a balcony overlooking a tree-shaded garden in an inner courtyard. It is as comfortable and roomy as any apartment that one could want in an American city. Both of these professors have summer houses in the country outside Berlin. In Halle a law professor graciously entertained us in his three-story home, surrounded by a modest-sized lawn and garden in a suburban residential area. By American standards it might be considered a slightly above average suburban home, but in the GDR—where housing is extraordinarily tight and a very large part of the population lives in apartments that are often small and cramped—this housing arrangement borders on the sumptuous. Each of these professors owns an automobile—a privilege enjoyed only by a minority of the population. Perhaps most surprising of all to me, in this "classless society" there are first-class and second-class accommodations on the trains—at different prices; moreover, one can reserve a seat by paying an extra fee. Prices of meals vary widely from one restaurant to another.

Despite the emergence of an upper economic stratum, a visitor can still discern that he is in a "workers' state" that is different from Western society. On the streets and in the restaurants and theatres, even in the largest cities, it is evident that the people are preponderantly the sons and daughters of the factory and the soil. On occasions and in places where in the Western world one would likely find only elegantly dressed men and women, one finds a majority of the men in work jackets and open collars and the women in rather ordinary dresses. Persons who have risen to high positions often seem to think it important to point out that their status is relatively new to them. It was not uncommon for a law teacher to say with pride that he was "born into a working-class family" or that he was "the son of a worker." Yet it seems likely that economic disparities will continue to grow and that over the next generation they could become substantial indeed. The political ramifications of this evolution should be interesting.

Yet the worker and the working class remain as the national image and ideal. Membership in that class determines important opportunities and benefits. This practice in the GDR resembles the "affirmative action" programs in the United States. Just as these programs have forced Americans to think about who is a "minority member," and should therefore get the benefit of preferential treatment, so in the GDR is there a need to define "worker." Does the working class, for example, include the secretary to the manager of an enterprise? Does it include a computer programmer at an industrial plant? The classification is evolving as conditions change and it runs the risk of being increasingly artificial. Moreover, the significance of the classification may be diminishing. Some law professors suggested that a working-class status is less important today in university admissions than it was some years ago.

There is in the GDR one glaring exception to the theory and the practice whereby all life is integrated into the collective system. That exception is the churches. The territory embraced by the GDR has been overwhelmingly Protestant since the time of Martin Luther. This makes the GDR unique among the communist countries of Europe. The Protestant membership of over 14 million shortly after the Second World War had shrunk by the 1980s to approximately 6 million. Roman Catholic membership is approximately 1.5 million. Estimates are that there are fewer than 1,000 Jews in the GDR. Marxism-Leninism is fundamentally atheistic; the existence of religious organizations and activities in the midst of such a regime is basically inconsistent with the system and its underlying principles. Yet the churches continue. For many years GDR authorities made life difficult for the churches and their members and ministers. This was partly because until 1969 the Protestant churches formed the last vestige of an undivided Germany; until then the Federation of Protestant Churches remained as one organization, encompassing both East and West. In that year the Federation divided, after intense pressure from the GDR government, resulting in the creation of the Federation of Protestant Churches in the GDR. This organization is a confederation of five different Protestant groups that exist primarily for historical reasons, deriving from the old territorial subdivisions. Altogether these denominations have about 5,000 congregations. In the last several years, an uneasy truce has been maintained between the Federation and the government.

The Federation occupies a four-story building on Auguststrasse, a relatively neglected street not far from the middle of East Berlin. It is only two blocks from the ruined Jewish synagogue on Oranienburg-strasse, which is maintained as a Jewish memorial. Some seventy staff members work in this headquarters building. To learn about the unique position of the Protestant church in this Marxist-Leninist land I interviewed two senior staff members at the Federation headquarters.

In the Federation headquarters building a considerable volume of mimeographed material is published for the church membership countrywide. This material is not subject to government censorship; however, if the Federation seeks to publish a book or other material for general circulation, the manuscript must first be submitted to the State Secretary for Church Affairs. This official, who works under the Council of Ministers, sometimes negotiates revisions in the text to make it acceptable; at other times he simply will not clear the material for publication. The mimeograph machines at the Federation's headquarters offer an escape from this censorship; one has the impression that distribution of this mimeographed material is not rigidly confined to church members. Apart from Federation publications, religious books of various sorts are available in some bookstores. Approximately 100,000 Bibles are published and sold annually in the GDR. These and other religious books are produced by a state publishing house acting in cooperation with the fourteen Bible societies that exist in the country.

To train Protestant ministers, theological faculties remain in four of the universities: Leipzig, Halle, Berlin, and Greifswald.

Their total enrollment was 453 in 1981. These state-supported programs are anomalies in an officially atheistic society. Their faculties are subjected to the same kind of government ministry control to which all faculties are subjected, and they must instruct extensively in Marxism-Leninism. Yet they train pastors for the Protestant churches. The Protestant churches themselves maintain three theological seminaries of their own—at Naumberg, Berlin, and Leipzig, together enrolling between 300 and 350 students. To become a pastor, one must complete the four-year theological program at either a university or a church-run seminary and then engage in a year's apprenticeship work in a parish, followed by a year of contemplation. At the end of that time an examination is administered by the churches to determine fitness to become a pastor. The state authorities dislike this church screening process, taking the view that the state-administered examination at the end of the four years is sufficient. The state is concerned that all persons who study theology become pastors because, in the view of the authorities, there is no other work in which they can safely be put. Nevertheless, the church continues to certify its own pastors. Protestant pastors in the GDR today number about 5,000.

According to one Federation staff member, the generation between the ages of thirty and fifty is lost to the church. Old people remain, and those now under thirty, especially teenagers, are coming back. This staff member thinks that young people are attracted to the church because it is the only place where they can escape the system, can talk freely, explore questions, and speak their minds. This official looks for a continuing membership decline over the next decade to perhaps four million but then a gradual rise. Another staff member is not as optimistic about future membership growth.

In addition to talking with Federation staff members I visited churches in different parts of the country. As in the United States, church life seems to be more vigorous in the small towns and villages than in the city centers. In Warnemunde, a fishing village and resort on the Baltic coast, on the Sunday morning of my visit, the church was filled almost to capacity with over 300 people of all ages. On a Saturday afternoon in Rostock, the GDR's major seaport, multiple bells announced a special service; parents and children by the dozens streamed toward the church—each child carrying a paper lantern and candle. At the church in Halle, where Martin Luther occasionally preached, a senior minister and two or three young assistants conducted services for 200 or more persons of varied ages. At the Marienkirche, the major Protestant church in the center of East Berlin, attendance varied from just over 100 to 300 or more, apparently depending on whether special music programs were offered. In some churches the congregation is so small that it no longer meets in the main sanctuary but meets instead in small rooms to the side or even in pastors' homes. Many church buildings were destroyed in the war and others are closed and dilapidated. But all in all one has the sense that many Protestant churches in the GDR are alive and functioning.

Perhaps the most significant aspect of the church scene in the GDR, at least from the standpoint of international politics and peace, is the tension between church and state relating to nuclear weapons. Church members have been involved in occasional peace demonstrations. To appreciate the significance of this, one must remember that public activities in opposition to any policy of the GDR or the USSR are generally unheard of. The church leadership has apparently been "called on the carpet" by GDR authorities concerning such activities. The churches' position seems to be one against all nuclear weapons in both East and West. A sermon at the Nicolai church in Leipzig one October Sunday was devoted to that theme. That position was enunciated at a countrywide meeting of the Protestant churches in Greifswald in 1984. A church staffer reported that the GDR authorities have tried to explain that there is a difference between nuclear weapons in the East and those in the West. However, this difference is not acknowledged by church members interested in the peace movement. Church members and pastors involved in this effort seem to be the only visible sign of opposition to any government policy in the GDR, and for that reason this movement is especially interesting. It may test the extent to which the church can survive and remain outside the system. A staff member explained that churches are the only organizations not integrated into the system because "the Gospel cannot be integrated."

In theory there is no religious discrimination in the GDR. However, active church involvement still seems to be an impediment to a career. Church staff members are unaware of any high-ranking official in the GDR who is an active church member. The CDU is the political party to which church members belong, but not all CDU members are actively affiliated with the church. Indeed, the CDU in the GDR is not the same as the CDU in the FRG. Dr. Heinrich Toeplitz, President of the Supreme Court, is a member of the CDU, but is not known to have any active church involvement. It taxes the imagination that a church member could go very far in a system whose basic premises involve a rejection of the existence of any divine authority.

Nowhere is this ideological incongruity portrayed in tangible form more dramatically than at Marx-Engels Platz. There, at the head of Unter den Linden, side by side, stand the Protestant Cathedral (Dom) and the Palast der Republik. The shining new palace, the seat of the highest state organ, symbolizes this new order, based on scientific materialism and on the premise, explicitly stated in its constitution, that "man is the centre of all efforts of socialist society and its state." Scarcely a hundred yards away is the Dom, erected in the 1890s to create a kind of mausoleum for the Hohenzollerns. Architecturally reminiscent of St. Paul's in London, it is gradually being reconstructed from its extensive wartime damage. One portion is already open for weekly services. The immense concourse under the dome is still undergoing restoration. On the outwide walls, at different points, are two inscriptions. They can be translated thus: "Lo, I am with you always until the end of the world." "Our faith is the victory that has overcome the world." These statements on the Dom, at the heart of the physical domain of Party and State, are utterly inconsistent with this temporal regime. They are seen daily by throngs of workers, bureaucrats, and high officials as they go back and forth to work or mill around at lunchtime along the Spree and on Karl-Liebknecht-Strasse. Not only is there no effort to hide these words, but restoration is going forward actively, probably with the assistance of state funding. These statements are unusually striking because there is no commercial advertising in the GDR. The only signs and publicly visible wording that one normally sees are the slogans on the Party-erected banners and billboards.

The state apparently permits churches to continue to function for two reasons. One is that such a substantial part of the population holds church membership that serious instability or unrest might result if an all-out effort were made to abolish the churches. The other is that the churches do a substantial amount of good works that actually serve the purposes of the regime; churches maintain hospitals and children's homes and perform other social-welfare functions, some of which are subsidized by the government. The government also contributes to the restoration of historical church buildings. Thus there is a peculiar, and somewhat uncomfortable, coexistence of church and state.

Of all the bizarre features of GDR life the most visible and dramatic is the existence of the city of West Berlin in the middle of its territory. There it sits, a city as large as East Berlin, surrounded by heavily guarded concrete walls and fencing erected by the GDR authorities. The citizens of the GDR can see it from the upper floors of buildings in East Berlin, from the trains as they pass between East Berlin and other points in the GDR, from the Cecelienhof in Potsdam, and from other points. They see the guard towers, the search lights, the bare dirt strips, and armed guards; they are told by their own government that all of this is necessary to prevent intrusions from their enemies. Yet surely they must know otherwise. Although they can see it and hear from it (on radio and televison), they cannot go into it. There are a few exceptions. Old-age pensioners can go and come, and a few especially privileged officials have occasional opportunities to visit, but for the masses it is a world beyond their reach. Passing through the barriers, the guards, and the checkpoints between the two Berlins brings home, as perhaps nothing else can, the reality of the division of Germany, and, indeed, the division of East and West. On Kurfürstendamm, in the center of West Berlin, next to the ruined tower of the Kaiser Wilhelm Memorial Church, a sunken fountain features splashing water and a fractured globe; it bears the legend, "The Divided World."

The existence of West Berlin is a constant reminder that something is askew in this part of the world. It symbolizes the division of Germany as a whole. The bizarreness of the situation suggests its artificiality, leaving the uneasy feeling that it cannot be permanent. Yet the reunification of Germany seems, in one light, to be nothing more than a pipe dream. The massive presence of the Soviet armed forces and the near-paranoid concern of the Soviet Union about its Eastern European interests seem to preclude the merging of the two German states. Moreover, after thirty-five years of intensive development as a Marxist-Leninist society, with two generations having been reared and trained in that system, it would be difficult to blend that society with Western-style parliamentary democracy and private enterprise.

But the whole situation is volatile and unpredictable. Events can move rapidly. At the end of November 1983, when I departed the GDR, no one suspected that a new, massive outmigration was about to begin. Yet over the next six months some thirty-thousand GDR citizens were allowed to leave for the West. The sharp division and isolation are being ameliorated in several ways. Volkswagen has undertaken to establish an engine plant in the GDR. The FRG underwrote the cost of an autobahn from Hamburg to Berlin and continues to extend sizable financial loans and credits to the GDR. Air service was instituted between Frankfurt and Leipzig in the fall of 1984. Although GDR authorities continue to maintain tight security at the border, they have removed automatic firing devices.

The future is unusually unpredictable. There could be a rush of ideas and events that would confound observers. After all, Hitler came and went in twelve years. It is possible that the spirit that animated the drive toward unification in the middle of the nineteenth century is not dead. Offsetting this, however, is the firmness of the Soviet Union's grip, as evidenced by the cancellation of Erich Honecker's trip to the West in September 1984.

In the meantime, the universities will almost surely continue their heavy and pervasive emphasis on Marxism-Leninism. The law sections will continue to train their students to man the justice system, to keep the dispute-resolution machinery functioning, to investigate illegalities and antisocial conduct, to prosecute crime, and to help keep the economy functioning. Law shows no sign of "withering away"; it remains as an important element of official control over society, though it affords relatively few individual rights in the Anglo-American sense. To serve Marxist-Leninist ends, university legal education and the two legal systems are firmly established. While the law students will be well-schooled in world affairs as seen through Marxist-Leninist eyes, they will, sad to say, know little of the real world as it is outside of the collectivist societies of Eastern Europe and the USSR.

As I think over the various emotions that one feels in the GDR—fascination, irritation, frustration, and an occasional bit of admiration—the one that dominates in my mind is sadness. It is not that the people appear sad—publicly they are rather cheerful and lighthearted—the sadness is in my own mind as I think about what life could be for them were it not for their system. The historical and cultural places they could visit, the literature they could read, the ideas to which they could be exposed, and the opportunities that they could pursue are probably not comprehended by most of them.

Does this society point the way to the future, as Marxists-Leninists assert? Standing against it is Western civilization, but it too is seriously flawed; it is threatened by an erosion of individual self-discipline, weakened adherence to moral standards, and fragmentation of family and community life. Will it nevertheless prevail? Do we have here an irreconcilable conflict, or can the fundamental differences be adjusted? Is it possible that some kind of Hegelian dialectic may yet work to bring traditional Western civilization and Marxism-Leninism together into a now indiscernible synthesis? These are the fundamental questions set before the world by the tumult of the twentieth century. The course of events yet to come in the two German states may yield insights into the answers that the world will eventually give to these questions. Thus what happens in East Germany—as well as in West Germany—should be watched with the utmost interest. There, in a microcosm of the divided world, may be both a barometer and a key, measuring and perhaps opening up the next age of mankind.

Appendixes

Glossary

Selected Bibliography

Index

A
Study Plan

Council of Ministers of the German Democratic Republic
Ministry for Higher Education

Study Plan
for the Primary Directions in Educations for Law
(Nomenclature No. 550)

Third Revised Edition

Authorized as an Obligatory Study Plan for Instruction at GDR Universities

This Study Plan is Effective as of September 1, 1982

Prof. Dr. h.c. Bohme
Minister of Higher Education

The study plan for the fundamental design of the teaching of law has been compiled by a work group connected with the Advisory Council for Political Science and Legal Education under the supervision of Prof. Dr. Willi Buchner-Uhder, Martin Luther University, Halle-Wittenberg. The plan has been modified by the advisory body at the universities and has been discussed with practicing associates of the authorized sections of the state and law faculty and synchronized with the appropriate government organs.

(References and suggestions for specific amendments are to be addressed to the Ministry for Higher Education, Department of Humanities.)

Contents

1. Aim and Main Topics of Instruction and Education
1.1 Aim of Instruction and Education
1.2 Main Topics of Courses
2. Characteristics of Special Professional Training
2.1 Specialization in Law (Justice) Nomenclature No. 55001
2.2 Specialization in Law (Economics) Nomenclature No. 55002
3. Development and Utilization of Studies
3.1 Resident Studies
3.2 Nonresident Studies
3.3 Suggestions for Continuing Education

1. Aim and Main Topics of Instruction and Education

1.1 Aim of Instruction and Education

In realization of the historical mission of the proletariat, the legal leading roll of the working class and its Marxist-Leninist party grows through ongoing construction of the already developed socialist society and the establishment of basic prerequisites for the gradual transition to Communism. Connected with this is the universal strengthening of the socialist state of workers and farmers as a form of dictatorship of the proletariat which represents the interests of all the people of the German Democratic Republic and guarantees freedom and human rights, further development and improvement of the socialist democracy, and the consistent realization of democratic centralism.

Inseparably bound up with the universal strengthening of the socialist state are the systematic improvement of the socialist judicial system and the guarantee of socialist legality. Socialist law serves as an expression of the power of the proletariat, the realization of the interests of the workers, and the protection of the socialist order and the freedom and human dignity of the citizens.

Accordingly, high and constantly improving standards have to be set for the political and ideological education and for the theoretical and practical training of the students who enroll in the GDR university courses of political science and law. The student's training and education is aimed at the attainment of a firm class-consciousness and stresses that all their future activities are perceived as political functions. The student is to develop into a socialist lawyer working within the socialist apparatus of state and economy. He must become a political functionary and public leader who is able and determined to protect the socialist order of state and society, to apply socialist law in the service of social progress, and to preserve the rights and interests of the people. This requires also the student's training in loyalty to the socialist fatherland, to proletarian internationalism, and especially to a firm friendship with the Soviet Union and with the other socialist countries. In conjunction with this the student is to be instructed in the ability and preparedness to represent at all times the policies of the Party and of Marxism-Leninism and also to aggressively dispute the bourgeois ideology and the policies of imperialism.

Socialist military training and the acquisition of military knowledge and capability are inseparable from the total process of education. The student is to be ready and able to defend the GDR and the community of socialist countries.

An essential basis of scientific studies and communist teaching is the study of the scientific ideology of the proletariat and of the policies of the revolutionary party. Because of the uniformity in the basic Marxist-Leninist doctrine concerning the study of law, the training and education in all phases of law study is to be characterized by a continual transmittance of political ideologies and the reconciliation of theory and practice. The basic Marxist-Leninist teaching emphasizes that throughout the time spent at the university, and particularly as pertains to the study of law, all must be synchronized with the three components of Marxism-Leninism and express steadfast adherence to their content and form in state and law.

The leading role of the Soviet Union in the community of socialist states and their social and economic integration, the continued gradual approach to one another by the countries belonging to the community of socialist states, as well as the immediate utilization of Soviet jurisprudence and its practical applications, require a working knowledge of, and fluency in, the Russian language, and also a solid perception of national and legal developments in the Soviet Union and in other socialist countries. The many and continually growing international activities of the GDR necessitate the learning of another foreign language and the understanding of national and legal developments in other countries.

Through the study of the works of Marx, Engels, and Lenin, through constant practice-oriented study of the resolutions of the CPSU (Communist party of the Soviet Union) and the SED (Socialist Unity Party of Germany), through comprehensive utilization of the Soviet social and legal systems, through participation in competitions among the student body and personal active engagement in leadership and planning for the socialist society, and through various intellectual-cultural activities, the future jurist is being trained into a well-rounded socialist personality. Lofty political-moral motivations are joined with the ability to apply socialist justice efficiently to the current level of social development. The students are to be encouraged to further their qualifications and readiness to participate in the analysis of theoretical and practical solutions of newly emerging political, economic, social, ideological, and intellectual-cultural problems, propagate Marxism-Leninism and the political tenets of the SED, and develop their knowledge of government and legal systems.

The training demands a thorough self-assessment; it leads to independent scientific studies and to a gradual integration of the student into research. In this way the high standard of university education is productively constructed to facilitate for the student an opportunity for independent research and effective and creative individual study. This fact increases the responsibility and role model of the teaching staff as well as the accountability of the student for his individual performance in the socialist youth organization. During the studies various connections to the working class, with social applications, are created and nurtured through practical training and social-political activites at the university; and in the spheres of government agencies and social organizations, through partnership agreements, mobilization of labor forces at crucial moments of need, *subbotniks* [A Russian word meaning a "voluntary" contribution of work for a day or other short period of time away from one's regular place of employment. —Ed.], and other forms of contributing. Subsequent to the university studies of either one of the branches of these subjects, at the beginning of the practical training—which lasts usually one year—a probationary period is added for more intensive training. During this time the students acquire advanced experience in social applications and specific knowledge in their area of responsibility.

The resident students and the nonresident students are to be impressed with the ever-growing demands of their socialist society through communist training and education; their abilities and accomplishments must urge them on to represent the Marxist-Leninist ideological beliefs, to adopt new political and technical knowledge, and to broaden their general educational development.

Law graduates will be employed predominantly as judges, procurators, notaries, lawyers and as jurists in the socialist administration of law as well as judges in the State Contract Court. Further possibilities of employment are offered as legal assistants in state organs, industries and other operations, and as associates in academic institutions.

1.2 Main Topics of Courses

The structure of the courses in their special departments of law is based on the necessity of providing a practical basic knowledge. The following subject matters pertain to this:

Dialectical and Historical Materialism
Political Economy of Capitalism and Socialism
Scientific Communistic Fundamentals of the History of the Workers' Movement
Special Courses on Selected Problems of Marxism-Leninism
Special Seminar on Classics of Marxism-Leninism
Marxist-Leninist Theory of State and Law
History of State and Law

History of the Perceptions of the Theory of State and Law
Constitutional Law of the GDR
Constitutional Law of the USSR and other Socialist States
Constitutional Law of Bourgeois States
Constitutional Law of Developing Countries
Administrative Law
System for the Administration of Justice
Economic Law
Scientific-Technical Protection Law
Labor Law
Agricultural Cooperative Law
Land Law
Environmental Law
Civil Law
Civil Procedure
Family Law
Copyright Law
Criminology
Criminal Law
Criminal Procedure
International Law
Private International Law/International Economic Law
Sports, Russian language and one other foreign language

By expanding on the basic instructions, a deepening and growing of learning abilities and skills of the students is promoted. (Refer to Part 2). The concentrated components of the courses are meant primarily to advance an ability to think in complex juristic terms and also to lead to the early structuring of professional motivation.

In the final phase of law studies, elective subjects are offered as incentives to individual development and to the particular needs of the student's special field of future activity. The entire course of studies is based upon an established system of teaching with the following objectives:

—Dialectical and Historical Materialism
—Political Economy of Capitalism and Socialism
—Scientific Communistic Fundamentals of the History of the Workers' Movement

This subject matter is offered in expanded lectures in compliance with the courses designated "Fundamental Teachings of Marxism-Leninism at Universities of the GDR." Marxism-Leninism is the ideological, theoretical, and methodological basis for the entire course of studies. Also belonging to these categories are the special lectures on particular issues of Marxism-Leninism in the final years of law studies. The following special courses are offered as *electives among required studies* in the seventh semester:

—History of the SED
—Cultural Theories and Ethics of Marxism-Leninism
—Fundamental Concepts of Marxist-Leninist Ethics and Socialist Morals
—Scientific Atheism
—Selected Issues of Intensive and Extended Socialist Productivity

In the fourth year of law study, special seminars on the classical works of Marxism-Leninism are offered. These seminars facilitate the introduction of important classical works in connection with party documents and also the competence of the students to apply these historical, political-economic, and strategic perceptions to the ongoing structuring of the developing socialist society and its state and legal order.

The goal of the instructions in the subject matter of *Marxist-Leninist Theory of State and Law* is to demonstrate the insights of basic developmental legalities of the socialist state and law as shown in the works of Marx, Engels, and Lenin and elaborated upon by the CPSU (Communist party of the Soviet Union) and its related parties. The students must comprehend that the socialist state is the chief instrument of the proletariat and its Marxist-Leninist party for the realization of its historical mission and for the enforcement of the objective legalities in socialism and communism. An overall impression of the governmental and judicial development of exploiting societies along with the struggle of the people against capitalistic states is to be explained. The essence of these studies is the legality of the rise, the implementation, and the development of the socialist state and its legal system as well as its nature and functions in directing its social process. It exists for the protection of the socialist community and for the comprehensive establishment and maturation of the socialist democracy as demonstrated in the historically shown developmental stages of socialism and communism. Bound up with this study is the constant review of imperialistic, revisionistic, and social-reform concepts of state and law. The Marxist-Leninist theoretical studies of state and law convey the basis for government and law courses and serve as a distinctive expression of ideological foundations for socialist personalities. In this way the students are trained to become militant jurists.

In the subject matter of *History of State and Law* the development of state and legal systems as well as their institutions are taught. Here it is also demonstrated how the ideologies are necessary manifestations of the general growth of society as compared to the maturation of productive powers of the people and their political and ideological struggle. Through this teaching the students are made to recognize the historically proven limitations of materialism in other state and judicial systems and to be aware of the necessity of overcoming them. Thus, the importance of utilizing socialist law in the construction of a state and its judicial system is a powerful instrument serving as the political and theoretical postulate. The history of the state and of the legal system in the GDR is especially important in this kind of education. The basis for this is the SED. The firmness with which the durable friendship with the Soviet Union is fostered contributes to an understanding of Soviet history of state and law.

The subject matter of the *History of the Perceptions of the Theory of State and Law* is concerned with the general historical developmental process in the method of theoretical thought pertaining to state and law. The historical-theoretical view illuminates the new fundamental quality of the Marxist-Leninist state and law theory; at the same time it proves the progressive, revolutionary, humanistic thinking of past ages has been dialectically invalidated by the Marxist-Leninist theory concerning state and law. The disclosure of the origins and the development of basic imperialistic, social-reformative, anarchistic concepts of state and law enables the student to arrive at well-founded ideological conclusions. Accordingly, this subject matter contributes to the historical and theoretical ideological content and enriches the training and education of socialist jurists.

The subject matter of *Constitutional Law of the GDR*—based upon the social development of the GDR—teaches the shaping and operation of the socialist state law of the GDR, especially the socialist constitution and the constitutional statutes which were issued for its ongoing implementation. Thus, the establishment of the socialist state and the social organizations was implemented according to the teachings of the Marxist-Leninist classical works and according to the doctrines of the SED.

The focal point of these studies is the exposition of the class character of the political power of the GDR and the further development of social democracy, the political and economic foundations, as well as the role played by science, education, and culture in the social and political growth of the GDR. Equally important is the political attitude and development of the citizens and of the communities of the socialist society, the formation and the system of government—based on the sovereignty of the working class, realized in the fundamentals of democratic centralism. The regulation of the constitutional law explaining the development of socialist legality and administration of justice is also imperative.

The subject matter of the *Constitutional Law of the USSR and other Socialist States* proceeds from the premise of the global historical importance of the Great Social October Revolution and the general validity of the experiences of the Soviet Union. This subject matter stresses the fundamental characteristics of the constitutional development in the USSR, the structure of society and state, the foundations of the economy, the attitudes, basic rights and duties of Soviet citizens as well as the education, position, duties and work systems of the most important governmental and administrative organs in the USSR. In addition, the students survey the constitutional development of other socialist countries.

The subject matter of the *Constitutional Law of Bourgeois States* elaborates on the effects and basic trends of the government system and of the states' monopolistic capitalism. The study deals with the most important concepts of imperialistic constitutional theories and with the chief methods of imperialistic government. Taking as an example the state and constitutional development of the USA, Great Britain, France, and the FRG (Federal Republic of Germany), the students become acquainted with the governmental system of the imperialist powers and are made aware of the anti-imperialistic struggle of the masses under the leadership of the Marxist-Leninist parties.

The subject matter of the *Constitutional Law of Developing Countries* deals with effects and basic trends of the government of developing nations. The study elaborates on the most important concepts of their constitutional theories and the chief methods practiced in their spheres of influence. Taking as examples those developing countries allied with the GDR, the students survey the political systems in these countries as well as the characteristics of their ongoing social development.

The teaching of the subject matter of *Administrative Law* is closely related to Constitutional Law. It proceeds from the unity of state power through people's representation and government apparatus and includes those conditions in society which are continually reconstructed by the processes of the ratifying legislative activities of government organizations and practical leadership concerning social conditions. The duties and the authority of government organs are discussed as well as the legal position of the citizens and the cooperation existing between the government organizations and the social organizations. Here too the most important administrative methods of leadership and the problems of management and authority within the government organs, as they pertain to the main spheres of society, are dealt with.

The subject matter concerning the *System for the Administration of Justice* is based upon the historical development as rooted in the constitutional law of the GDR and as contained in its socialist legal system. It discusses the basic principles of the people's sovereignty, the unity of socialist governmental power, and the democratic centralism of legal regulations pertaining to position, function, development, organization, and administration in the state and social courts. It also deals with the work of the procurator's office and with the lawyers as well as with activities of investigating organs and of notaries.

The training in *Economic Law* covers the socialist state's system of economic planning pertaining to structure and production in industrial organizations. The students are made to understand the effects of international economic integration as it influences the domestic economy of the family of socialist states. The studies must emphasize the connection between economic law as an instrument of the political control of society and the economic management of a growing socialist attitude toward production. This will lead to systematic improvement of the material and cultural level of the people and enhance the development of awareness and personality of the workers employed within the economic system. The objective in teaching Economic Law is to make the students understand the entire subject matter in relation to its separate parts and to acquaint them with the principal legal issues pertaining to administration, planning, organization, and management as well as their methodological ramifications.

The subject matter of *Scientific-Technical Protection Law* deals with society's concerns with new acquisitions, inventions and patents, forms of industry, the diverse utilization of scientific-technical products, licensing matters, and the rationalization of scientific-technical functions. The separate area of trademarks is included in this course.

The subject matter of *Labor Law* deals with the legal regulations pertaining to the working conditions of workers, employees, and members of the intelligentsia which have been compiled in collaboration with the trade unions of the socialist state. These regulations represent the doctrines of the political-governmental organs of the leading working class. In this course it will be demonstrated how the socialist labor law is being used as an instrument of management for the development of socialist democracy in the enterprises. It shows how the growth of socialist personalities will be encouraged by conscious acts in enterprise and in the collectives in an atmosphere free from exploitation and supported by camaraderie among the workers. Knowledge of management principles to be used in the work process for labor law conditions, for problems of legality concerning capacity for work, and matters of morale and discipline will be attained as well as knowledge of improvements of working and living conditions of the workers.

The subject matter of *Agricultural Cooperative Law* deals with the legal regulations issued by the socialist government influencing the agricultural cooperatives and the legal status of cooperative farmers and workers of the agricultural cooperatives. This is an example of the useful application of the Leninist plans for cooperatives and encourages the deepening relationships between the leading working class and the class of cooperative farmers. The subject matter demonstrates how the agricultural cooperative law is instrumental in protecting and strengthening the democratic labor unions and how it promotes conditions of cooperative ownership and work situations in order to foster the development of socialist personalities. Here also the progress and consolidation in agricultural cooperative plant and animal production as well as the growing conversion to modern industrial methods of production are made clear, leading to ever closer cooperation.

In the subject matter of *Land Law* the legal regulations issued by the socialist government pertain to land protection, land ownership, and real estate transaction. It will be shown how to organize the planned and rationally executed use of land according to the needs of society and how the ratio of private ownership and cooperative use of arable land can be formulated. Special emphasis is given to the rights and duties of government organizations, socialist operations, and citizens as they work for the protection and profit of all of society.

The teachings in the subject matter of *Environmental Law* deal concisely with all legislative functions of government and society pertaining to the duties and legal implications of state organizations which are involved in the planning for, and protection of, a healthful and natural environment for all humankind.

The subject matter of *Civil Law* is concerned with the student's acquisition of a basic knowledge of governmental and legal management and the legal structures of those social relationships in which the citizens are directly involved and which serve important material and cultural needs. This deals chiefly with the involvement expected of the citizens in general and specifically at work places in regard to attitudes toward one another as well as the safeguarding of life, health, and socialist and personal property. This subject deals also with special rights and duties arising out of interactions resulting from supply of goods and rendering of services and with living arrangements.

The teachings in the subject matter of *Family Law* deal with the basic significance of socialist family relations, the common responsibility of state and society to nurture and preserve these, and the legal rights of individual family members. The central point of these studies is the legal status of matrimony and the relationships between parents and children as well as the influence exerted by the socialist government and its social dynamics for the preservation and strengthening of the socialist family. Also included in this course are legal regulations about support and income as they pertain to family relationships or changes and dissolutions within the family.

The subject matter of *Civil Procedure* is taught in close connection with Civil Law, Labor Law, and Family Law. It communicates the class-related social function of socialist law in the above-mentioned areas as a special form of government involvement for the protection of the rights of citizens and the duties expected of them. Here the focal point is the development and strict enforcement of socialist legality, the growth and perfection of socialist democracy, and objective truth as a prerogative for a well-founded educational legal system. Civil

Procedure also deals with functions and work methods of arbitration.

The subject matter of *Copyright Law* acquaints the students with the methods and means used by the socialist government in the interest of society regarding creation and distribution of intellectual-cultural works of literature, art, and science. Consideration is also given to rights and duties of authors and of the institutions distributing their work and to their correlated legal protection. This course also deals with the fundamentals of international copyright law.

The subject matter of *Criminology* deals with criminality as an acknowledged social and historical occurrence. The teaching of this subject demonstrates the social character, structure, and evolution of criminality as well as the prospect of its eradication. Thus, it shows also in this area the superiority of socialism and communism as compared to all other social structures. The basis for understanding the problems and possibilities of socialist criminal law and the gradual elimination and final conquest of crime through the historical process of constructing a socialist society, and subsequently a communist society, is the discovery of a strategy built upon the perceptions of Marx, Engels, and Lenin. The teaching of criminology includes the introduction to methods of crime prevention and of the practical organization of crime prevention in the GDR. In the analysis of imperialistic teachings and other bourgeois views about criminality the students affirm their own Marxist-Leninist positions and can then further develop their abilities to differentiate between these concepts.

The subject matter of *Criminal Law* elaborates on the necessity of protection, through criminal law in the socialist state, of the people's property and of the citizens' rights and interests as a prerequisite for the realization of the socialist state. Utilizing the experiences in the Soviet Union and in other Socialist countries, and in essential isolation from the bourgeois theories of criminal law and its practical application, the focal point of this course is the emphasis put on the nature of class consciousness coupled with the duties as detailed in socialist criminal law. It also deals with the understanding of the hypotheses, contents, sizes, limits, and different responsibilities as illustrated in the criminal law in general and in the various types of offenses. In addition, the objective of individualizing and implementing punishment through expedient application of criminal law is taught.

The teaching of the subject matter of *Criminal Procedure* is closely allied with that of Criminal Law. It conveys, based on class-consciousness, the social function of the socialist procedure against criminality in a special form of socialist governmental activity in order to enforce personal responsibility regarding criminal law and also to prevent and control crime. Important here is the strict adherence to socialist legality, the development and improvement of socialist democracy, the guarantee of uncovering objective truth, especially as a prerequisite to legal decision-making and to the rights of the people.

In the subject matter of *International Law* the students get acquainted with the class character, peculiarities, themes, and basic principles of international law, territorial concerns, international organizations, and laws regarding diplomatic and consular matters. The students are also taught that the international politics of the GDR conform to democratic human rights and to the principles of socialist international law. Here also the struggle of the members of the community of socialist countries for the establishment of a collective European security system and for worldwide disarmament is emphasized.

The studies concerning *Private International Law* cover mainly those matters of civil and family law concerned with aliens, and with citizens residing in foreign countries or with those people whose legal affairs occur in foreign countries. Because of the increasing international exchange of merchandise and cultural activities, the GDR has created regulations designating which special civil law is to be applied. Furthermore, the students will be instructed in general principles relating to legal-political fundamentals which have developed in the science of private international law, in order to arrive at correct political decisions.

The studies of *International Economic Law* deal chiefly with basic knowledge concerning the development and construction of socialist economic integration. Deriving from legal aspects pertaining to socialist economic integration and from legal structures for the regulations of integrated connections, emphasis is placed upon the coordination of planning, mutual planning of material production, specialization and cooperation, scientific-technical collaboration, and foreign trade as the most essential areas of integration. The basic legal regulations of foreign trade which govern the state's monopoly of foreign trade and monetary value are used as examples for the main forms of international business contracts.

Sports and *Language Courses* are given in accordance with stipulations by the Ministry for Higher Education. Required foreign languages are Russian plus one other foreign language. Nonresident students do not participate in sports. Their study in foreign languages is limited to Russian.

The *Socialist Military Training* is an integral part of communist education and serves to develop and strengthen the defense readiness of the students. Its systematic absorption during the entire course of studies is a task to which all other schooling must contribute.

In the area of *Civil Defense* the students are taught basic principles and preventive measures to protect the workers and the economy against weapons of mass destruction, sea disasters, and other catastrophes. Special seminars—based on laws and regulations—deal with the responsibility of state organs, factories, and other work places as well as social organizations in the field of population protection and economic protection.

A civil defense course adapted to the professions within the approved educational framework is compulsory; it is integrated with the lectures covering:

—Constitutional Law of the GDR
—Constitutional Law of Bourgeois States
—Administrative Law
—Economic Law

2. Characteristics of Special Professional Training

In the basic directions for the teaching of law the instructions for resident studies are carried out in the following special areas:

—Specialization in Law (Justice)
—Specialization in Law (Economics)

For nonresident courses the subjects of Justice and Economics will be taught together. Specialization will be made possible near the end of all studies.

The training in special areas consists of an intensification and expansion of knowledge, abilities, and skills in the particular fields of principal specialization. It contains further special subject matter necessary for the intended area of practice. The content of such specialized courses depends on the profile of the various sections.

Because of the "arrangement in the sections for the use of time" [Special Section Time] the students can intensify the study in certain areas at the appropriate sections of the universities so that they are able to get a comprehensive overview of the complex treatment of problems in government and law. Together with the appropriate practice partner the director of each section decides on the use of this time.

2.1 Specialization in Law (Justice)

The goal of specialization here is to train a law student in such a way that he can adapt socialist law into protective rules for state and law in an ever-developing socialist society. This requires the following abilities beyond basic legal knowledge:

—heightened awareness of theoretical foundations and of practical structures of organizations and activities in the courts, procurators' offices, and at state notaries as well as the counseling offices that work to guarantee the socialist statutes and the rights of the people

—deep understanding of social processes which have been established with the help of socialist organs of justice—this pertains especially to individual consumption, to the conditions essential for work and life of the working classes, and to human relationships

—theoretical and practical methodological mastering of the role played by socialist organs of law and justice as they prevent and control violations of law and as they insure order and security in all social matters

—a comprehensive view of respective developments in other socialist countries, and of relevant legal issues and relations with other governments, especially in the areas of civil law, family law, and criminal law

—a professionally oriented utilization of further knowledge in other important areas of socialist law—civil law, family law, and criminal law belong also in this category

—special knowledge in forensic sciences (forensic science, forensic psychology, psychiatry, and forensic medicine) as well as the law of sentencing

The students must become socially effective and irreproachable leaders within the government (process of procedure). They must be able to arrive at appropriate governmental decisions (verdicts, indictments, etc.) and to analyze the effect of socialist tenets and their legal application. It is important for the students to become competent in explaining convincingly socialist law to the workers and to help them with the attainment and enforcement of their rights.

The specialized education includes mainly the following subject matters:

—system for the administration of justice
—civil law, family law, labor law, agricultural cooperative law, and land law (including procedural law)
—criminal law and criminal procedure
—international law

Here too are added special classes which are part of the "time utilization at the disposal of each section" [Special Section Time]. They are offered to those future jurists who will be working in the courts, in procurators' offices, and at state notaries. Along with this, courses from which students may choose and faculty teaching arrangements are available. In this area of specialization belong studies in criminal law and criminal procedure, civil law and civil procedure, and also specific courses in criminology, sentencing, notary law, forensic psychology, forensic psychiatry, etc.

The law graduates who take these courses will be placed chiefly as judges, procurators, notaries, lawyers, or as functionaries in corresponding places within the government apparatus.

2.2 *Specialization in Law (Economics)*

The goal of this specialization is to train a law graduate in such a way that he can enforce and further develop the policies of the state's economy and society as they pertain to the economy based on the decrees of the party of the working class. This demands, in addition to the basic education in law:

—special knowledge of the use and effect of economic-political methods and of the various phases and areas in the economic reproduction process
—thorough knowledge of scientific-technical legal protection
—heightened awareness of the interactions of regulations within the state and of the developing law of international economic integration of socialist countries
—special professional orientation in other important areas of socialist law, especially in economic law
—further knowledge about the laws of countries belonging to the family of socialist states in matters of economy
—a comprehensive view of the law in the areas of economy in capitalist countries
—a thorough understanding of the science of economy

In connection with the application of law, the students must become able to analyze the effects of legal regulations. They must also learn to work with, enforce, and further develop the regulations of enterprises and conglomerates. In this area of specialization belong:

—Administrative Law
—Economic Law
—Scientific-Technical Protection Law
—International Economic Law, Finance Law, and Monetary Law

Here too are added special classes which are part of the "time utilization at the disposal of each section" [Special Section Time]. These are offered to those students whose future field of activity will be in industry, in trade and building matters, and in other areas of the economy, as well as jurists active in foreign economies. Along with this, courses from which students may choose and faculty teaching arrangements are available. In this area of specialization belong studies in economic law, international economic law, and also courses in administrative law, trade law, construction law, etc.

The law graduates taking these courses will be placed chiefly as legal administrators in the areas of socialist economy and as contract judges as well as legal administrative assistants in the central or regional state organs and establishments.

3. Development and Utilization of Studies

3.1 *Resident Studies*

The application—that is, admission to university education—is under the directive of the Ministry for Higher Education, which governs selection and admission to resident studies at the universities of the GDR.

There are special matriculation conditions for the study of law (Justice). The applicants are urged to collect practical experience in government, in socialist economy, and in work with social organizations before they enter into their studies. The entire length of study is four years. During the time of preparation for the first year of study the students get an initial impression of the standards set for socialist jurists. Thus their motivation for study is fortified. This preparation occurs at suitable places such as regional procurators' offices, regional courts, and legal departments of People's Owned Enterprises (VEB).

A crucial part of the study is the *independent academic work* of the students. Through intensive independent studies—supported by courses in the applicable areas—the student enriches his studies with the appropriate works of Marxist-Leninist classics, with party regulations and legal directives and also with textbooks, academic periodicals, and other special literature. In this way the student deepens and complements the studies of the classroom. The active application of attained knowledge and its strengthening and intensification, as well as the active participation of the students, is reenforced by attendance at seminars or other classroom exercises.

During the course of studies, previously determined free time is to be utilized in special ways for the improvement of qualified, independent academic work. Aside from using this free time for the preparation of written academic work, it is to be applied to specified areas of study and to attainment of a thorough knowledge of languages. Here each student determines his own work time.

Individual course plans will be offered to especially gifted students who also can occasionally change universities or do part of their studies in socialist foreign countries. In the first year at the university the students will become acquainted with various ways of individual academic study and also with research in special sections. This will foster self-reliant academic work. The students are also trained for independent academic work by joining collectives for students. Finally the student's expertise in independent academic work methods, as well as the preparation for his thesis, is tested through annual examinations (or other comparable work) which must be defended. It is obligatory to write one paper on Marxism-Leninism, that is, on Marxist-Leninist theories of state and law. (The themes of the theses are established through coordination with the research programs of the appropriate section.)

During the education of the socialist jurist it is important that he take part in social-political matters, that he is active in public life, and is engaged in the realization of socialist democracy and in the acquisition of expertise and ability regarding political public appearances.

Another important aspect of the education is practical training. It coordinates the student's education and training at the university with practical socialist aspects, and it unites theory and practice. The students get a chance to use in actual practice their theoretical knowledge, to learn advanced practical methods, and to be active as propagators of socialist law even during their time of study.

During the second year of studies a four-week-long practical service period in local organizations of government takes place for all participants in the studies of law. This has as its goal the intensification of the student's practical training in state and administrative law, of work in government organization, and learning from the experience accumulated in local organs of government.

While the students of law are involved in their practical training they will have the opportunity to attend conferences, that is, consultations with state and social courts. The selection of areas for practical participation in local organizations of government depends on the educational goals in the subject taken.

In the third year of studies a twelve-week-long practical training period is required for (a) Students of law (Justice) in the courts, at the state notaries, and in the procurators' offices. This has as its aim the student's practical training in criminal law, civil law, family law, and labor law. It also acquaints the student with work methods used in the courts and in the procurators' offices. (b) Students of law (Economics) at People's Owned Enterprises and at the State Contract Court. Here the goal is to heighten the student's practical education in the areas of economic law and labor law. It also involves the students in the work methods of administrative, that is, legal organs in People's Owned Enterprises and in the functions of the State Contract Court.

The responsibility for setting up learning situations for the practical training periods and the task of supervising these are dependent on suitable arrangements made by the section with the government organizations and with the enterprises.

The examinations and measures of achievement are administered according to the criteria for examination[1] and theses.[2] The completion of university education is evidenced by the issuance of the academic degree of *Diplom jurist*. This entitles the graduate to call himself professionally *Diplom jurist*.

[1]At this time the directive on the administering of examinations at places of higher education—order of examinations—is applicable as of January 3, 1975.

[2]At this time the directive for certification—certification order—is applicable as of January 28, 1976.

Examinations in the Subject Matter of Law (Justice)

Intermediate Examinations	
Dialectical and Historical Materialism	2d semester
Marxist-Leninist Theory of State and Law	2d semester
Constitutional Law of the GDR and Constitutional Law of the USSR and other Socialist States	2d semester
Criminal Law/Criminal Procedure	4th semester
Political Economy of Capitalism and Socialism	4th semester
Civil Law/Civil Procedure	5th semester
Final Examinations	
History of State and Law	3d semester
Administrative Law/System for the Administration of Justice	4th semester
Agricultural Cooperative Law/Land Law/ Environmental Law	5th semester
Labor Law	5th semester
Family Law	6th semester
Private International Law/International Economic Law	6th semester
International Law	6th semester
Scientific-Technical Protection Law	7th semester
Economic Law	8th semester
Language Studies: Russian, Second Foreign Language	3d semester
Comprehensive Examinations	
Marxism-Leninism	8th semester
Marxist-Leninist Theory of State and Law/ History of the Perceptions of the Theory of State and Law	8th semester
Constitutional Law	8th semester
Civil Law	8th semester
Criminal Law	8th semester
Certificates of Attendance	
Practice Exercise in Administrative Law	3d semester
Practice Exercise in Criminal Law	4th semester
Practice Exercise in Civil Law	5th semester

Special Seminars on Marxist-Leninist Classics and Two other Exercises, i.e., Special Seminars	7th semester
Special Course on Selected Problems of Marxism-Leninism	7th semester
Sports	8th semester

Examinations in the Subject Matter of Law (Economics)

Intermediate Examinations

Dialectical and Historical Materialism	2d semester
Marxist-Leninist Theory of State and Law	2d semester
Constitutional Law of the GDR and Constititional Law of the USSR and of other Socialist Countries	2d semester
Political Economy of Capitalism and Socialism	3d semester
Economic Law	4th semester

Final Examinations

History of State and Law	3d semester
Administrative Law	4th semester
Civil Law, Family Law, and Civil Procedure	5th semester
Criminal Law and Criminal Procedure	5th semester
Agricultural Cooperative Law and Land Law	5th semester
Labor Law	6th semester
Finance Law	6th semester
International Law	7th semester
Scientific-Technical Protection Law	7th semester
Language Studies: Russian, Second Foreign Language	3d semester

Comprehensive Examinations

Marxism-Leninism	8th semester
Marxist-Leninist Theory of State and Law/ History of the Perceptions of the Theory of State and Law	8th semester
Constitutional Law	8th semester
Economic Law	8th semester
International Economic Law, Finance Law, and Monetary Law	8th semester

Certificates of Attendance

System for the Administration of Justice	2d semester
Practice Exercise in Administrative Law	3d semester
Practice Exercise in Civil Law	3d semester
Practice Exercise in Economic Law	6th semester
Special Courses on Marxist-Leninist Classics and Two other Exercises, i.e., Special Seminars	7th semester
Special Course on Selected Problems of Marxism-Leninism	7th semester
Sports	8th semester

3.2 Nonresident [Part-Time] Studies

The application—that is, the admission to nonresident studies—is dependent on the authorization of July 1, 1973, from the Ministry for Higher Education dealing with nonresident and evening study at the universities and technical schools.

Prerequisite for the application and the admission to nonresident study is a certificate for university study and usually also completed training and several years of practical work in a trade. The student must have been actively involved within the structure of the socialist society, which includes the readiness to defend accomplished socialist gains. The admission also depends on the results of interviews. A qualifying contract will have been arranged between the designating officials and the official at the enterprise regarding the admission to nonresident study. The enterprises which employ the nonresident students vouch for an effective professional utilization and placing of the student after the successful completion of his studies.

Nonresident study has as its basis a self-education dependent upon textbooks, correspondence lessons, written instructions, and other didactic-methodological material. The intensive individual study, with its required papers, is supplemented by study group sessions. Individual study is conducted, supported, intensified, and controlled through seminars, exercises, lectures, written exercises, and examinations.

To promote independent and academic work methods, the nonresident students must write two scientific papers, one of which is to be submitted before the end of the second school year. The nonresident students learn the Russian language before and during the time of study in the related educational field.

After the four years of prescribed studies are finished there is a fifth year of study in which special knowledge and abilities are taught in those areas which are relevant to the present or future professional placement of the various groups of nonresident students. They will learn about the most recent results of research. During this year also the nonresident students write their second scientific paper. There follows a phase of research for thesis purposes. The entire time for nonresident study lasts five and a half years.

The examinations and measures of achievement are administered according to the criteria for examinations. The completion of university education is evidenced by the issuance of the academic degree of *Diplom jurist*. This entitles the graduate to call himself professionally *Diplom jurist*.

All courses cease with the end of the 10th semester. In the 11th semester the thesis is written and defended. The nonresident students are excused from their regular places of work in order to attend planned courses, to prepare and take required examinations, and to write term papers as well as to research, write, and defend the thesis. The amount of time off from work can be determined from the Hour Tables.

Examinations for Nonresident Studies in the Subject Matter of Law (Justice/Economics)

Intermediate Examinations	
Dialectical and Historical Materialism	1st year
Political Economy of Capitalism and Socialism	1st year
Marxist-Leninist Theory of State and Law	1st year
Constitutional Law in the GDR	2d year
Final Examinations	
Administrative Law	3d year
Civil Law/Civil Procedure	3d year
Economic Law	4th year
Labor Law	4th year
Agricultural Cooperative Law and Land Law	5th year
Criminology, Criminal Law, and Criminal Procedure	2d year
Comprehensive Examinations	
Marxism-Leninism	2d year
Marxist-Leninist Theory of State and Law	5th year

Special Education in Jurisprudence	5th year
Constitutional Law	2d year

Courses to be Attended

History of State and Law	2d year
International Law	3d year
Family Law	3d year
One other course determined from the *Study Plan*	5th year

3.3 References for Continuing Education

Some professional demands for the mastering of new challenges in the practical work of the socialist state and economy require further education subsequent to the completed university studies. Special subjects of continuing education are:

—work-related education dealing with state and legal organs and with People's Owned Enterprises as well as conglomerates

—postgraduate studies of jurists in the administration of justice with approval of their appropriate central organs (Ministry of Justice, Procurator General's Office) and with the support of university professors

—postgraduate studies of jurists (Economics) at the Law Section of the Martin Luther University, Halle

—postgraduate studies of leading cadres in the economy and in the government apparatus at the Law Section of the Humboldt University, Berlin

—continued education in special courses dealing with patent law, design law, and trademark law as well as with new acquisitions. These courses are offered at the Humboldt University, Berlin.

Details explaining the courses for postgraduate studies can be found in the catalogue dealing with continuing education: *Informator* of the Ministry for Higher Education.

[The remaining 7 pages of the printed *Study Plan* contain tables that set forth in detail the Justice Curriculum, the Economics Curriculum, and the Curriculum for Nonresident Study. Those tables are omitted from this translation. The key information in those tables concerning the Justice Curriculum and the Economics Curriculum is presented in Appendixes B and C.]

B
The Law Curriculum (Justice) by Semester

For the schedule of examinations, see the *Study Plan*.

Course	Hours per week
1st Year	
Semester 1	
Dialectical & Historical Materialism	4
Political Economy of Capitalism & Socialism	4
Marxist-Leninist Theory of State & Law	4
History of State & Law	4
Constitutional Law of the GDR	4
Criminology	2
Russian Language	2
Other foreign language	2
Sports	2
Semester 2	
Dialectical & Historical Materialism	4
Political Economy of Capitalism & Socialism	2
Marxist-Leninist Theory of State & Law	4
History of State & Law	2
Constitutional Law of the USSR & Other Socialist States	3
Administrative Law	2
Criminal Law	5
Russian Language	2
Other foreign language	2
Sports	2
Special Section Time	1
2d Year	
Semester 3	
Political Economy of Capitalism & Socialism	3
History of State & Law	2
Constitutional Law of Developing Countries	1
Constitutional Law of Bourgeois States	2
Administrative Law	2

Civil Law	2
Criminal Law	5
Criminal Procedure	2
Introduction to Psychology	2
Russian Language	1
Other foreign language	1
Sports	2

Semester 4

Political Economy of Capitalism & Socialism	2
System for the Administration of Justice	3
Labor Law	4
Land Law	4
Civil Law	4
Criminal Procedure	2
Forensic Science	2
Sports	2
Special Section Time	2

[Practical training period—4 weeks]

3d Year

Semester 5

Scientific Communistic Fundamentals of the History of the Workers' Movement	4
Labor Law	2
Agricultural Cooperative Law	3
Environmental Law	2
Civil Law	4
Civil Procedure	2
Family Law	1
Criminal Law	2
International Law	2
Sports	2
Special Section Time	2

Semester 6

Scientific Communistic Fundamentals of the History of the Workers' Movement	6
Civil Law	3
Civil Procedure	3
Family Law	3
International Law	3
Private International Law/International Economic Law	5
Sports	2

Special Section Time	2
[Practical training period—12 weeks]	
4th Year	
Semester 7	
Special Course on Selected Problems of Marxism-Leninism	2
Special Seminar on Classics of Marxism-Leninism	2
Marxist-Leninist Theory of State & Law	2
Economic Law	4
Scientific-Technical Protection Law	3
Copyright Law	1
Criminal Law	2
Sports	2
Special Section Time	8
Semester 8	
Scientific Communistic/Fundamentals of the History of the Workers' Movement	2
History of the Perceptions of the Theory of State & Law	4
Economic Law	2
Forensic Science	1
Sports	2
Special Section Time	9
[Work on 4th year paper—5 weeks]	

C
The Law Curriculum (Economics) by Semester

For the schedule of examinations, see the *Study Plan*.

Course	Hours per week
1st Year	
Semester 1	
Dialectical & Historical Materialism	4
Political Economy of Capitalism & Socialism	4
Marxist-Leninist Theory of State & Law	4
History of State & Law	2
Constitutional Law of the GDR	4
Civil Law	3
Russian Language	2
Other foreign language	2
Sports	2
Semester 2	
Dialectical & Historical Materialism	4
Political Economy of Capitalism & Socialism	5
Marxist-Leninist Theory of State & Law	4
History of State & Law	2
Constitutional Law of the USSR & Other Socialist States	2
Administrative Law	2
System for the Administration of Justice	1
Civil Law	2
Russian Language	2
Other foreign language	2
Sports	2
2d year	
Semester 3	
Political Economy of Capitalism & Socialism	4
History of State & Law	3
Constitutional Law of Bourgeois States	2
Administrative Law	2
Economic Law	5

Civil Law	3
Criminology	2
Socialist Enterprise Economics	2
Russian Language	1
Other foreign language	1
Sports	2

Semester 4

Scientific Communistic Fundamentals of the History of the Workers' Movement	5
Constitutional Law of Developing Countries	1
Administrative Law	2
Economic Law	6
Labor Law	4
Civil Law	2
Family Law	2
Criminal Law	4
Sports	2

[Practical training—4 weeks]

3d Year

Semester 5

Scientific Communistic Fundamentals of the History of the Workers' Movement	3
Economic Law	3
Labor Law	3
Agricultural Cooperative Law	3
Land Law	4
Environmental Law	2
Civil Procedure	3
Criminal Law	3
Criminal Procedure	2
Sports	2

Semester 6

Scientific Communistic Fundamentals of the History of the Workers' Movement	3
Economic Law	2
Scientific-Technical Protection Law	3
Labor Law	2
Finance Law	3
International Economic Law	3
Special Section Time	8
Sports	2

[Practical training—12 weeks]

4th Year

Semester 7

Special Course on Selected Problems of Marxism-Leninism	2
Special Seminars on the Classics of Marxism-Leninism	2
History of the Perceptions of the Theory of State and Law	3
Economic Law	2
Scientific-Technical Protection Law	3
Copyright Law	1
International Law	3
Private International Law	1
International Economic Law	2
International Finance and Monetary Law	2
Special Section Time	2
Sports	2

Semester 8

Marxist-Leninist Theory of State and Law	3
International Finance and Monetary Law	2
Special Section Time	12
Sports	2

[Work on 4th year paper—5 weeks]

D
Law Textbooks

Each of the following is a legal textbook (*Lehrbuch*) written by a group of legal scholars under the aegis of the GDR Ministry for Higher Education and (unless otherwise indicated) published by the *Staatsverlag*, a state publishing house in East Berlin. The year of publication and the number of pages are shown with each title.

Administrative Law, 1979, 686 pp.
Agricultural Cooperative Law, 1976, 460 pp.
Civil Law, Part I, 1981, 399 pp.
Civil Law, Part II, 1981, 350 pp.
Civil Procedure, 1980, 581 pp.
Constitutional Law of Bourgeois States, 1980, 489 pp.
Constitutional Law of the GDR, 1977, 557 pp.
Constitutional Law of the USSR, 1982, 264 pp.
Copyright Law, 1980, 212 pp.
Criminal Law—The General Part, 1976, 603 pp.
Criminal Law—The Special Part, 1981, 271 pp.
Criminal Procedure, 1977, 623 pp.
Family Law, 1981, 351 pp.
General History of State and Law: From the Origins of States up to the Rise of Capitalism, 1980, 416 pp.
International Law—Part I, 1981, 351 pp.
International Law—Part II, 1982, 286 pp.
Labor Economy, 1981, 712 pp. (Berlin: *Verl. Die Wirtschaft*)
Labor Law, 1983, 539 pp.
Land Law, 1976, 763 pp.
Marxist-Leninist Theory of State and Law, 1980, 672 pp.

E
Law Summaries

Each of the following is a summary (*Grundriss*) written by one or more legal scholars and (unless otherwise indicated) published by the *Staatsverlag*, a state publishing house in East Berlin. The year of publication and the number of pages are shown with each title.

Agrarian Law for Political and Economic Functionaries, 1976, 187 pp.

Civil Law, 1977, 1978 (Published in 10 parts as follows)

1. Basic Issues of Socialist Civil Law
2. Property Law: Use of Real Estate for Residential and Recreational Buildings
3. General Contract Law
4. Rent
5. Purchase
6. Services, Communities, Reciprocal Help, and Donations
7. Contracts Dealing with Accounts, Savings Accounts, Credits, and Loans
8. Protection of Life, Health, and Property from Damage
9. Inheritance Law
10. Civil Law Matters in Reference to Foreign Countries

Economic Law for Political Science, 1978, 227 pp.

Environmental Law, 1982, 237 pp.

German History: Class Conflict, Tradition, Socialism, 1979, 839 pp. (*Dt. Verl. der Wissenschaften*)

International Law, 1983, 286 pp.

Labor Law, 1979, 288 pp.

F
Law Commentaries

Each of the following is a commentary (*Kommentare*) published by the *Staatsverlag*, a state publishing house in East Berlin. The year of publication and the number of pages are shown with each title.

Commentary on the Civil Code of the GDR, 1983, 528 pp.

Commentary on the Documents of the Constitution of the GDR, 1969, vol. 1, 416 pp.; vol. 2, 550 pp.

Commentary on the Family Code of the GDR, 1982, 256 pp.

Commentary on the Identification Statute of the Agricultural Cooperative, Section for Animal Production, 1981, 217 pp.

Commentary on the Identification Statute of the Agricultural Cooperative, Section for Plant Production, 1980, 236 pp.

Commentary on the Law Dealing with Disorderly Conduct, 1961, vol. 1.

Commentary on the Law of Fire Protection in the GDR, 1977, 128 pp.

Commentary on the Law Concerning International Economic Contracts, 1978, 475 pp.

Commentary on the Law for Local People's Representation and for Their Organizations in the GDR, 1977, 352 pp.

Commentary on Regulations About the Duties and Work Methods of the State Contract Court, 1971, 575 pp.

Commentary on Regulations About the Problems, Rights, and Duties of People's Owned Enterprises and Combines, 1975, 220 pp.

Commentary on Traffic Laws, 1980, 282 pp.

Contract Law: Commentary on the Law of the Contract System Within the Socialist Economy, 1975, 752 pp.

Criminal Law of the GDR, 1981, 688 pp.

Criminal Procedure in the GDR, 1968, 544 pp.

The General Terms of Contract of the RGW 1968 in the Practice of Decision Making by Socialist Courts of Arbitration in Regard to Foreign Trade, 1975, 495 pp.

G
History of State and Law of the GDR

Summary (*Grundriss*) published in the GDR by *Staatsverlag*, Berlin, 1983

Table of Contents

		Page
Preface		9
Introduction		12

The Emergence of the State and the Rights of Workers and Farmers

Chapter 1

The Antifascist Democratic Upheaval and the Emergence of the Workers' and Farmers' State and Its Law (1945-1949)		24
1.1	The liberation of the German people from Hitler fascism—the concept of the working class for the establishment of the antifascist democratic republic—the taking over of the supreme governmental powers of the anti-Hitler coalition	24
1.1.1	The liberation of the German people from Hitler fascism and the historical responsibility of the working class	24
1.1.2	The concept of the Communist Party of Germany (KPD) and the Socialist Party of Germany (SPD) for the establishment of the antifascist democratic republic and of the socialist state	26
1.1.3	The taking over of the supreme governmental power by the anti-Hitler coalition—the stipulations of the Potsdam Conference	29
1.2	The origin and structure of antifascist democratic state organs and their function in the process of societal restructuring, 1945-1946	34
1.2.1	The origin and structure of antifascist democratic state organs, 1945-1946	34

1.2.2 Agrarian reform and antifascist democratic state organs 39
1.2.3 The function of the antifascist democratic state organs with the launching of the economy—first steps to restructure the production relationship 42
1.2.4 The cultural-educational activity of the antifascist democratic state organs 45
1.2.5 The commencement of the establishment of antifascist democratic justice 49
1.3 The foundation of the Socialist Unity Party (SED)—requirement for further social upheaval 52
1.4 The further structuring of the antifascist democratic state authority (1946-1948) 53
1.4.1 The expropriation of the monopolistic-capitalistic Nazi and war criminals—the origin of the economic basis of antifascist democratic state authority 53
1.4.2 The first democratic elections in the fall of 1946 56
1.4.3 The constitutional proposals of the Socialist Unity Party and the constitutions of the provinces 60
1.4.4 The further development of the state and legal-political concepts of the Socialist Unity Party and the governmental institutions in the fight against the imperialistic striving for restoration 63
1.4.4.1 The further preparation of state and legal-political concepts of the Socialist Unity Party 63
1.4.4.2 The further shaping of state authority 64
1.4.4.3 The beginning of the People's Congress movement 65
1.5 The development of state and law in the years before the founding of the GDR 68
1.5.1 Changing international and national conditions of the development of state and law 68
1.5.2 The Socialist Unity Party's political concepts of state and law 69
1.5.3 The reorganization of the German Economic Commission (DWK) 71
1.5.4 The significance of the People's Congress Movement for the foundation of the GDR 72

State and Law in the Creation of the Fundamentals of Socialism

Chapter 2
The Founding of the German Democratic Republic 78
2.1 Founding of the state 78
2.1.1 The initiative of the Socialist Unity Party and the formation of the highest state organs 78

2.1.2 The political and socioeconomic fundamentals of the GDR 83
2.1.3 The dissolution of the Soviet Military Administration in Germany (SMAD) 84
2.1.4 The international effect of the formation of the state 85
2.2 Character and historical place of the formation of the state 86
2.3 The constitution of the GDR of October 7, 1949 87

Chapter 3
The Development of State and Law in the Process of the Socialist Transformation in Preparation and Execution of the First 5-Year Plan (1949-1955) 91
3.1 The development of the political power of the working class and their institutions of state and law 91
3.1.1 The consolidation of the GDR in the class struggle 91
3.1.2 The organization of the central state institutions 93
3.1.3 The development of socialist law and the legislation of the People's Chamber 97
3.1.4 Foreign policy of the GDR 103
3.2 The people's elections of October 15, 1950 104
3.3 State and law in the beginning of the period of the first 5-year plan 107
3.3.1 The conclusion of the 2-year plan 107
3.3.2 The first 5-year plan (1951-1955) 108
3.4 The second party conference and the development of state and law 111
3.4.1 The establishment of national-political tasks for state and law by the second party conference of the Socialist Unity Party 111
3.4.2 The development of the local people's representatives 112
3.4.3 Changes in the central state organs 117
3.4.4 The further development of justice, the procurator's office, and the fundamentals of the administration of justice 118
3.4.5 The socialist reformation of agriculture 123
3.4.6 The extension of protection and security functions of the socialist state 125
3.4.7 The continuation of the socialist construction—the improvement of working and living conditions 127

Chapter 4
State and Law in the Socialist Reformation Until the Victory of Socialist Production Standards (1955-1961) 130

4.1 The development of the international power relationship, the conclusion of the treaty GDR–USSR of September 20, 1955, and the extension of the security function of the socialist state 130
4.2 The orientation of the Socialist Unity Party on the further construction of the foundations of socialism until the victory of socialist production standards 133
4.3 The stabilization of socialist state authority and the development of socialist democracy 135
4.3.1 The further development of the system of people's representatives and its organs 135
4.3.2 The further development of the economic guidance of the socialist state 141
4.3.3 The Conference of Babelsberg 145
4.3.4 The statute of the Council of Ministers of 1958 and the dissolution of the *Land* chambers 146
4.3.5 The formation of the Council of State of the GDR 147
4.4 The development of state and law in the further socialist reformation of socioeconomic relationships 150
4.4.1 The strengthening of the publicly owned sector of the people's economy 150
4.4.2 The further socioeconomic reformation in agriculture and its termination 153
4.4.3 The incorporation of the middle classes into the construction of socialism 156
4.5 The socialist legal order at the end of the transformation period 160
4.5.1 The legal arrangement of the working and living conditions of the citizens 160
4.5.2 Agricultural Cooperative Law 161
4.5.3 The protection of the workers' and farmers' authority 162
4.6 The securing of the state border of the GDR on August 13, 1961 168

State and Law in the Evolution and Formation of the Developed Socialist Society

Chapter 5

Socialist State and Socialist Law in the Sixties 172
5.1 A new period of social development—its external and internal conditions 172
5.2 The development of state and law after the sixth and seventh party conferences of the Socialist Unity Party 176

5.3 State and law in the management of socialist processes 179
5.3.1 Socialist democracy and development of the people's representatives 179
5.3.2 Management and planning of agriculture 181
5.3.3 Management of agriculture 186
5.3.4 Mangement of education and culture 187
5.3.5 The formation of the workers' and farmers' inspection in the GDR 191
5.3.6 The development of the socialist administration of justice 192
5.3.7 The reliable protection of socialism as a governmental task 195
5.4 The GDR in the socialist state community—its contribution to socialist foreign policy 196
5.4.1 Treaties of friendship and cooperation 196
5.4.2 The socialist foreign policy of the GDR in the struggle for peace and international detente 197
5.4.3 The cooperation of the GDR in the Council for Mutual Economic Assistance 198
5.5 The design of the socialist legal order 200
5.6 The constitution of the German Democratic Republic of 1968 206
5.7 Constitution, law, and socialist legitimacy 208

Chapter 6
The Further Development of Socialist State and Law in the Seventies 210
6.1 The external and internal requirements for the further development of the socialist society—the orientation through the party of the working class 210
6.2 The development of the socialist state and the state and legal management of social processes 214
6.2.1 Power of the working class and shaping of the political system 214
6.2.2 The perfection of socialist democracy and the further development of the activity of the people's representatives and their organs 215
6.2.3 Management and planning of agriculture 220
6.2.4 State management of agriculture—environmental protection and the regulation of land use 223
6.2.5 Shaping of social policy 226
6.2.6 State management of education, science, and culture 228
6.2.7 Development of state and social control 229
6.2.8 The protection of legitimacy; the perfection of the socialist administration of justice 230

6.3	Foreign policy and economy of the GDR in the community of the socialist states	234
6.3.1	The further strengthening of the alliance with the USSR and other socialist states	234
6.3.2	Socialist economic integration and the contribution of the GDR	235
6.3.3	Worldwide international recognition of the GDR—its contribution to détente in Europe	237
6.3.4	Development of relationships with other nonsocialist states	239
6.4	Further shaping of socialist law in the developed socialist society	240
6.4.1	The constitution of the GDR	240
6.4.2	Systematic development of socialist law—socialist legal order and socialist legitimacy	241
Final Comments		248
Subject Index		253

H
Constitutional Law of the GDR

Textbook (*Lehrbuch*) published in the GDR by *Staatsverlag*, Berlin, 1977

Table of Contents

		Page
Introduction		5
Chapter 1		
The Objective and Social Function of the Constitutional Law of the GDR		15
1.1	Objectives, sources, and the system of constitutional law	16
1.1.1	The objective of constitutional law	16
1.1.2	The sources of constitutional law	27
1.1.3	The system of constitutional law	30
1.2	The constitution as the core of constitutional law	32
1.2.1	The fundamental thesis of Marxist-Leninist constitutional teaching	32
1.2.2	The socialist nature of the constitution of the GDR	38
1.3	The Marxist-Leninist political science of the GDR	42
1.3.1	The responsibility of political science	43
Chapter 2		
The German Democratic Republic—a Sovereign Socialist State		46
2.1	The formation of the socialist state authority	47
2.1.1	The founding of the GDR as the realization of the working class's historic mission—comprehensive support of the Soviet Union	47
2.1.2	The problems of the constitution in the antifascist democratic upheaval: the significance of the constitution of October 7, 1949	65
2.1.3	The unity of people's sovereignty and state sovereignty	73
2.1.4	Development of socialist state authority	76
2.1.5	The constitution of April 6, 1968, and its further development	84
2.2	The international position of the GDR and the basic constitutional elements of its foreign policy	88
2.2.1	The GDR in the socialist state community	88

2.2.2 The solidarity with the people's anti-imperialistic battle 92
2.2.3 The principle of peaceful coexistence 93
2.3 Territory and the territorial sovereignty of the GDR 95
2.3.1 Territorial sovereignty 95
2.3.2 The borders of the GDR 101

Chapter 3
Foundations of the Socialist, Social, and State Order of the GDR 105
3.1 The socialist state of the GDR—a form of dictatorship of the proletariat 107
3.2 Further political bases of the socialist society and the government system 113
3.2.1 The position and relationships of classes and social strata in the socialist society 113
3.2.2 The position and relationships of political parties and societal organizations 115
3.2.3 The people's representatives in the political organizations of the socialist society 119
3.3 The economic basis of the socialist order of society and the state 126
3.3.1 The forms of socialist property and their constitutional regulation 127
3.3.2 The personal property of the working population 135
3.3.3 The constitutional regulation of state administration and planning of the economic system 137
3.4 Science, education, and culture as the basis of the socialist order of society and state 141
3.5 The military protection of the socialist order of society and the state 143
3.5.1 The necessity and the international and state law basis of military protection 143
3.5.2 The GDR as a member of the socialist military coalition 145

Chapter 4
Citizenship in the GDR 148
4.1 Content, character, and origin of GDR citizenship 149
4.1.1 The content and concept of socialist citizenship 149
4.1.2 The international character of citizenship 154
4.1.3 Origin and development of GDR citizenship 159
4.2 Acquisition and loss of GDR citizenship 159
4.2.1 Acquisition 159
4.2.2 Loss 165
4.3 The position of citizens of other states and stateless persons in the GDR 171

4.3.1	The position of citizens of other states and stateless persons	171
4.3.2	Asylum	173

Chapter 5
The Basic Rights and Basic Responsibilities of GDR Citizens 175

5.1	The socialist basic rights concept in the constitution	176
5.1.1	The class nature of basic rights and responsibilities	176
5.1.2	The basic rights and responsibilities, and the development of the socialist personality	181
5.1.3	Origin	
5.1.4	Basic rights, basic responsibilities, and socialist morality	190
5.1.5	The unity of socialist basic rights	194
5.2	The political, socioeconomic, and cultural basic rights and responsibilities	197
5.2.1	Political rights and responsibilities	197
5.2.2	Socioeconomic rights and responsibilities	207
5.2.3	Intellectual-cultural rights and responsibilities	213
5.3	Guarantees of the basic rights	219
5.3.1	Political and ideological guarantees	219
5.3.2	Economic guarantees	222
5.3.3	Legal guarantees	232
5.4	The socialist basic rights of GDR citizens and democratic international law	227

Chapter 6
Elections and Suffrage in the GDR 230

6.1	The foundations of the socialist election system	231
6.1.1	The social function of elections	231
6.1.2	The socialist election system—its principles and fundamentals	237
6.2	Preparation and execution of the elections of the people's representatives	244
6.2.1	The responsibilities of the people's representatives in the preparation and execution of the elections	244
6.2.2	The conduct of the elections by the election commissions	246
6.2.3	The democratic process of nominating candidates	248
6.2.4	The election process and ascertaining election results	251

Chapter 7
The State System of the GDR 255

7.1	The GDR as a socialist unitary state	255
7.1.1	The socialist unitary state as a state form	255
7.1.2	The principles of the state form	259

7.2 Political-territorial structure 262
7.3 Organization of the state authority 269
7.3.1 The people's representative organs 269
7.3.2 The collective head of state 275
7.3.3 The Council of Ministers and its organs 276
7.3.4 The local councils and their special organs 277
7.3.5 The courts 279
7.3.6 The procurator's office 281
7.3.7 The organs of national defense, security, and order 282

Chapter 8
The People's Representatives 289
8.1 The social function and the constitutional position of the representatives 290
8.1.1 The social function of the representatives 290
8.1.2 The constitutional position of the representatives 292
8.1.3 The responsibility to support the representatives 297
8.2 Privileges of the representatives and successor candidates 299
8.2.1 The rights and responsibilities of the representatives 299
8.2.2 The rights and responsibilities of the successor candidates 309
8.3 Guarantees and legal protection of the representatives 310
8.3.1 Socioeconomic guarantees 310
8.3.2 Legal protection of the representatives 312
8.4 Commencement and termination of the representative function 314
8.4.1 Commencement of the representative function 314
8.4.2 Termination of the representative function 315

Chapter 9
The Central Organs of GDR State Authority 317
9.1 The People's Chamber as the highest organ of state authority 318
9.1.1 The function of the People's Chamber as an expression of the working people's sovereignty 318
9.1.2 The responsibilities and privileges of the People's Chamber 324
9.1.3 The meetings and activity of the People's Chamber 329
9.1.4 The chairmanship and committees of the People's Chamber 332
9.1.5 The democratic procedure of legislation 336
9.2 The Council of State 339
9.2.1 The functions of the Council of State as an organ of the People's Chamber 339

9.2.2	The functions and privileges of the People's Chamber	341
9.2.3	The responsibilities and privileges of the Council of State and its chairman	343
9.3	The National Defense Council	349
9.3.1	The function and constitutional position of the National Defense Council	349
9.3.2	The responsibilities and privileges of the National Defense Council	351
9.4	The Council of Ministers	353
9.4.1	The function of the Council of Ministers as an organ of the People's Chamber and the government of the GDR	353
9.4.2	The responsibilities and privileges of the Council of Ministers	358
9.4.3	The fundamental operating principles of the Council of Ministers	361
9.4.4	The organs of the Council of Ministers	366
9.4.5	The administration, coordination and control of the county councils by the Council of Ministers	372
9.4.6	The function of the workers' and farmers' inspection as an organ of the Central Committee of the Socialist Unity Party and the Council of Ministers	374
9.5	The Supreme Court	379
9.5.1	The constitutional position of the Supreme Court	379
9.6	The Procurator General	387
9.6.1	The constitutional position of the Procurator General	387
9.6.2	The responsibilities and privileges of the Procurator General	389

Chapter 10

The Local Organs of GDR State Authority		393
10.1	The local people's representatives—the organs of the socialist state authority in their jurisdiction	395
10.1.1	The constitutional position and the fundamental responsibilities of the local people's representatives	395
10.1.2	Meetings of the local people's representatives	401
10.1.3	Commissions of the local people's representatives	406
10.2	The local councils as organs of the people's representatives	410
10.2.1	The constitutional position, the competence, and the operation of the local councils	410
10.2.2	The organs of the local councils	416
10.2.3	The operation and organization of the local councils	419

10.3 The cooperation of the local people's representatives with other organs of state and with operations and organizations 421
10.3.1 The cooperation of the local people's representatives and their councils with the courts, the procurator's office, the organs of security and order as well as with the workers' and farmers' inspection (ABI) 421
10.3.2 The cooperation of the local people's representatives and their organs with operations, combines, organizations, and associations which are not under their control 424
10.4 The formation of associations through the local people's representatives 427
10.4.1 The administrative councils 427
10.4.2 Communal associations 431

Chapter 11
The Constitutional Position of the Assistants in the State Organs 437
11.1 The social function and the constitutional position of the assistants 438
11.1.1 State activity—service for the interests of the people 438
11.1.2 The principles of the socialist state activity 440
11.2 The rights and responsibilities of the assistants and leaders 447
11.2.1 The rights and responsibilities of the assistants 447
11.2.2 The special rights and responsibilities of the leader 451
11.2.3 The support and legal protection of the assistants in the execution of their state functions 453
11.3 The accountability of the assistants 454
11.3.1 Disciplinary accountability 455
11.3.2 Material accountability 455
11.3.3 Criminal accountability 456

Chapter 12
The Guarantee of Socialist Legality 457
12.1 The nature, the significance, and the guarantees of socialist legality 458
12.1.1 The nature of socialist legality and its Marxist-Leninist foundation 458
12.1.2 The growing significance of socialist legality in the further formation of the developed socialist society 463
12.1.3 The guarantees of socialist legality 468
12.2 Socialist legality as a basic principle of the state organ's function 473
12.2.1 Content and extent of the state organ's responsibility for the strengthening of socialist legality 473

12.2.2	Persuasion and pressure as fundamental state methods to insure socialist legality	477
12.2.3	Requirements of state guidance to guarantee socialist legality	481
12.3	The protection of socialist legality in state decisions	492
12.3.1	The legal character and the procedures of state decisions	492
12.3.2	The enactment of legal provisions	496
Bibliography		500
Subject Index		531

I
International Law

Summary (*Grundriss*) published in the GDR by *Staatsverlag*, Berlin, 1983

Table of Contents

		Page
Introduction		13
Abbreviations		15
1	Nature and Concept of the International Law of the Present. The Position of the Basic Principles in the System of International Law	19
1.1	The international law of the present and its conceptual elements	19
1.2	The social foundations and the function of international law	21
1.2.1	The existence of states with different social orders and peaceful coexistence	21
1.2.2	The necessity of legal regulation of international relations	23
1.3	The class character of international law	24
1.3.1	The nature of bourgeois international law until 1917	24
1.3.2	The shaping and nature of the general democratic international law	25
1.3.3	The new types of relationships between socialist states and their regulation of international law	29
1.4	Characteristics of international law	30
1.4.1	Subjects of international law	30
1.4.2	The agreement character of international law	32
1.4.3	Sources of international law	33
1.4.4	Enforcement of international law	35
1.4.5	The relationships between international law and common law	35
1.5	The basic principles of international law today	37
1.5.1	Nature and function of the basic principles of the general democratic international law	37

1.5.2	The basic principles of the United Nations Charter	41
1.5.3	The socialist principles of international law and their relationship to general democratic international law	45
1.6	Concept of international law today	47
	Examination questions	
2	Subjects of International Law. The Principles of	48
	Sovereign Equality of States and Noninterference	49
2.1	Concept and forms of international law subjects	49
2.2	States as fundamental subjects of international law	52
2.2.1	The existence of states as prerequisite of international law	52
2.2.2	The sovereign equality of states	53
2.2.3	The legal subjectivity of international law of federated states	56
2.3	The subjectivity of international law of nations	56
2.4	The principle of noninterference in international matters	59
2.5	Recognition under international law	60
2.5.1	Concept and legal effects of recognition under international law	60
2.5.2	The recognition of states and their subjectivity in relation to international law	61
2.5.3	Forms and procedures of recognition	64
2.5.4	Recognition of governments	65
2.5.5	Recognition of organs of the national liberation movement	65
2.6	State succession	67
2.6.1	State succession as an institution of international law	67
2.6.2	The main types of state succession	67
2.6.3	Materials of state succession and their regulation by international law	70
2.6.3.1	Succession in treaties	70
2.6.3.2	Succession in national capital, national archives, and national debts	72
2.6.4	Regarding the state succession of the GDR and FRG	73
	Examination questions	
3	The Basic Principle of Loyalty and the Legal	75
	Sources of International Law	76
3.1	The basic principle of loyalty	76
3.2	Concepts and forms of the legal sources of international law	78

3.2.1	The agreement as legal source of international law	78
3.2.2	The norm of common law as legal source of international law	79
3.2.3	The resolutions of international organizations	79
3.3	The codification of international law	79
3.4	The agreement of international law	80
3.4.1	Nature and significance of the international law agreements	80
3.4.2	The forms of the international law agreement	82
3.4.3	Conclusion and the effective date of international law agreements	83
3.4.3.1	The authority	83
3.4.3.2	The agreement negotiations	83
3.4.3.3	The signing of international law agreements	84
3.4.3.4	Reservation and one-sided declaration	85
3.4.3.5	Acceptance, agreement, and entry into multilateral contracts	86
3.4.3.6	The ratification of international law agreements	86
3.4.3.7	The taking effect of international law agreements and their transformation into domestic law	87
3.4.4	Application and interpretation of international law	90
3.4.4.1	Application of international law agreements	90
3.4.4.2	Interpretation of international law agreements	91
3.4.5	International law agreements and third-party states	91
3.4.6	Amendment and alteration of international law agreements	92
3.4.7	Invalidation, termination, and suspension of the effectiveness of international law agreements	92
3.4.7.1	Invalidity of international law agreements	92
3.4.7.2	Termination and suspension of the effectiveness of international law agreements	93
	Examination questions	93
4	Basic Principles of Equality and Rights of Self-Determination of Nations, Human Rights, and Population	96
4.1	Basic principle of equality and self-determination of nations	96
4.1.1	Nature and significance of this basic principle	96
4.1.2	The shaping of an international law principle	98
4.1.3	The right of self-determination of nations as a fundamental collective human right	100
4.2	The general place of human rights in international law	102

4.2.1	Human rights, securing of peace, and enactment of the right of self-determination	102
4.2.2	The guarantee of human rights and the prohibition of intervention	104
4.2.3	International cooperation in the promotion of human rights and the role of the United Nations	105
4.3	Regulations in international law in individual areas of cooperation in the field of human rights	108
4.3.1	The prevention of genocide	108
4.3.2	The prohibition of discrimination	108
4.3.2.1	Prohibition of race discrimination	108
4.3.2.2	Prohibition of apartheid	110
4.3.2.3	Protection of minorities	110
4.3.2.4	Equal rights of women	111
4.3.3	The unity of political, economical, social, and cultural rights	112
4.4	The personal and territorial sovereignty of the state with regard to the population	113
4.4.1	Personal sovereignty and citizenship	113
4.4.1.1	Acquisition and loss of citizenship	114
4.4.1.2	Nationality of judicial persons, ships, and aircraft	115
4.4.2	Diplomatic immunity	115
4.4.3	The legal status of foreigners	116
4.4.4	The right of sanctuary	117
4.5	International cooperation in the fight against crime	118
4.5.1	International crimes	118
4.5.2	Other felonies prosecuted according to universal principle	120
4.5.3	Extradition	120
	Examination questions	121
5	Territory in International Law	123
5.1	Fundamentals of general international law for the peaceful utilization of state and nonstate territory	123
5.2	The international law status of state territory	125
5.2.1	Concept of state territory	125
5.2.2	The legal character of state territory	125
5.3	Principle of territorial integrity of the state	126
5.4	State border and border regime	128
5.4.1	General legal fundamentals	128
5.4.2	Principle of the immunity of state borders	129
5.4.3	The border regime	131
5.4.4	Territorial sovereignty and transit traffic	133
5.5	The legal status of the polar regions	134

5.5.1	The legal regime of the Arctic	134
5.5.2	The international law regime of Antarctica	135
5.6	International maritime law	136
5.6.1	Regarding the development of international maritime law	136
5.6.2	Inland waters	137
5.6.3	Territorial waters	138
5.6.3.1	Extent of territorial waters	138
5.6.3.2	Right of peaceful passage	141
5.6.4	Connected zone	142
5.6.5	Straits (channels)	142
5.6.6	Economic zone	143
5.6.7	Mainland base	143
5.6.8	The open sea	144
5.6.9	The sea bed	146
5.7	International aviation rights	147
5.7.1	National sovereignty over air space	147
5.7.2	International air traffic	148
5.8	Space rights	150
	Examination questions	151
6	Diplomatic and Consular Rights	152
6.1	Class content and responsibilities of diplomatic and consular rights	152
6.1.1	Diplomacy as a part of foreign policy	152
6.1.2	State organs for foreign relations	154
6.2	Diplomatic missions in other states and with intergovernmental organizations	156
6.2.1	Permanent diplomatic missions	156
6.2.2	Nonpermanent diplomatic missions	160
6.2.3	Immunities and privileges of diplomatic missions and their members	161
6.3	Consular missions	163
	Examination questions	166
7	International Organizations. Their Role in the Realization of the State's Responsibility of Mutual Cooperation	167
7.1	The responsibility of the states in mutual cooperation as the basic principle of international law	167
7.1.1	Content and goal of the basic principle	167
7.1.2	Forms of intergovernmental cooperation	168
7.2	The legal status of international organizations	170

7.2.1	Fundamentals of international law in the activity of international organizations	170
7.2.2	The subjectivity of international law	170
7.2.3	The legal character of resolutions	171
7.2.4	Regarding the problems of supranationality	173
7.3	The United Nations	174
7.3.1	The founding of this organization	174
7.3.2	Goals and principles	175
7.3.3	Main tasks	176
7.3.4	Membership	177
7.3.5	Main organs	178
7.3.6	The resolutions of the General Assembly and the Security Council	182
7.4	Special organizations	183
7.5	Organizations of socialist countries	186
7.5.1	Responsibilities in strengthening socialist state unity	186
7.5.2	The organization of the Warsaw Pact	187
7.5.3	The Council for Mutual Economic Assistance	188
7.6	The imperialistic pact system	191
7.7	Selected regional organizations	192
7.7.1	The Organization of African Unity	192
7.7.2	The Arab League	193
7.7.3	The Organization of American States	194
	Examination questions	194
8	The Prohibition of Violence by International Law and Its Enforcement	195
8.1	Formation and content of the prohibition of violence	195
8.1.1	Regarding the historic origins of the prohibition of violence	196
8.1.2	Comprehensive prohibition of violence as a basic principle of current international law	197
8.1.3	Definition of aggression	198
8.2	The right of states to individual or collective self-defense	200
8.3	The formation of selective safety systems	202
8.3.1	Possibilities within the UNO	203
8.3.2	Regional safety systems	204
8.3.3	A system of collective safety in Europe	205
8.4	Regarding the agreements for nonaggression	207
8.5	Regarding neutrality	207
8.6	Regarding the movement of the nonaligned	209

8.7	Disarmament as a form of enforcement of the prohibition of violence	210
	Examination questions	215
9	Peaceful Regulation of International Disputes	216
9.1	Peaceful dispute settlement as a principle of international law	216
9.1.1	Place and function of the principle of peaceful dispute settlement in current international law	217
9.1.2	The content of the principle of peaceful dispute settlement	217
9.1.3	The UN Charter and peaceful dispute settlement	219
9.1.3.1	Regarding the term *international dispute* in the UN Charter	219
9.1.3.2	The jurisdiction of the Security Council and the General Assembly within the framework of peaceful dispute settlement	220
9.2	The means of peaceful dispute settlement	221
9.2.1	Diplomatic means	221
9.2.1.1	Negotiations	221
9.2.1.2	Good offices	223
9.2.1.3	Mediators	223
9.2.1.4	Investigations	224
9.2.1.5	Settlement	224
9.2.2	Judicial means	225
9.2.2.1	International courts of arbitration	225
9.2.2.2	Permanent international courts	226
9.2.3	Other peaceful means of our choice—combined means	227
	Examination questions	230
10	Violations Against International Law and Responsibility of International Law	231
10.1	Nature and concept of responsibility of international law	231
10.1.1	The position of responsibility in international law	231
10.1.2	The violation of international law as sole prerequisite of responsibility	232
10.1.3	Regarding the position of codification	234
10.2	The kinds of violations of international law	235
10.2.1	International crime	237
10.2.2	International offenses	238

10.3	The state as subject of violation of international law	239
10.3.1	The attitude of state organs	240
10.3.2	The attitude of state organs in connection with the actions of noninternational law subjects	241
10.4	Contents and forms of responsibility	242
10.4.1	The content of responsibility	242
10.4.2	The forms of responsibility	243
10.4.2.1	Self-defense	244
10.4.2.2	The kinds of reparations	245
10.5	Regarding the application of norms in responsibility	246
	Examination questions	248
11	Rules of International Law in International Armed Conflicts—Humanitarian International Law	249
11.1	Place and development of the rules of humanitarian international law in current international law	249
11.1.1	Fundamental position and function of humanitarian international law in the current system of international law	249
11.1.2	The development of rules of international law about warfare and for the protection of war victims	251
11.2	The principles and rules of humanitarian international law	253
11.2.1	The international conflict as a case of main application	254
11.2.2	Separate rules in the case of noninternational armed conflicts	254
11.2.3	Status of combatants and prisoners of war	254
11.2.4	Means and methods of warfare	255
11.2.5	Protection of the civilian population and civilian property	256
11.2.6	Protection of wounded, sick, and shipwrecked persons	257
11.2.7	The treatment of prisoners of war	259
11.2.8	Regulations concerning the termination of international armed conflicts	260
11.2.9	Neutrality in international armed conflicts	260
11.3	The enforcement of the regulations of international armed conflicts	261
11.3.1	Responsibility for war crimes and the system of penal sanctions in the Geneva Agreements and in Protocol I	261
11.3.2	The prohibition of reprisals	262
11.3.3	The system of the protecting power	263

11.3.4	The role of the Red Cross movement	263
	Examination questions	264
12	Fundamentals of International Law for Security in Europe	265
12.1	Problems of the postwar development in Europe	265
12.1.1	The Potsdam Agreement as the basis of international law for a European regulation of peace and for the guarantee of security in Europe	265
12.1.2	The significance of the peace treaties with Germany's former allies and the international treaty with Austria for the guarantee of peace in Europe	267
12.2	The basic questions for security in Europe	267
12.2.1	The characteristics of the quadrilateral treaty for West Berlin	267
12.2.2	The relationships between the GDR and the FRG	271
12.2.3	The significance of the Final Act in Helsinki for peace, security, and cooperation in Europe	275
	Examination questions	278

Selected collective representation of international law 279

Recommendations for belletristic readings 279

Index 280

Documents

UN Charter

Declaration on the Principles of International Law concerning friendly relations and cooperation among states in accordance with the Charter of the UN, October 24, 1970.

The Vienna Convention on the Law of Treaties, May 23, 1969.

Definition of Aggression, December 14, 1974.

J
Constitutional Law of Bourgeois States

Textbook (*Lehrbuch*) published in the GDR by *Staatsverlag*, Berlin, 1980

Table of Contents

Page

Introduction 11

Chapter 1
Subject and Sources of the Constitutional Law of Bourgeois States 13
1.1 The object of the constitutional law of bourgeois states 14
1.2 The sources of the constitutional law of bourgeois states 17
1.3 The Marxist-Leninist science of constitutional law of bourgeois states and the system of presentation in this textbook 19

Chapter 2
Economic Foundations of the Modern Bourgeois State and Political Organization of the Bourgeois Society and Constitutional Law 23
2.1 The economic foundation and the bourgeois state 24
2.2 The civil state in imperialism and changes in bourgeois constitutional law 29
2.3 Political organization of the civil society and constitutional law 33
2.3.1 The employers' associations 35
2.3.2 The political parties 38
2.3.3 The unions 42
2.3.4 The bourgeois mass media 44

Chapter 3
The Constitutions of Bourgeois States 48
3.1 Concept and class character of bourgeois constitutions 49
3.2 Fundamentals of bourgeois constitutions 53
3.3 Passage and change of bourgeois constitutions 56

Chapter 4
Forms of Bourgeois States 59
4.1 The concept of forms of the bourgeois state 60
4.2 The forms of government of the bourgeois state 63
4.3 The organization of government in bourgeois states 66
4.4 The political regimes in bourgeois states 73

Chapter 5
Election and Suffrage in Bourgeois States 79
5.1 Concept and functions of elections 79
5.2 The mechanism of a state's exclusive control to plan elections 82
5.3 Suffrage and principles of elections 88
5.4 Election systems 91
5.5 The basic position of communist parties to take part in elections 95

Chapter 6
The Bourgeois Parliament 96
6.1 The political significance of the bourgeois parliament 97
6.2 Transformation and changes of the bourgeois parliament 98
6.3 Formation, structure, and authority 100
6.4 Functions and variations of the bourgeois parliament 104
6.5 Bourgeois parliament and exclusive control 107
6.6 Crisis and mobility of the bourgeois parliament 108

Chapter 7
Head of State and Government in the Bourgeois State 109
7.1 Head of state 110
7.1.1 Concept and forms of the head of state 110
7.1.2 The functions of the head of state 111
7.2 The government 115
7.2.1 The concept of government in the bourgeois state 115
7.2.2 One-party governments and coalition governments 117
7.2.3 The mechanism of government 118
7.2.4 The emergence of new forms of power concentration relating to a state's exclusive control 119
7.2.5 The influence of intergovernmental organs on bourgeois governmental systems 121

Chapter 8
Regional and Local Administrative Organs and Self-Administering Organs 123
8.1 The system of regional and local organs in the bourgeois state 124
8.2 The nature of regional and local self-administration 125

8.3 The administrative structure of regional and local self-administering units 129
8.4 The relationships of regional and local organs to the organs of the central state authority 130
8.5 "Reforms" relating to state monopoly in the area of regional and local organs of the bourgeois authority 132
8.6 The position of anti-imperialistic democratic powers in questions of regional and local self-administration 134

Chapter 9
The Civil Justice System 137
9.1 Concept and function of justice in the bourgeois state 138
9.2 The fiction of the independence of the judges in the bourgeois state 140
9.3 Concrete manifestations of imperialistic justice 143
9.4 The judicial function of "controlling the law" 147

Chapter 10
Imperialistic Forces, Police, and Secret Services 153
10.1 Constitutional aspects of the extension of imperialistic forces, police, and secret services 154
10.2 The specific functions of imperialistic forces, police, and secret services 158

Chapter 11
Civil Service in the Bourgeois State 166
11.1 Concept and function of public service 167
11.2 The structure of the civil service and the position of its members 170
11.3 The bureaucracy of civil service 174
11.4 The intensification of contradiction in the civil service 177

Chapter 12
Basic Rights in the Bourgeois State 179
12.1 Capitalistic government and basic rights 180
12.2 The bourgeois regulation of basic rights 182
12.3 Restrictions and cut-backs of constitutional rights in imperialism 186
12.4 The fight to defend and extend democratic rights 190

Chapter 13
Fundamentals of the Constitution of the USA 193
13.1 Introduction 194
13.2 The Constitution 194

13.3 The position of the parties, employers' association, and trade unions 198
13.4 Election system and suffrage 203
13.5 The central governmental organs 206
13.6 State organs and local organs 212
13.7 The basic rights 213
13.8 The Constitution of the United States of America [full text] 216

Chapter 14
Fundamentals of the Constitution of Japan 231
14.1 Introduction 232
14.2 The Constitution 232
14.3 The position of the parties, employers' associations, and trade unions 235
14.4 Election system and suffrage 238
14.5 The central state organs 240
14.6 The local organs 243
14.7 The basic rights 245
14.8 The Constitution of Japan 247

Chapter 15
Fundamentals of the Constitution of the Federal Republic of Germany (FRG) 256
15.1 Introduction 257
15.2 Origin and character of the Basic Law 257
15.3 Parties, employers' associations, and trade unions 262
15.4 Election system and suffrage 266
15.5 The central federal organs 268
15.6 The local organs 274
15.7 Citizenship and basic rights 276
15.8 The Basic Law of the FRG 279

Chapter 16
Fundamentals of the Constitutional Law of Great Britain 308
16.1 Introduction 309
16.2 The Constitution 310
16.3 The position of the parties, employers' associations, and trade unions 311
16.4 Election system and suffrage 317
16.5 The central state organs 319
16.6 Regional and local organs 322
16.7 The basic rights 324
16.8 Constitutional documents of the United Kingdom of Great Britain and Northern Ireland 326 (excerpts)

Chapter 17
Fundamentals of the Constitutional Law of France 343
17.1 Introduction 344
17.2 The Constitution 344
17.3 The position of the parties, employers' associations, and trade unions 346
17.4 Election system and suffrage 350
17.5 The central state organs 353
17.6 Regional and local organs 356
17.7 The basic rights 358
17.8 The Constitution of the French Republic 360

Chapter 18
Fundamentals of the Constitutional Law of Italy 374
18.1 Introduction 374
18.2 The Constitution 375
18.3 The position of the parties, employers' associations, and trade unions 377
18.4 Election system and suffrage 382
18.5 The central state organs 384
18.6 Regional and local organs 387
18.7 The basic rights 390
18.8 The Constitution of the Republic of Italy 393

Chapter 19
Fundamentals of Constitutional Law of the Northern European States—Denmark, Norway, and Sweden 411
19.1 Introduction 412
19.2 The Constitutions 413
19.3 The position of parties, employers' associations, and trade unions 416
19.4 Election systems and suffrage 422
19.5 The central state organs 425
19.6 Regional and local organs 433
19.7 The basic rights 434
19.8 The Constitution of the Kingdom of Sweden 437

Chapter 20
The European Communities—Consequences for the Constitutional Law of Member States 454
20.1 Tendencies of the internationalization of economic power and its influence on the political superstructure 455
20.2 The interlacing of the European Community's apparatus with national executive powers and political nongovernmental organizations 462

Chapter 21
State Question, Bourgeois Constitutional Law, and the Fight for Social Progress 471
Subject Index 479

K
The United States Constitution as Seen in the GDR

The following is an English translation of a chapter from the textbook *Constitutional Law of Bourgeois States,* which is devoted to the Constitution of the United States (see Appendix J for complete table of contents). Efforts have been made here to provide a literal translation from the German. This tends to result in verbose and awkward English. Moreover, words such as *Parliament* and *Ministry* that are used in the German text—and retained here—are not terms used in American law and government.

Chapter 13—Fundamentals of the Constitution of the USA

13.1 Introduction

13.2 The Constitution

The Constitution of the USA is the oldest still valid bourgeois constitution. It was adopted by the Constitutional Convention in Philadelphia on September 17, 1787. Its predecessor was the Articles of Confederation. They were adopted in 1777, became effective on March 1, 1781, and can be called the first constitution of the USA. The USA went down in political history as the first confederation. Not until 1787 did the Constitution embody the federal-state structure.

The Constitution was a work of the representatives of the monied aristocracy and the slave owners who were ruling the southern states. In its political and legal design it mirrors the compromise between bourgeois trade and industry and the plantation owners. It sanctioned the fundamental results of the War of Independence (1775-1783). Among them were the national independence from British colonial power and the constitutionalizing of the bourgeois national state in the form of the republic. Yet the Constitution failed to prohibit slavery; in this way it reflects legally the failure of the revolution, which was not able to resolve the problem of slavery in the interest of the slaves.

Like the Revolutionary War of Independence and the Declaration of Independence on July 4, 1776, the Constitution of the USA of 1787 has to be included in the historical events which have been of paramount significance for the progress of mankind. This evaluation has to reflect the understanding that the Constitution of the USA and its inherent principles present the generally characteristic mark of bourgeois constitutions and constitutional principles. They are political-legal instruments for the realization of bourgeois governmental authority, they mask the bourgeois class dictatorship, and in the fundamental questions of the political organization of society they pass off from the start appearance as reality.

The principle of people's sovereignty (Preamble and 10th Amendment), which was the first in history to be incorporated in a constitution, remained an interpretation from the outset. Its proclamation happened, thanks to the strict rejection of the monarchist principle. With regard to its realization, the creators of the Constitution had no illusions. As representatives of the aristocratic upper class they expressed themselves not only explicitly, but also quite disparagingly, against a people's government.

Likewise, the principle of majority rule and the related principle of the selection of political offices by election remained as nothing more than an interpretation from the outset. Even though virtually only 2 percent of the population was allowed to vote during colonial times, the Constitution did not expand suffrage. Under the actual economic and political power relationships, the subsequent introduction of general suffrage (initially reserved predominantly for white males and limited by numerous restrictions which have been partially maintained until recent times) never even comes close to providing validity to the principle of majority rule.

In the face of the undivided rule of the bourgeoisie the principle of separation of powers had, from the start, interpretational value. The purpose was to divert the center of attention away from the actual property and power relationships and toward the illusion of a democratic distribution of authority among the various central representatives of the uniform bourgeois power structure (legislative, executive, and judicial). This distribution of authority assumed a specific arrangement. According to this the organs of the fundamental state activities were, on the one hand, bound to cooperate on certain questions (e.g., legislation and the signing of treaties). On the other hand, however, a system of checks and balances was created to exclude an imbalance by one institution or the other.

During the course of capitalist development the distribution of authority changed fundamentally. Clear examples are the adoption by the Supreme Court of rights not sanctioned in content or wording in the Constitution, entry of parties into the political system, and the process of concentration of state authority with the president, which mainly occurred during the imperialistic phase of American capitalism.

Thus the difference between the states (including slavery in the southern states) and the internal autonomy of individual states (already organized under a constitution) had to be recognized to facilitate the fight against British colonial power and to strengthen the rule of the bourgeoisie. Capitalist development in the form of monopolies led to a steady strengthening of central authority. This coincided with the development of gigantic economic regions, which transcended the borders of individual states, and the need of the big monopolies, which subjugated the states' economies without respect to borders and authorities. It also coincided with a necessary requirement for uniform and concentrated execution of power in all social areas which emerged with the continual interlacing of monopolistic rule and imperialistic state power. Thus the principle of federalism originally proclaimed in the Constitution was being constantly undermined. Externally this process appeared to be the adaptation of the principle of federalism—constitutionally based on legal decisions of the Supreme Court—to altered social conditions.

The Constitution of the USA is fundamentally different from other bourgeois constitutions, whether they be old or new. Excluding the Preamble, it originally consisted of 7 Articles. The Articles are divided into sections, the sections into clauses. An important part of the Constitution is the Amendments. As of 1977, a total of 26 Amendments had been passed. These have successive numbers and partially replace the original constitutional text. The first ten Amendments can be attributed to the original constitutional text. Passed in 1791, they contain the

Bill of Rights. Some individual states made this a condition for the ratification of the federal Constitution. Of significant importance is the 13th Amendment which prohibits slavery and which took effect in 1865.

With regard to the special features of the USA's Constitution, they above all strongly emphasize regular procedures. They sketch only a general scheme of the governmental power mechanism and—next to their regulations and amendments—they recognize developmental processes (which initially took place outside the constitutional regulations) as belonging to the constitutional law of the USA. This touches the pivotal question of American constitutional law, which is that fundamental mechanisms and institutions of the political system have developed outside the constitutional texts and are continuously being updated. This procedure is termed as constitutionally effective (compare Chapter 3) or, using the terminology of the bourgeois constitutional doctrine, as the "living constitution." This constitutional effectiveness has always changed according to the needs of the ruling class.[5] For this purpose, the ruling circles avail themselves especially of the most important governmental institutions controlled by them: the Congress, the President, and the Supreme Court. In doing this these institutions far transcend the limits set by the text of the constitutional documents and cause changes that go beyond this text and partially even eliminate it.

Examples:
By virtue of its legislative authority (and with the full support of the Supreme Court) Congress took over jurisdiction to enact the entire legislation on the economy as it deemed necessary in the interest of state-monopolistic regulations. The constitutional legitimacy was produced by an extensive interpretation of Article 1, Section 8, Clause 3 of the Constitution (the so-called Interstate Commerce Clause). According to it, the Congress has the right to "regulate commerce among the several states."

During the economic processes in the imperialistic phase of capitalism the president continually appropriated new authority through actions and acts, and this effected the adequate concentration and centralization of governmental powers at the top of the executive branch.

The constitutional argument to justify many of these actions is the theory of the inherent powers of the presidency. These are

[5]A. A. Mischin, *Gosudarstwennoe Prawo SSA,* Moskau 1976, n. 30.

> authorities which, no doubt, are not granted to the president by the Constitution but which grow out of the requirements of his office and are necessary for his administration. One such authority is his privilege to "protect American life and property" in foreign countries, which is not covered by his competence as supreme commander of the armed forces (the war powers). As history shows, this right was the pretext for numerous military interventions by USA imperialism.
>
> By its own decisions, and by disregarding the Constitution, the Supreme Court in 1803 claimed judicial review. Thus it controls the constitutionality of the laws of the federation and the several states. Thereby, and by deciding other constitutional questions, it so substantially influences legislation that it is often considered to basically play the role of a third chamber of the legislature and even that of a permanent constitutional convention. Its influence is so strong that one of its judges said, "The Constitution is what the judges say it is."

Inherent parts of the Constitution are policies in the form of customs. They include, for example, the obligation of the members of Congress to reside in their respective voting districts and also the affiliation of the Speaker of the House of Representatives with the majority party. Finally, it must not be overlooked that constitutional practice is deeply influenced by the party system. Neither the original constitutional text nor the Amendments mention the parties with even one word. The party conventions, in which the presidential candidates are nominated, are part of the customs, while many other elements of the party system have developed out of practice and habit.

13.3 The Position of Parties, Employers' Associations, and Unions

The imperialistic power system, and thus the constitutional practice of the USA, are important parts in the shaping of the two-party system consisting of the two big parties of the monopolistic capital. According to the 1971 program of the Communist party of the USA, this system is one

> of the most ingenious constructions of the monpolistic capital for the pursuit of political business and to camouflage its stranglehold. . . . Each one of the two big parties appears as a mixture of controversial group and economic interests, cemented by the interest of expediency in regard to the struggle for the presidency during elections. But precisely this mixture, which is passed off as proof

> for its alleged democratic character, is the instrument for the political domination by the centralized economic power of the giant monopolies. . . . The present two-party system is the vise that aids the monopolistic power to forcibly control class conflicts and social movements, thus securing its own rule.[6]

The two big monopolistic parties are the Republican party and the Democratic party. The Republican party was established in 1854 by opponents of slavery. During the Civil War it was known as the Union party, striving for the restoration of the Union. In the imperialistic phase of capitalism it became the party of monopolistic capital. It represents the interests of the big industrial concerns and high finance. For about two decades rival wings have been fighting for the leadership. The designation "liberal" for one of the wings is purely manipulative to mislead the voters.

The Democratic party, founded in 1800, was previously called the Republican party. It received its present name under Andrew Jackson in 1828 and, until 1940, shaped itself as the representative of the interests of plantation and slave owners as well as with parts of the bourgeoisie in the North. In imperialism it also became a party of the monopolistic capital. It mainly represents those circles of the monopolistic bourgeoisie that can be found in commerce, light industry, and in the southern states. Groupings in it are the so-called Dixiecrats, that is, monopolistic-bourgeois circles and other racist powers of the southern states, and circles of the monopolistic bourgeoisie of the East Coast and Midwest, which give the impression of "liberal" positions. The Democratic party represents itself in its internal political image as being open to innovations and reforms and receives many votes from the working population as well as the Afro-American population.

Even though the deep crises in which the political system of the dictatorship of the USA monopolistic capital finds itself also affects the two-party system, and it is primarily mirrored in the immense dwindling of the citizen's trust in the two monopolistic parties, there is no acute threat to their existence. There are no signs that a third party could succeed in breaking the predominance of the twin parties of the monopolistic capital in the near future. There are many reasons for this, the crucial

[6]*The New Program of the USA Communist Party,* Berlin 1971, pp. 97 ff.

one being the lack of a workers' party with mass character. The historical reasons cannot be pursued here in detail. Therefore it will only be pointed out that capital has succeeded in the past century in gaining "the organized support of bourgeois political parties by the working classes."[7] This bond of the majority of workers and the unions with the bourgeois two-party system did in no way relax under state monopolistic conditions. The fundamental factors were the unions, most of which committed themselves (with the help of a corrupt union bureaucracy) on a course of class cooperation and anticommunism. Another factor was that the development of the awareness of the working class could be slowed down with the help of limited social concessions. Especially since the social legislation by Franklin D. Roosevelt in the framework of the "New Deal" they succeeded to camouflage until the present the Democratic party as the party of the working people—as the party of the little man without reducing in any way this party's close cooperation with the monopolies.

Another fundamental reason for the superiority of the two big monopolistic parties is the relative majority election system which hopelessly discriminates against candidates who are not nominated by one of those two parties.

The Communist party belongs to the small parties which present their own candidates at the presidential elections. It is the only party in the country to represent an antimonopolistic alternative.

The Communist party was founded in 1919 (in 1921 it united with the Communist Labor party of the USA) and gained maturity and strength during a decade-long battle against the omnipotence of capital, while being exposed to a tide of reprisals and persecutions.

During the years of the Cold War, several laws put the Communist party and its members under legal exceptions. Some of those are the McCarran Act of 1950, the McCarran-Walter Act of 1952, and the Brownell-Butler Act of 1954. The Subversive Activities Control (McCarran) Act (law to control subversive activities), also known as the Internal Security Act (law for internal safety), required the registration of "communist leaders and organizations" because of "subversive activities." The

[7]W. Z. Foster, *History of the USA Communist Party,* Berlin 1956, p. 15.

Immigration and Nationality (McCarran-Walter) Act made possible the deportation of, and the ban on immigration of, communists. Finally, the Communist Control (Brownell-Butler) Act extended the obligation for registration to all members of the Communist Party and divested the party of all political rights in the nation and in the several states.

These actions were similar to an actual party ban. In 1949 and 1951 eleven and thirteen members, respectively, of the Communist party's committee were sentenced to long terms of imprisonment. Such trials took place until the beginning of the sixties. Organized by committees of the Congress, anticommunist inquisition procedures (McCarthyism, named after Senator McCarthy, the chairman of such a committee) resulted in a system of intimidation, mass insinuation, and the expulsion of progressive citizens from their jobs.

Even though by the middle of the sixties, and partly even until the beginning of the seventies, the antidemocratic provisions against the legality of the Communist party were declared unconstitutional at the federal level, the party is still exposed to constant defamations. In a number of states it is still prohibited at the present time.

The Communist party sees itself as a part and as a result of the strengthening democratic movement in the USA. It makes it its business to create a broad antimonopolistic coalition and to expand during this process its influence, especially on the federal level, thus developing step by step into a party of the masses.

As in all capitalist states, the bourgeois parties are important stepping stones to governmental power for policy and legislation. Leading positions in the two monopolistic parties merge with important leading functions on the various levels of the government, particularly in the executive and legislative branches. In the USA, of course, there are special features in the relationship between parties and government and between parties and monopolies. They are supported by the federal organization of the government, in the structure of the parties, and in the paramount political position which is occupied by the presidents or the presidential candidates within the parties.

The following facts about the status of the parties (in particular the two big monopolies) will contribute to the understanding of this situation.

First. As a rule, the legal provisions of the party system, as well as suffrage and election procedures are the responsibility of the several states. Only sections of the party system are controlled by the federal government. Thus the principle of federalism is very effective in the party system.

Second. These legal provisions are very complicated and are organized in very different ways. They mainly affect the nomination of candidates for electoral offices, the financing of parties (particularly in election campaigns), and they establish the fundamentals of the internal party activity as well as exceptional rules which were aimed solely against the Communist party.

Third. The two big monopolistic parties do not have registered members who are committed to a party organization. They have adherents who acknowledge one of them, mostly because of traditional and local factors. Every citizen of voting age who registers either as Democrat or Republican in the governmental registration office of the respective voting district is ordinarily considered a "member."

Fourth. The core of adherents of the two big monopolistic parties is composed of party staff, professional politicians, and persons who, with the help of the party, were able to take over a governmental elective office.

Fifth. Both parties have developed identical structures of organization in the precinct or in the rural community. The second highest organizations are those on the city and county level and, finally, those on the state and national level. One typical organization is the committee. An internal party hierarchy which corresponds to this organizational structure does not exist; no organization is subject to directions.

Sixth. This proves that both parties are being held together by the endeavor of those groups of people who built its core to gain governmental elective offices. In the years of a presidential election only a united performance promises the victory of the respective presidential candidate. For this reason the existence of numerous "liberal," "conservative," and other groups in both parties does not jeopardize the party as such.

These factors, which were outlined rather incompletely, determine two fundamental characteristics of the relationships between state and parties. First, the two big monopolistic parties are a major market for the staffing of the numerous elective functions in legislative organs, for the offices in the executive apparatus, and in the administration of justice. Second, the party leaders do not play a role in the drafting of governmental policy—in that respect they differ from the leadership of bourgeois parties in Western Europe. Such political practice means that the president, who is also the leader of the victorious party in the presidential election, is not bound to any decisions of the party leadership on the national level (the National Committee). Thus he cannot be held liable to realize the platform announced during the election campaign. (Party programs like West European models of bourgeois parties are not common.)

In the relationships between monopolies, parties, and government the loose party structure does not impair the realization of monopoly interests in any way. These interests are put forward by those institutions which are actually exercising the political decisional authority. In the USA these are not the party leaders, but the president and his staff (who are tightly linked to big business), the chairmen of the congressional committees (rarely the parliamentary leaders), and lastly, the senators and the members of the House of Representatives. Their political stance and social position ensure that the interests of the monopolistic capital are being considered and represented. The most crucial means to make the wishes of the monopolies clear to the parties, their candidates, and the holders of public offices who intend to run for re-election, and the carriers of parliamentary mandates, are the donations of huge sums of money that are necessary for every election campaign. Return services are expected and demanded, and in the interest of monopoly profits they are furnished in many ways—extending from tax legislation to actions in foreign policy. Thus the loose structure of the two big monopolistic parties and the relative independence of their politicians from the party apparatus are not synonymous with a lack of internal stability. The amalgamation of politics and business, the interlacing of both parties with capital, and the crucial institutions of the government decisively explain the firm positions of those parties in the political power mechanism of the USA.

Countless organizations and unions and their associations try to influence government decisions in the USA. Bourgeois politicians deal with an unmanageable wealth of publications coming from what they call "the pressure groups." They deny almost without exception under their "theory of union" (which they developed) the basic difference in the class character and in the actual influential possibilities that exist between the various organizations. It is precisely the pro-imperialistic course of the leading umbrella union of the American unions, its close connection with the Democratic party, and the undeniable existence of its own lobby which aided the bourgeois politicians not to differentiate between the organizations and associations and to ascribe the same characteristic for all of them. In the USA the individual business monopolies and the employers' groups have a stronger and more direct influence on the key institutions of the government power mechanism than in other countries of state monopolistic capitalism, without resorting in every case to the employers' associations. Notwithstanding, such associations gain more and more importance. On the basis of the economic power that is concentrated in them, they have significant influence on politics. They are—just like territorial and functional groupings of capital—part of the existing political system.

The largest association—with regard to the number of its members—is the Chamber of Commerce. Four thousand local Chambers of Commerce and a further 25,000 firms are affiliated with it. Some American sources list a total of about 3 million firms and individual members. Like the Chamber of Commerce, the National Association of Manufacturers, which counts 20,000 firms, represents the employer's interests and a position that is hostile toward unions. Not to be underestimated is the Committee for Economic Development, through which the leading big combines are represented by 200 representatives.

Associations, groups, foundations, institutes and other organizations of the monopolistic capital of the USA have influence on the executive, legislative, and judicial branches and prepare important governmental decisions. Among themselves they fight bitter battles over the most varied areas of influence and their strongest positions.

A crucial institutional instrument of influence is so-called lobbying. As a "progressive" form of influence there is in the USA the "cooperative" lobbying to speed up or block legislation in certain areas. The often open or concealed criminal practices of the lobbyists have not been stopped with the federal Regulation of Lobbying Act of 1946. Data from the Department of Justice prove the ineffectiveness of the law. In a period of twenty-two years there have been five cases that went before courts and only one conviction.

Trade unionism in the USA is, in its mass, under the influence of a union leadership which is, unlike in any other imperialistic country, linked to the state monopolistic power system. According to the USA Communist party, "It is not a matter of the usual class collaboration, but an absolute opposition to the interests of the workers' class collaboration with the most reactionary, ultra-right, racist, antidemocratic, and defense-oriented circles of the monopolistic capital."[8]

This leadership conducts the largest federation of trade unions in the USA, the American Federation of Labor/Congress of Industrial Organizations (AFL/CIO) which has a membership of about 130 associations (about 150 million members). The tendency of increasing strike actions, and also of a growing opposition of the union rank and file, with actions partly directed against the line of the leadership, and with the objective to pursue a more class-conscious union policy, has indeed intensified in view of the aggravated manifestations of crisis. Nevertheless, the AFL/CIO even today is to be valued as a power system in the political mechanism of the USA. Regardless, the unionist rights are very limited. Important instruments here are the Taft-Hartley Law (Labor Management Relations Act) of 1947 and the Landrum-Griffin Law (Labor Reform Act) of 1959. One of the most adverse regulations for workers, the Taft-Hartley Law authorizes the President of the USA to compel in the district courts the suspension of a strike for a maximum of 80 days, when he considers the "national safety and welfare" endangered.

13.4 Election System and Suffrage

In the USA 530,000 offices are staffed through elections—about 100,000 yearly. The nomination of candidates by the parties plays an important role. For form's sake eligible citizens take part in the nomination of many candidates. This procedure creates many illusions about the democracy that apparently exist in the USA. Together with the periodic activating of the citizens by the Democratic or Republican party for the elections, it also promotes an attitude which causes a high percentage of USA citizens to perceive themselves as, and pose even today,

[8]"For Peace, Freedom, and Socialism!" Political Main Resolution of the XXI Party Conference of the USA Communist Party, in *Party Conference of the USA Communist Party*, Berlin, 1977, p. 147.

as "Democrats" or "Republicans" and to vote accordingly, thus contributing to the strengthening of the two-party system. At the same time, so-called absenteeism is increasing, meaning that the number of eligible citizens who are actually going to the polls is becoming less and less. In the November elections of 1978 only 78 percent of those eligible voted. The growing apathy of the population toward the elections expresses the far-reaching crisis of faith in the two monopolistic parties and the legislative representatives, who up to now have not known how to use the popular masses in their favor.

Elections are largely conducted by the system of the relative majority vote. Conduct and implications of the relative majority vote have been explained in chapter 5.

In the USA there exists, with certain reservations, general suffrage which had to be achieved with great struggle. During the middle of the last century most of the states abolished the property qualifications for male white citizens; the women's right to vote was enforced after World War I (19th Amendment, 1920); the tax qualification was abolished on the federal level in 1964 (24th Amendment, 1964); the voting age was decreased to eighteen years (26th Amendment, 1971); and finally, the civil rights movement of the sixties (which also put into effect the Voting Rights Act, enacted in 1965 and amended in 1970) led to a significant reduction of discrimination against Afro-American citizens at elections.

The prerequisites for holding office are regulated differently. A presidential candidate must be at least thirty-five years old, be an American citizen by birth, and have resided in the USA for at least fourteen years. For the office of senator only those candidates are eligible who are 30 years old, have been American citizens for at least nine years, and at the time of the elections have their residence in the respective state which they are "representing."

One of the fundamental, and at the same time politically most significant, characteristics of the USA elections is the procedure for nominating candidates which can be presented here only in rough outlines. First of all, it is emphasized again that the election legislation lies in the jurisdiction of the several states and, therefore, varies considerably. Presently two procedures are of interest, according to which the candidates of the two parties are nominated at different levels in the states:

the party convention procedure and the primary procedure. Both are procedures by which candidates of one party are nominated.

Every citizen who publicly confirms his party membership can participate in nominating candidates. Since in the USA "membership" in one of the monopolistic parties does not require an organizational commitment, participation in nominating candidates is not subjected to strict standards. In some states the citizen declares his membership in a party with registration in the election office, in others by showing up for, and participating in, the nomination procedures, and in still others by declaring to have supported the nominated candidate in the last election and/or having the intention to do so in the upcoming election.

The nomination through the convention procedure is basically a form of an indirect nomination by assemblies of delegates. At the lowest level (urban district or rural community) all "members" of a party participate in preliminary elections. Out of this emerge delegates who elect delegates in conventions on the respectively higher levels until, for example, in elections for the nomination of presidential candidates, the delegates of the individual states directly participate in the nomination in the national party convention. This procedure, which is often used in the selection of party candidates for less important functions in the states, districts, cities, etc., is more and more losing significance.

Instead, the primary procedure is increasingly successful, not only for nominating the presidential candidates but also for nominating senators, members of the House of Representatives, members of state legislatures, governors, mayors, etc. The primary election—this being said expressly in order to prevent any misunderstandings—is also the election, by the voters of a party, of candidates for an office or of delegates who nominate the candidate. There are different forms of preliminary elections, one being the closed primary in which only party adherents participate. In some states the open primary is used. This enables every eligible citizen to participate in the primary election without being forced to publicly acknowledge adherence to a particular party. This form also includes the modifications whereby the voter is handed the primary ballots of all parties and then only fills out the ballot of his preferred party.

Finally, in some states there is the form of a combination of convention and primary procedure. This means that party conventions or party committees suggest a candidate for each office respectively, who then jointly, with other competing candidates, face the voters.

Those candidates who emerge victorious from the primaries (which, by the way, are supported and supervised by the government) face each other later in the state elections as the candidates nominated by the parties.

The question as to how the presidential primaries and the nomination conventions of the two big monopolistic parties are integrated into this already confusing complex is answered in rough outlines as follows: the presidential primaries are keyed to appoint delegates for the National Convention of the respective party. In states which are not conducting presidential primaries the convention procedure is applied as a principle. However, after presidential primaries it is always announced that, for example, of all the Democratic party's candidates, candidate *A* won over candidate *B*. Such an announcement is based on a so-called presidential preference primary which also encompasses the delegate primary. Through those the voters announce which candidates they prefer. This is the party adherent's demonstration of opinion to make the candidate who was victorious in the preference primary the presidential candidate of the party. Yet the final nomination of the presidential candidate is carried out by the delegates at the National Convention.

The voting on the presidential candidate about to be nominated is the actual closing ceremony of the national convention (at the conventions of the big monopolistic parties). This takes place by the informal votes of the delegations of the several states and by the respective chairman of the delegation who announces the results to the conventions. Often it requires several votings for a candidate to receive the necessary simple majority. This procedure, as well as other activities which in the party conventions play a role in closely related political events and oversized shows, must not be overvalued. The actual decisions are made behind closed curtains. There the representatives of big business, together with the party managers, do everything possible in tactics, maneuvering, and corruption in order to place the "desired" candidate onto the party's escutcheon.

The party conventions are followed by the actual presidential election. This is preceded by an election campaign in which the candidates of the two monopolistic parties are so exclusively pushed into the foreground that alternatives for them are practically manipulated away. The election of the president does not occur directly, but through electors in the several states. This means that (in no way intended by the Constitution) the candidate who receives the majority in the respective individual state gets all electoral votes of this state. This explains the often fundamental differences between the proportional shares of votes of presidential candidates and their shares in the totality of the electoral votes.

Presidential Elections 1960 to 1976

1960	Kennedy
1964	Johnson
1968	Nixon
1974	Ford
1976	Carter

This sketchy representation of the nominating procedure and also the procedure for the public election of the president shows that a "democratic shaping of the will" is out of the question.

13.5 The Central Governmental Organs

In the governmental mechanism of the USA the president embodies the highest power. He and his staff form the center of the governmental monopolistic execution of power. The process of power concentration has been favored by a series of constitutional and political factors. According to the Constitution (Article 2, Section 1, Clause 1) the executive power lies with the president. The function as head of state is united with the function of a minister-president, the latter of which exists in the bourgeois nonpresidential governmental system. The president is independent from, and not accountable to, parliament. He cannot be forced to resign, for example, through a vote of no confidence. The only possibility to remove him from office is impeachment.

An impeachment occurs only if in the impeachment procedure the proof of the elements of an offense of high treason, bribery, or such grave abuse of power has been made that it goes beyond political misjudgments. The impeachment procedure is a kind of judicial procedure carried out by Congress. It has been carried out against a president only once (Andrew Johnson, 1868) and without success. Richard M. Nixon could only avoid its initiation by resigning from presidential office (1974).

Only the president appoints the ministers (the heads of the departments). They are bound to his instructions and can be dismissed by him at any time. Consequently there is no joint passing of a resolution or a majority decision of the cabinet which is directed at the view of the president. The president is also not subject to control by the leading groups of the party which nominated him and whose leader he is. His executive power is unlimited.

The presidential power, which is largely independent from parliament and vested with numerous rights, turned out to be an appropriate institution during the transition to governmental monopolistic capitalism, in order to widen enormously the executive rule against the people and against traditional parliamentary institutions. The first big attempt in widening the executive's power proceeded hand-in-hand with the politics of the "New Deal." G. Hall describes this process as follows:

> President Roosevelt was a war President. At the same time, when he saw himself forced into projects of social welfare programs he, indeed, initiated many of these authoritative governmental concepts, especially in his second term in office. President Truman added the "state of national emergency" as a shield behind which the executive appropriated to itself additional authorities; and every president has contributed considerably to this police-state structure. Every president has since added bricks to the building of a state in a state.[9]

The expansion of the presidential power developed largely at the expense of the competence of Congress, to which, according to the law, is assigned the legislative power. Yet it is estimated unanimously that 80 percent of the most important laws that pass initially come from the White House. To carry through their processing the president uses the most diversified methods. They extend from the activities of contacts in the individual ministries to influential representatives ("the executive as the most significant lobby in Washington") and regular meetings

[9] G. Hall, "Watergate and the Fascist Danger," *Political Affairs*, August 1973, p. 10.

of the president with the leading powers in Congress, as well as utilization of his patronage opportunities (opportunities to distribute positions and to grant privileges).

The recognition of the president's role in the legislative initiative began with the Budget and Accounting Act of 1921. It provided for financial programs to have their starting point with the president. At the same time this law also became the base from which an extensive influence of the president on the budget law developed. Based on the constitutional regulation, according to which the president ensures "that the law be faithfully executed" (Art. 2, Sec. 3), he can issue executive orders. In practice he often outmaneuvers and amends the legislation of Congress. Since Franklin D. Roosevelt's term of office the president and his successors make more and more extensive use of this right. This is testified to by the fact that on 15 August, 1971 Executive Order No. 11615 was issued.

One privilege granted by the Constitution in order to influence legislation is the president's right to veto, which has its roots in the principle of "checks and balances" (Art. 1, Sec. 7, Cl. 2). This allows him to block the enactment of a law. Only a two-thirds majority in both Houses of Congress (which have to consult again after the veto) can eliminate the veto. In this way the presidents of the USA have been able to defeat many laws.

How often the right to veto is practiced depends on many political factors. Franklin D. Roosevelt made the most use of this right (631 times). The reasons were not so much the length of his office term but the lack of ability of the congressional majority to understand the measures that were initiated in the course of the "New Deal," under the conditions of that period, as an action program aimed at saving the capitalist system.

The president, however, does not only act as chief executive and as "supreme legislator" but also has concentrated in his hands the entire foreign policy. In this area he also largely eliminates parliament and avoids the constitutional regulation according to which the Senate has to ratify treaties. Most international agreements are mainly closed by only the president in the form of an executive agreement. An idea of the extent of the shifting of this privilege is seen in the fact that the ratio of 60 treaties versus 27 executive agreements (1789 to 1839) has reversed itself into a ratio of 5,653 executive agreements versus 310 treaties (1940 to 1970).

Finally, the president holds the supreme command over the armed forces. Under war powers only the personal taking-over of the command authority was constitutionally contemplated. In the meantime the authorities of the president were expanded with regard to their contents so that with the transition of capitalism into its imperialistic phase and the therefore growing aggression of the USA he more and more openly claimed the right to trigger armed conflicts without consulting Congress. Only with the defeat of USA imperialism, which appeared in the course of the Indo-China aggression of the USA, Congress tried to limit the war powers (War Powers Act of 1973) and the actual extent of presidential authority. These activities, however, did not cause fundamental changes concerning the president's position.

Finally, this exceptionally extensive predominance of the president, and the growing power of the executive, are made visible by the degree to which the central governmental executive apparatus has been enlarged. Thus, according to calculations in 1975, the president leads an executive apparatus which consists of about 2,000 organizational units of the federal administration—ministries, governmental administrations, authorities, offices, commissions, and others—in which almost 3 million civil employees and over 2 million military employees are active. Consequently the twelve departments existing in 1978 are only part of a much more comprehensive governmental mechanism. A decisive role for the realization of the aggressive and expansionist foreign policy of USA imperialism is played by the Ministry of War (called the Pentagon, after the structure of the building in which it has its seat) and the State Department.

The ministers of the departments carry the title Secretary—with the exception of the minister of justice who has the title of Attorney General.

The central governmental terminal for the executive is the immediate personal staff of the president, which decides on all fundamental questions of internal and foreign policy, legislation, and the budget. The organizational form of this terminal is the Executive Office of the President. A number of councils and offices are combined in it. They have arranged a widespread system of relations, which is effective inside and outside the government mechanism and represents a particularly distinct form of the fusion of the imperialistic government. These organs not only extensively prepare fundamental political decisions in all the important social areas, but in many cases they are practically making decisions.

The criminal conduct of some of the president's advisors, who had decisive functions in some of these organs in connection with the Watergate proceedings and the massive critique on the apparatus of the White House connected with it, motivated Carter to make changes. In spite of dissolving one or the other structural unit in the Executive Office—e.g., the Domestic Council—these changes proved to be a mere exchange of forms and designations. They touch neither the presidential center of power as a whole nor its decisional elements.

Among the key decisional elements are the following:

—The National Security Council is the most important organ of the foreign and military policy of the USA (compare chapter 7), by which the infamous CIA, convicted of numerous criminal actions, was tied even closer.

—The Office of Management and Budget which not only establishes the yearly budget plan but is, concerning the disposal of financial means, superior to all other executive organs.

—The Council on Economic Policy is the core of a group for economic policy, in which all cabinet members and the leaders of the other offices as well as the advisors of the president are included.

One of the most marked changes (1978) in the area of executive agencies which are directly under the president's control—there are about 50—is the organization of the International Communications Agency (ICA). It is not merely a simple replacement for the prevailing propaganda institution, the United States Information Agency (USIA). This is not only outwardly visible by the name of this super-institution, its yearly budget of 413 million dollars, and its 9,000 employees, but also by the fact that the Department of Cultural Affairs in the State Department is under its control. The establishment of this institution gives evidence of the intensified and concentrated efforts of USA imperialism to further extend and strengthen its world-wide subversive ideological activities.

The parliament in the USA is Congress. It consists of two Houses—the House of Representatives and the Senate. The House of Representatives has 435 members who are elected for 2 years; the Senate has 100, two of whom "represent" each state. The length of the senator's mandate is constitutionally limited to 6 years, with the understanding that every other year one-third of all senators will be newly elected.

According to the Constitution, Congress is legislative. Compared to other bourgeois parliaments it is a quite active organ of the state-monopolistic shaping of will (compare chapter 6). Notwithstanding its secondary role compared to the executive and its core (the presidental power), Congress as well has at its disposal important levers to influence the central state apparatus.

In contrast to many other bourgeois parliaments no communist or social-democratic representatives belong to the USA Congress. Thus the legislature is completely ruled by capital. This fact deeply influences content and procedure of legislation and other parliamentary activities. Controversies consequently mirror partially—not fundamentally—different monopolistic interests, influences, and needs of nonmonopolistic bourgeois circles, as well as the class collaboratist attitude of the unions. In this connection it is important how far individual groupings are able to realize certain interests by means of the presidental apparatus or will try to utilize it in case of unsuccessful efforts in Congress. Thus Congress proves to be an institution in which disagreements over divergent positions are settled within the ruling class. The lack of firm party discipline makes it easy to win influential representatives of both parties for the adoption or rejection of bills. It is also beneficial to the president when he, as a member of a party, has to reckon with a congressional majority of the other party. Yet it must be kept in mind that in the USA there are no close ties between the majority party and the administration, typical in a bourgeois parliamentary system.

The relationship between the two Houses of Congress is characterized by both independently carrying on their course of business, proceeding according to their own rules, and conducting independent examinations. The legislative activity, however, is divided between the two chambers. Each chamber has the right of veto against the other concerning the draft of a bill that was approved by it.

The main work is done in the committees of Congress. For this reason they are often referred to as the "small legislatures."

There are different types of committees. One of them is the standing committee. The following are considered the most important: the permanent Rules Committee, the Appropriations Committee, the Committee on Foreign Affairs in the House of Representatives, as well as the Committee on Foreign Affairs, Finance Committee, and the Appropriations Committee in the Senate. With the Congressional Budget Reform Act of 1974 a permanent Budget Committee for both houses was created, among other reasons, to counteract the fullness of power of the Office of Management and Budget. The standing committees, particularly the ones in the House of Representatives, have great influence; they debate all bills, expedite or reject them altogether, slow down their processing (so-called pigeonholing), or change them beyond recognition. Select or special committees are the second type. They are formed to investigate certain problems and are dissolved after the conclusion of their activity. Joint committees are the third type. They consist of the same number of senators and members of the House of Representatives and are formed to treat especially significant questions. They have primarily an advisory character. Finally, there are the conference committees. These consist of members of both chambers and have the function to work on a mutual draft of a bill in the case of differing views. Numerous subcommittees (the House of Representatives has more than 130) must be included in this system.

This system of committees is most tightly connected to an extensive parliamentary service and the institution of lobbyists. In its framework, that special mechanism of the American parliament becomes effective, and with its help government drafts—with the concrete conception of the monopolies and other capitalist power groups, as far as they have not been seized by the government—are voted on and often are modified substantially.

In the system of the central state organs in the US the Supreme Court has a key position. This is not due to the fact that this court is the last instance in a three-level organization of the federal courts (next to which exists a second, self-contained court organization in the individual states with a Supreme Court respectively at the top). The special position of the Supreme Court is moreover attributed to the function of the constitutional jurisdiction (compare chapter 9). Very soon after the enactment of the Constitution the Supreme Court monopolized the right of judicial review. Laws of the individual states, federal laws (examination for their constitutionality—norm control), and other constitutional questions are subjected to it.

The Supreme Court has taken, and takes, corresponding to the respective demands of the bourgeois class dictatorship, substantial influence in the shaping of the governmental power mechanism by interpreting the Constitution or evaluating constitutional rights respectively and establishes latitude of action and authorities of other governmental organs by making use of its constitutional-judicial function. It also proved to be a decisive instrument in strengthening the central power at the states' expense and in safeguarding the interests of capital in questions of bourgeois rights and freedom and, above all, in social legislation. Since procedures and decisions externally appear as court procedures and court decisions, they have the appearance of rule of law, thereby having a considerable illusory effect on the citizens of the USA.

The flexibility of the Supreme Court in conducting its constitutional function demonstrates that by this function it is an immediate instrument of politics. Consequently, in its activity and its decisions the differences between the various groupings of the bourgeoisie (today largely the monopolistic bourgeoisie), are mirrored the differences which are guided at various times under different external and internal conditions for the most effective methods to secure the rule of capital.

13.6 State Organs and Local Organs

The constitutions of the fifty states in their baseline are similar to the federal Constitution. Accordingly, the system of the state organs mirrors the governmental system on the federal level.

The parliaments of the states are designated as legislatures (lawmaking bodies). They consist of two chambers. As on the federal level they are mainly called Senate and House of Representatives. Only in Nebraska does the state legislature consist of one chamber.

The highest representative of each state is the governor. With regard to his executive authorities he is comparable to the President of the USA. Next to him there are other high-ranking officials who preside as heads of administrative departments of the states. Yet the governor, according to the typical state constitutional text relating to his authorities, is "assigned the highest executive power." His duty is conducting the entire administration and he has the command authority over the National Guard; in the filling of offices he has the final word, and, as a rule, he has a veto power over the laws of the respective state. However, the most important instrument of his authority is his privilege, which exists in almost all states, to control the state budget.

The organization of courts is similar to that created for the federal courts. There exists (with many variations) generally a three-level system. Last instance is the Supreme Court. At the state level the right of judicial review is also recognized. Consequently, the state courts are able to reject the application of state laws on the ground that they violate the constitution of the respective state or the federal government. They are also able to declare federal laws unconstitutional. Such judgments, however, are subject to the decision in the last instance of the Supreme Court of the US.

Initially the states had large competences in the federal system. In the course of the process of centralization not much was left. Admittedly the Tenth Amendment of the Constitution still decrees that the states ("or the people") are reserved all jurisdiction which the Constitution does not expressly transfer to the United States or withdraws from the states, meaning all but the competences of the federation listed in Article 1, Section 8 of the Constitution. However, under the pressure of monopolistic development and the growing missions of the imperialistic state, the federation not only appropriated to itself further additional competences, but also furthermore limited the initial competences of the states. The main device for the centralization proved to be the subsidies that the federal government grants the states (grants-in-aid). Conditions are attached to their payments (e.g., the receiving state is bound to the instructions of the federal agency in the respective area of the subsidies), aherence to which the agency of the central authority controls rigidly and is therefore in the position to intensify pressure on the states.

Regardless of the constant strengthening of the central authority at the cost of the states, their development still has great significance for the bourgeoisie. Were it not for the fact that regional monopolies and other groups of capital owners significantly influence state legislation and administration, the ruling circles could not solve the manifold tasks which evolve from the domestic, economic, and social situation of the country; they would also disregard the specifics of living conditions in the states and on the local level.

On the local level there are over 78,000 administrative units in the USA: cities, counties, townships, school districts, water control districts, and others. Their number per state (except Alaska and Hawaii) is somewhere between 6,000 (Illinois) and

100 (Rhode Island). Under constitutional law they have in common their authority derived from that of the respective state in which the state power is concentrated. Local organs fundamentally exist only as authorities of states and exercise only authorities conferred on them by the states. This representation illustrates the limited latitude of the local government. Finally, it can only be stated that the organs with regard to their structure differ extraordinarily in their authorities, their extent, and the relationships between them.

13.7 The Basic Rights

In the stronghold of world imperialism, the incompatibility of democratic rights and freedoms with state monopolistic capitalism makes itself felt as never before. Under the authority of monopolistic capital the USA deviated far from the legally binding statement of the Declaration of Independence according to which freedom and the pursuit of happiness is numbered among the inalienable human rights.

Thus about 26 million US citizens live below the official poverty level (1978). Unemployment is chronic. According to the situation in February 1978, the unemployment rate was 6.2 percent; for adolescents it was 17.3 percent; 10.3 million Americans were at that time unemployed or were working part-time. Industrial accidents and illnesses increased alarmingly. In 1974 the private sector of the economy alone officially registered 5,915,800 cases. In the same year 17.6 million workers were denied unemployment compensation, 19.5 million US citizens did not receive health insurance, and 5.8 million were without Social Security.

An idea of the severity of the problems of town centers and housing is conveyed by the fact that one family out of six lives in dilapidated or overcrowded houses, that 10.5 million citizens have to spend 25 percent of their income for rent (1975), and that there exist extreme differences between the living conditions in the suburbs and the town centers. The population in the town centers is 40 times as high as in the suburbs, but 95 percent of the Afro-American town population lives in the inner cities.

The USA has the highest criminal record in the world. In 1976 the highest murder rate in 200 years was reached. The police registered 11.3 million crimes and 20,510 murder victims.

The earnings of the largest criminal organization in the world, the Mafia, from selling illegal narcotics, their proceeds from gambling casinos, blackmail and other kinds of the so-called Black Business amount annually to more than 9 billion dollars—twice the amount which the government spends on police, justice, and other organs commissioned with the task of law enforcement. There are 20 million marijuana smokers and 4 million drug addicts.

A little less than 1 million US citizens over twenty-five have never attended school. Hundreds of thousands of children between the ages of six and thirteen do not receive schooling. There are 23 million so-called functional illiterates who, if need be, are able to decipher street signs but cannot read any instructions or newspapers.

This still incomplete insight into the social conditions recognizes, if only partially, the actual position of the US citizen in state and society. It also shows that in the USA basic social rights are nonexistent. Such basic rights are proclaimed neither in the Bill of Rights of the USA Constitution nor in the basic rights listed in the constitutions of the several states, issued after the Declaration of Independence. The reason for this is that these documents were created in the preindustrial phase of USA imperialism. Since the later unsuccessful effort to adopt the basic social rights in the Constitution of the USA, the status of this question remains unchanged: the Supreme Court in connection with the decision *San Antonio School District* v. *Rodriguez* (1979) gave to understand that neither social importance nor the judge's opinion about the significance of a law would be a standard for it to be recognized as "fundamental" and therefore as a basic right. Whether it be guaranteed explicitly or implicitly by the Constitution would be conclusive. The Constitution, however, would guarantee no one a right to education, housing, or social welfare.

The practical handling of those rights and freedoms which were enacted in 1791 as the Bill of Rights, also does not convey a different impression of decline and deformation of society.

For example, now as before, the race problem has not been solved. Racism exists in all areas of social life, not only as ideology but also, above all, as concrete discrimination against Afro-Americans and other portions of the population considered "nonwhite." Progress has been made in a long and bitter battle against race discrimination. For example, several legal acts could be enforced, especially regarding the rights of Afro-Americans, to actively participate in elections. On the other hand, however, appearances of racism in the educational system demonstrate, for example, how far social reality deviates even today from the prohibitions and rules pronounced in laws of judicial decisions. Twenty years after the fundamental decision of the US Supreme Court about the unconstitutional segregation of races in public schools (1954), 40 percent of all Afro-American students were taught in classes in which they were almost completely separated from "white" students. In addition, the US Supreme Court, with the decision *Bakke* v. *The University of California* (1978), in which it attacks the admissions quota for the enrollment of Afro-Americans in universities, paved the way for new discrimination and the withdrawal from obligations, which were hard fought for during the sixties in the area of civil rights.

The course of monopolistic capital into development as a police state in which the guaranteed rights of freedom are more or less suspended is manifested more clearly in the overpowering surveillance and spy system, which consists of more than a dozen of the most varied services and organizations. The infamous Secret Service, CIA, and the Federal Bureau of Investigation (FBI) are among them. Their information affects 200 million persons, whose fingerprints they have stored; and with their comprehensive, detailed knowledge of all citizens in decision-making functions—members of Congress included—they are able to exercise continuous control. The expression that the USA is a "Dossier Society," invented by a US Senator, is not at all exaggerated; nor is the realization that US citizens live in fear of "Big Brother"—the customary term there for the investigation system.

Thus today in the USA, the crisis of basic rights is in no way overcome—a crisis which, after the McCarthy era, even representatives of bourgeois constitutional law were themselves forced to concede.

[At this point the text of the U.S. Constitution is set out in German.]

L
Case Exercises

The following are English translations of case exercises used in the Humboldt University Law Section in the fall of 1983 in the course entitled "System for the Administration of Justice." These exercises were distributed to students and were the basis for discussion in seminars.

Case I
Citizen *A* owns a piece of land along the edge of a lake which he uses for recreational purposes. All the land around the lake has been decreed a regional recreation area by the appropriate district council. The property belonging to *A* is being included in the landscaping for the public recreation area. The efforts of the district council to come to a legal civil agreement with *A* (exchange, shared use, purchase) remain unsuccessful. Consequently, the district council revokes *A*'s property rights but allows compensation. With reference to Article 11 of the Constitution and sec. 22 Civil Code (guarantee and protection of personal property), and also sec. 33 II Civil Code (ceding of personal property), *A* sues the district council in the district court.

—How should the district court decide?
—Is the action of the district council legal?

Case II
A and *B* decided to exchange apartments. They had completed and signed the necessary forms for apartment dwellers and had also collected the necessary signatures from the rental agency. The consent of the agency for apartment control had been legally requested.

In the meantime *B* explained to *A* that for personal reasons he was no longer interested in the apartment exchange and that he had already notified the agency for apartment control and explained his reasons. *A* is unwilling to go along with this change of affairs and sues *B* in the district court. He asks that *B* be required to go along with the initial agreement.

—Is the district court in a position to negotiate and decide this conflict?

Case III

During his employment as tax preparer the accused had for several years falsified tax assessments for his private business and for a number of his clients. He did this by entering only partial income or none at all into the books and by exaggerating business expenses as well as falsifying the totals of the accounts. Thus, he avoided payment of adequate taxes for himself and for some of his clients.

During the main trial it became difficult to ascertain the actual amount of money owed in this case of tax evasion. The indictment states the sum of 199,614 marks, which was arrived at through the addition of the money requested by the tax authorities. This request was made, after the discovery of the crime, by the finance section at the city administrative office—that is, from its tax department. The decrees from the tax authorities had been legalized. A tax expert, whom the court asked to testify, arrived at a much higher sum. To prove his contention he produced tax documents and copies of legal tax decrees and also those tax forms that had been falsified by the accused.

—Is the court bound by the findings of the tax authorities, or can it order the accused to pay the higher sum recommended by the tax expert?

—What would the legal situation be if the estimate of the tax expert, supported by this documentation, had been lower than that of the tax department?

—What preventive measures can the court take when it finds that there are shortcomings within the tax system, in the control over accurate tax declarations, in the clarity of tax adjustment requests, and in the thoroughness of tax investigations?

Case IV

C, a musician, signed a contract with the state symphony orchestra, *S*—represented by the appropriate local authority—concerning his employment as a cello soloist. The orchestra's work regulations, which are binding for all of its musicians, require them to own two special suits which they are to purchase themselves and which are to be kept in good condition. For the expenses arising out of this regulation, the work contract stipulates a sum of 20 marks per month as a flat rate to be paid to each musician for clothing.

The legal regulations in the GDR dealing with income and wages for the members of theater and cultural orchestras specify that a compensation of 10 marks be paid monthly for the purchase and use of special clothing (formal wear, dinner jacket, or some kind of uniform).

After consultation with the finance revision board, the orchestral administration paid *C* only 10 marks as of August 1, because it assumed that the finance organ had stipulated 10 marks as the highest sum to be paid for special clothing. *C*, on the other hand, maintains that the regulation allows for 10 marks for each of the two suits and that he therefore should be paid 20 marks, as agreed to in his work contract.

C turns to the appropriate conflict commission. The chairman would like to know whether this commission is authorized to schedule a hearing for *C*, in spite of the ruling of the finance revision board, or if its decision is binding for all involved.

Case V

Citizen *A*, who has been released from prison, appeals to the procurator in a letter in which he explains that he has met with difficulties after being hired by People's Owned Enterprise *V*. The local manager had refused to place him in the position of a machine mechanic even though open slots existed and even though he, *A*, had submitted the papers establishing his technical qualifications in this field. The manager insisted that *A* should be placed in a lower income bracket and work as a shipment clerk until he had proved his worth. The procurator sends *A*'s letter to the director of People's Owned Enterprise *V* and asks him to take care of the complaint in accordance with grievance regulations and with sec. 7, the Law of Reinstatement.

—Did the procurator act correctly?

Case VI

During a conversation at a People's Owned Enterprise, the procurator discovers that the distributor for the trade organizations of industrially manufactured goods has refused to sell replacement parts for defective washing machines, refrigerators, or other appliances. Even though the sales representative had in each case acknowledged the defect, he told the customers that they must turn for help to the factory, that is, to the next higher contract work shop.

—How should the procurator react to this information?

Case VII

At the conclusion of a proceeding, *B*, a businessman from *O*, is fined 100 marks by the city Administration for Trade and Supply. *B* objects, claiming the penalty is too high (violation of standards of secs. 13 and 14, OWG). In spite of this objection, neither the city council nor the mayor takes any action to change the sentence. Consequently, *B* turns for help to the district procurator.

—Is it permissible for B to turn for help to the procurator after exhausting appeals within the local legal system?

—What should the procurator decide to do in this case?

M
GDR Laws in English Translation

The following is a list of GDR codes and other laws pertaining to the courts and other organs in the system for the administration of justice that have been translated into English and printed in *Law and Legislation in the German Democratic Republic.* The citation to this publication appears to the right of the title of each law.

Constitution of the GDR, as amended 1974	2/78, p. 43
Law on the Constitution of the Courts, 1974 [Court Organization Act]	1-2/77, p. 17
Civl Procedure Code, 1975	1-2/77, p. 67
Criminal Procedure Code, as amended 1979	1-2/80, p. 19
Civil Code, 1975	1-2/76, p. 13
Introductory Law to the Civil Code, 1975	1-2/77, p. 57
Family Code, as amended 1975	1-2/82, p. 37
Introductory Law to the Family Code, as amended 1975	1-2/82, p. 76
Labor Code, 1977	1/78, p. 13
Penal Code, as amended 1979	1-2/79, p. 37
Social Courts Act, 1968	1/69, p. 57
Notary Public Act, 1976	1-2/82, p. 87
Law on the Procurator's Office, 1977	1-2/77, p. 43
Law on the Collegia of Advocates, 1980	1-2/81, p. 23
Model Statute on the Collegia of Advocates	1-2/81, p. 29
Regulation on the Tasks and Activities of Non-Associated Advocates, 1980	1-2/81, p. 38

An English translation of the law governing the Arbitrage Commission (described in Chapter 11) is in *Commercial Business and Trade Laws,* Vol. 1, Booklet 11, pg. 99 (Oceana Press, Mineola, N.Y., 1985), under the title of "Rules of the Court of Arbitration attached to the Chamber of Foreign Trade of the GDR of 1 Feb. 1975." An English translation of these rules also appears in *Law and Legislation,* 1-2/84, p. 104.

Glossary

The following is an alphabetical list in English of GDR state organs, courts, other entities, and terms mentioned in this book, followed by the original German. This list is provided because German-English translations vary, and it will be useful for anyone delving further into this subject to know the translations used here. The university law courses are listed separately following the alphabetical list.

Academy for State and Law *Akademie für Staat und Recht*
Academy of Sciences *Akademie der Wissenschaften*
Arbitrage Commission *Schiedsgericht der Kammer für Aussenhandel*
Assistant *Assistent* (Assistants and Higher Assistants are sometimes collectively referred to as *Wissenschaftliche Mitarbeiter*)
Central Committee *Zentral Kommittee*
Certificate of Class Attendance *Testat*
Collegium *Kollegium*
Commentary *Kommentar*
Comprehensive Examination *Haupt Prüfung*
Council for Legal Education in Ministry for Higher Education *Wissenschaftlicher Beirat für Staats und Rechtswissenschaften im Ministerium für Hoch- und Fachschulwesen*
Council of Ministers *Ministerat*
Council of State *Staatsrat*
CountyAssembly *Bezirkstag*
District *Kreis*
District Assembly *Kreistag*
District Court *Kreisgericht*
Docent *Dozent*
Federal Republic of Germany (FRG) *Bundesrepublik Deutschland (BRD)*
Final Examination *Abschluss prüfung*
Free German Youth *Freie Deutsche Jugend (FDJ)*
German Democratic Republic (GDR) *Deutsche Democratische Republik (DDR)*
Higher Assistant *Oberassistent*
Intermediate Examination *Zwischenprüfung*
Judge *Richter*
Jurist *Jurist*
Justice, Administration of *Rechtspflege*
Law enacted by People's Chamber *Gesetz*
Law promulgated by Council of Ministers *Statut*

Law Section *Rechtswissenschaftssektion*
Lawyer, or Advocate *Rechtsanwalt*
Lawyers Association *Die Vereinigung der Juristen*
Lecture *Vorlesung*
Library *Bibliothek*
Ministry for Higher Education *Ministerium für Hochund Fachschulwesen*
Ministry of Justice *Ministerium der Justiz*
Notary *Notar*
Part-time Study *Fernstudium*
People's Chamber *Volkskammer*
Practical Training *Praktikum*
Procurator General *General Staatsanwalt*
Protestant Church *Evangelische Kirche*
Regulation issued by a Ministry *Ordnung*
Research Student *Vorschungsstudent*
Social Court *Gesellschaftliches Gericht*
Socialist Unity Party of Germany *Sozialistische Einheitspartei Deutschlands (SED)*
State Contract Court *Staats Vertragsgericht*
Student Residence Hall *Studentenwohnheim*
Study Plan *Studienplan*
Summary or Outline *Grundriss*
Supreme Court *Oberstes Gericht*
Textbook *Lehrbuch*

University Law Courses

Administrative Law *Verwaltungsrecht*
Agricultural Cooperative Law *Landes Produktion Gemeinschaftsrecht*
Civil Law *Zivil Recht*
Civil Procedure *Zivilprozessrecht*
Constitutional Law of Bourgeois States *Staatsrecht Bürgerlicher Staaten*
Constitutional Law of Developing Countries *Staatsrecht Junger Nationalstaaten*
Constitutional Law of the GDR *Staatsrecht der DDR*
Constitutional Law of the USSR and other Socialist States *Staatsrecht der UdSSR und anderen Sozialistischer Staaten*
Copyright Law *Urheberrecht*
Criminal Law *Strafrecht*
Criminal Procedure *Strafverfahrensrecht*
Criminology *Kriminologie*
Dialectical and Historical Materialism *Dialektischer und Historischer Materialismus*
Economic Law *Wirtschaftsrecht*

Environmental Law *Landeskulturrecht*
Family Law *Familienrecht*
Finance Law *Finanzrecht*
Forensic Science *Kriminalistik*
History of the Perceptions of the Theory of State and Law *Geschichte der Staats- und Rechtstheoretischen Anschauungen*
History of State and Law *Staats- und Rechtsgeschichte*
International Economic Law *Internationales Wirtschaftsrecht*
International Finance and Monetary Law *Internationales Finanz und Wahrungsrecht*
Introduction to Psychology *Einführing in die Psychologie*
Labor Law *Arbeitsrecht*
Land Law *Bodenrecht*
Marxist-Leninist Theory of State and Law *Marxistische-Leninistische Theorie des Staates und des Rechts*
Political Economy of Capitalism and Socialism *Politische Okonomie des Kapitalismus und Sozialismus*
Private International Law *Internationales Privatrecht*
Scientific Communistic/Fundamentals of the History of the Workers' Movement *Wissenschaftliche Kommunistische Grundlehren der Geschichte der Arbeiterbewegung*
Scientific-Technical Protection Law *Wissenschaltlicher-Technischer Rechtsschutz*
Socialist Enterprise Economics *Sozialistische Betriebswirtschaft*
Special Section Time *Zetfonds zur Verfügung der Sektion*
Special Courses on Selected Problems of Marxism-Leninism *Speziale Kurse zu ausgewälten Probleme des Marxismus-Leninismus*
Special Seminar on Classics of Marxism-Leninism *Spezialseminare zu Werken der Klassiker des Marxismus-Leninismus*
System for the Administration of Justice *System der Rechtspflege*

NOTE: The translations used here are those likely to be most meaningful to Americans, taking into account: (1) current German to English translation practice in the GDR, and (2) prevailing practices among Western scholars in translating GDR material into English.

Selected Bibliography

Although English-language material on GDR law is slim, published material in English on the GDR in general has increased over the years as scholarly interest in that country has grown. A good bibliography is *Politics, Economics, and Society in the Two Germanies, 1945-75: A Bibliography of English Language Works*, compiled by Anna J. Merritt and Richard L. Merritt (University of Illinois Press, 1978). For a listing of GDR fiction, see *Literature of the German Democratic Republic in English Translation*, edited by Margy Gerber and Judith Pouget (University Press of America, 1984).

Two relatively recent books provide comprehensive descriptions of the GDR: David Childs, *The GDR: Moscow's German Ally* (George Allen and Unwin, London, 1983) and Eugene K. Keefe, ed., *East Germany: A Country Study* (Area Handbook Series, Government Printing Office, Washington, D.C., 1982). See also Henry Krisch, *The German Democratic Republic: The Search for Identity* (Westview Press, Boulder, 1985).

Law and Legislation in the German Democratic Republic, an English-language publication of the Lawyer's Association in the GDR, includes English translations of GDR laws (See Appendix M) and articles about the legal system written by GDR lawyers.

The *Statistisches Jahrbuch der Deutschen Demokratischen Republik* is the official statistical compilation published annually in the GDR. It contains data on the courts and their business.

Die Volkskammer der Deutschen Demokratischen Republik is a GDR publication listing all members of the People's Chamber with photographs and some biographical information about each.

A history of the German legal system and a description of the GDR system are sketched in volume 1 of *Manual of German Law* by E. J. Cohn (The British Institute of International and Comparative Law, Oceana Publications, Inc., 1968).

Two informative books on the German universities in the late nineteenth century are *The German Universities* by Friedrich Paulsen (Charles Scribner's Sons, New York, 1906), and *The American and the German University: One Hundred Years of History* by Charles Franklin Thwing (The Macmillan Company, New York, 1928).

The process leading to the fixing of the Allied Occupation Zones is described in *The Wartime Alliance and Zonal Division of Germany*, by Tony Sharp (Oxford, Clarendon Press, 1975). Also of interest in connection with the zonal division is *Eisenhower and Berlin, 1945: The*

Decision to Halt at the Elbe, by Stephen E. Ambrose (W. W. Norton, New York, 1967).

American legal periodicals contain little on GDR law. The most extensive writing has been done by Professor Inga Markovits of the University of Texas Law School. Her published writings on the subject include: Civil Law in East Germany—Its Development and Relation to Soviet Legal History and Ideology, 78 *Yale L.J.* 1 (1968); Socialist vs. Bourgeois Rights—an East-West German Comparison, 45 *U. Chi. L. Rev.* 612 (1978); Law or Order—Constitutionalism and Legality in Eastern Europe, 34 *Stan. L. Rev.* 513 (1982). She has also produced an unpublished manuscript entitled "Pursuing One's Rights Under Socialism" (Feb., 1985). Of general interest is Davies, Arrest and Pretrial Detention under the New Criminal Procedure Code of the German Democratic Republic, 13 *Col. J. Transnational Law* 269 (1974).

Index

Academy of Sciences, 58, 96, 100
Academy for State and Law, 58, 92, 93, 96, 103, 165, 179; origin, 92–93; purposes, 98–100
Advocates, *see* Lawyers
American (or Americans): views of GDR, 1; drawing of occupation zones, 22–28; classroom, compared to GDR, 83, 84; college papers, 85; state court system, 117; legal procedure, 119; lawyers, 120, 146, 162–63, 174; appellate court, 123, 125; juries, 143; dispute-resolution procedures, 144, 190–91; bar associations, 147, 170; admission to bar, 148; notary public, 152; government, GDR students' knowledge of, 188–89; jurisdictions, 191; flag on billboard, 195; GDR view of role in WW II, 196–97; view of Marxist-Leninist democracy, 199; comprehension of Marxist-Leninist system, 201
American law schools, 96–97, 103, 104, 106, 107, 112; hiring of law professors, 94; law faculties, 184; lack of stated mission, 183–84; clinical education, 187; critical legal studies, 187; comparative, foreign, and international law, 187–88
Amstgericht, 117–18
Arbitrage Commission, 165–67, 181
Association of the Blind and Partially Sighted, 6, 200–201
Aussen Wirtschaft, 102

Baedecker, 9, 19, 35, 60
Berlin, East, 34, 35–42; Alexanderplatz, 6, 195; traffic, 6; living quarters, 6; U.S. Embassy in, 32; USSR Embassy in, 33; military parades, 194; street named for noncommunist, 197; hotels, 198; theological seminary, 205; churches, 206, 207
Berlin, University of (Humboldt University), 17, 54–59, 93, 133, 197; American students, 17; buildings, 55
Berlin Wall, 30–32, 200
Berlin, West: physical presence in GDR, 32–34, 208
Betreuer, 5
Bezirksgericht, *see* County courts
Bismarck, Otto von, 18, 36
Bolivar, Simón, 56
Bonhoeffer, Dietrich, 197
Bucholz, Erich, 103

Case exercises, 84, 302–5
Central Committee of SED, 38, 41
Central Contract Court, 159–68
Christian Democratic Union (CDU), 39, 127, 206–7
Churches, 137, 197, 203–8; *see also* Federation of Protestant Churches

Churchill, Winston, 26
Civil cases, 122, 129, 156
Civil Code of GDR, 118, 180, 302
Civil defense, 84, 227
Combines, 160
Communism, 22; *see also* Marxism-Leninism
Communist party, 21, 30, 193, 195, 197, 216
Constitution, GDR, 33, 38–39, 133, 184–85, 302, 306; textbook on, 253
Constitution, U.S., 39, 78, 85, 271–72; as seen in GDR, 275–301
Contract judges, 230; *see also* County contract court
Council for Legal Education, 44, 102, 182
Council for Research, 103
Council of Ministers, 47, 99, 135, 157, 160, 173; compostion of, 40–41
Council of State, 41, 46, 135, 136, 154, 173; composition of, 40–41
Counties, in GDR, 41–42
County contract courts, 162–64
County courts (*Bezirksgericht*), 117; jurisdiction, 123; judges, 124, 133–34; organization, 124–26; procedure, 124–26; presidium, 126; work distribution plan, 126; cassation, 129
Court Organization Act of 1877, 18
Court Organization Act of GDR, 117–19, 306
Criminal cases, 121, 123–25, 129, 144, 151, 156
Criminal (penal) code of GDR, 118, 306
Democratic centralism, 34–35, 214
Diplom jurist, 72, 91, 232, 236
Dispute-resolution system, 168, 190–91
District courts (*Kreisgericht*), 117, 302, 303; organization, 119; procedure, 119; judges, 120, 132; third-party participation, 121; cases, 122; review of notaries, 153
Districts, 41

East Germany, *see* German Democratic Republic
Economic law, 47, 75, 159–68, 222
Economics curriculum, 75, 80, 159, 227, 229–30; subjects in, 241–42
Einheit, 96
Eisenhower, Dwight D., 26–27
Engels, Friedrich, 8, 22, 77, 110, 189, 197, 216, 219, 225
European Advisory Commission, 22–27
Examinations, 85–87, 233–35, 236–37

Family Code of GDR, 48, 118, 306
Family law cases, 121–22, 129, 156
Fascism: memorial to victims of, 37, 194; attributed to Western countries, 193
Federal Republic of Germany (FRG), 59, 78, 101, 102, 104, 221; judicial structure, 18; area of territory, 28; treaty with GDR, 32; continuity with earlier Germany, 33, 177; court

FRG (*cont.*)
system, 117–118, 124, 125; supreme court, 127; judges, 134; law graduates, 139; Minister of Justice, 154; prosecutor, 155; role of jurists, 173; lawyers per capita, 174; seen as fascist in the GDR, 193; war memorials, 194; items sold in intershops, 198; FRG currency in GDR, 199; future of, 210; constitution, 272
Federation of Protestant Churches, 5, 204–5; *see also* Churches
First World War, 21
Foreign language study, 78–80
Foreign students, 113–14; at Leipzig, 63; at Halle, 68
France, 78, 221; occupation zones, 25; radio from, 32; history book on, 190; constitutional law of, 273
FRG–GDR Transit Agreement of 1971, 32
Frederick the Great, 20, 28, 35, 37–38, 54, 55; back in fashion, 197
Free German Youth (FDJ), 94, 106–8, 109, 110, 112, 137, 179, 199, 200
Free University of Berlin, 59, 92
Friedrich Schiller University, *see* Jena, University of

GDR–FRG border, 24, 31
German Democratic Republic (GDR): people, 4, 5, 202–3; hotels, 5, 198; restaurants, 5; radio and TV, 6, 32, 190; travel in, 6–7; area of territory, 28; loss of population, 30; diplomatic recognition, 32; relation with Soviet Union, 32–33; intershops, 198–99; integrated society, 201; access to FRG, 209; *History of State and Law*, 247–52
German Reich: territory, 15; universities, 17–20, 28; university enrollment, 17; American students in, 17; legal education, 17–18; Civil Code, 18; Civil Procedure Code, 18, 306; Commercial Code, 18; Criminal Code, 18; Criminal Procedure Code, 18, 306; judges, 18; Ministry of Justice, 19–20; legal system, 18; state court systems, 18–19
Great Britain, 20, 22, 78; drawing of occupation zones, 23–27; radio and TV from, 32; court systems, 125; lawyers per capita, 174; history books on, 189; communist newspaper, 190; lay magistrates, 191; GDR view of role in WW II, 196; constitutional law, 272

Halle, city of, 7, 64–65, 69, 197, 200, 205
Halle, University of (Martin Luther University), 64–69; living quarters, 6; American students, 17; murals, 53
Hegel, G. W. F., 10, 55, 189
Helmholtz, statue of, 55
Heusinger, Hans-Joachim, 135

Hitler, Adolph, 22, 36, 192, 209
Ho Chi Minh, exhibit on, 56
Honecker, Erich, 40–41, 209
Humboldt, Alexander, statue of, 55
Humboldt, Wilhelm, statue of, 55
Humboldt University, *see* Berlin, University of

Imperial Supreme Court, 59; establishment, 18; building, 19
Institute for the Theory of State and Law, 100
Interhotels, 7, 198
International Association of Democratic Lawyers, 171
International law, 187, 226, 260–68
International Research and Exchanges Board (IREX), 2
Intershops, 198–99
Interviews, 2, 5, 7, 11
Isvestia, 57

Jena, city of, 3, 27, 69–70
Jena, University of (Friedrich Schiller University), 3, 69–72, 154, 159
Judges, 18, 20, 131, 229; political affiliations, 136; number and training, 138; women, 138–39; compensation, 139; typical background, 179; *see also* Berlin, University of; Justice Curriculum; Law sections; Lay judges
Justice curriculum, 75–80, 159, 227, 213–37; examinations, 85–86; subjects in, 238–40

Karl Marx University, *see* Leipzig, University of
Kreisgericht, *see* District courts

Labor cases, 122, 129, 144, 156
Labor Code of GDR, 118, 306
Landgericht, 117
Law and Legislation in the GDR, 172–73
Law books: commentaries, 88; summaries, 88, 187; *see also* Textbooks
Law curriculum, 72–86, 103, 187–89, 213–37; comparison to American, 191; case exercises, 302–5; *see also* Justice curriculum; Economics curriculum
Law degrees: *Diplom jurist*, 72, 91, 232, 236; *Doktor Jurist*, 91; *Doktor Scientiae Jurist*, 91
Law libraries: Berlin, 57–58; Supreme Court, 58; Halle, 68–69; Jena, 71; Leipzig, 62–63
Law sections
- relations with state organs, 44–45
- organization, 56
- Berlin, 56, 84, 93
  - weekly schedule, 80, 81
- Leipzig, 62, 93, 161, 164
- Halle, 66–68, 93, 95
  - law teachers, 68
  - weekly schedule, 80, 82
- Jena, 70–71, 154, 157
  - law teachers, 71
- special section time, 79, 228, 230
- exercises and examinations, 85
- councils, 93–94
- directors, 94–95
- practice partners, 105, 111, 182
- admissions, 105–7
- women, 108
- academic calendar, 110–11
- placement, 112

Law sections (*cont.*)
training, 179
see also Civil defense; Legal research; Practical training
Law students, 17; at Humboldt, 58–59; at Leipzig, 63; at Halle, 68; at Jena, 71; weekly class schedules, 81–82; Free German Youth (FDJ), 87; research students, 90–91, 98; admissions, 105–7; practical training, 111; stipends, 108; marriage, 108; women, 108; housing, 109; janitorial duties, 111; civil defense training, 111; placement, 111, 131–32; number, 13; part-time, 113; political nature of education, 183, 209; views of West, 188
Law teachers: professors in German Reich, 17–18; departmental organization, 56–57, 93; publications, 62, 97; teaching loads, 86, 90; professors, 89–94; assistants, 89–90; docents, 89–90, 94; honorary professors, 90; salaries, 90; education, 92; pre-1945, 92; vacancies, 94; SED members, 95; foreign travel, 95–96; research, 97; working conditions, 104; implementation of curriculum, 182; standard of living, 202; conversations with, 185; objectivity of scholarship, 186
Lawyers, 48, 144, 146–52, 222, 229; collegia of advocates, 146–48, 306; fees and earnings, 149; types of cases, 149–50; number of matters handled, 150–51; criminal cases, 151; obligations, 151–52; availability of and demand for, 152; employed by enterprises, 167; unions, 169; per capita, 174; education, 179; *see also* Lawyers' Association
Lawyers' Association, 127, 168–74, 200
Lay judges, 118, 119, 124, 140–43, 145
Lectures, 80, 83, 96
Legal research, 96–104; research plan, 97, 103; *see also* Publications
Leipzig, city of, 18, 27, 28, 59–61, 63–64, 93; Karl Marx Platz, 195; hotel, 198; Library of the Association for the Blind and Partially Sighted, 200; theological seminary, 205; church, 206; air service from Frankfurt, 209
Leipzig, University of (Karl Marx University), 59–64; living quarters, 7, 8; American students, 17
Lenin, V. I., 10, 78, 110, 189, 197, 216, 219, 225
Liberal party, 135
Libraries (other than law): Humboldt, 57; German State Library, 57; Academy of Sciences, 58; Leipzig University, 62; in Leipzig, 63; Halle University, 66; university libraries, newspapers in, 191; Library of the Association for the Blind and Partially Sighted, 200
Liebknecht, Karl, 197
London Protocol of 1944, 24–28, 35, 197

Luther, Martin, 28, 203, 205; in Halle, 65; 500th birthday celebration, 102, 197–8
Luxemburg, Rosa, 197

Martin Luther University, *see* Halle, University of
Marx, Karl, 8, 22, 77, 102, 110, 189, 216, 219, 225; bust of, 53; inscription by, 55; picture of, 56; name in slogans, 195; leading historical figure, 197
Marxism-Leninism, 86–87, 92, 120, 137–38, 171, 173–74, 178–79, 183–84, 186–90, 201, 207, 209–10; general description, 7–9, 21–22, 30, 48, 54; Library of, in Halle, 53; orientation of Study Plan, 73–78, 213–37; courses in, 77–78
Mass organizations, 39, 200
Melanchton, Philipp, 66; bust of, 54
Militarism, 194
Military training, 107, 194, 227
Ministry of Justice, 4, 40–42, 44–46, 48, 103, 126, 130–32, 134–36, 147–48, 150, 153–54, 158, 161, 182
Ministry for Higher Education, 2, 5, 40, 42–44, 72–73, 87, 94–96, 98, 102, 159, 182, 186, 230, 235, 237
Mommsen, statue of, 55
Morning Star, 190

National Defense Council, 41
National Front, 39, 142, 145
Nazi party, 21, 92–93, 192–94
Neue Justiz, 100–101
Neues Deutschland, 57
Nonresident studies, 227, 235
Notaries, 152–54, 222, 229, 306

Oberlandesgericht, 117–18
Oberstes gericht, see Supreme Court of GDR
Occupation zones, 23–28

Palast der Republik, 38, 40
People's Chamber, 45, 46, 135, 136, 154, 173; location, 38; function, 39–41
People's-owned enterprises, 47, 143, 159–60, 164, 230, 232, 304; *see also* State-owned enterprises
Photocopying, 4
Politburo, 38, 41, 46, 173
Practical training, 85, 112, 231
Pravda, 57
Procurator General, 4, 42, 44, 46–48, 103, 128, 130, 154–56, 158, 182
Procurators, 123, 154–59, 222, 229, 304, 305, 306
Publications, 97, 99–110; university newspapers, 110, 194; Lawyers' Association information bulletin, 171; religious, 204

Quadripartite Agreement of 1971, 32

Red Army, 7, 22, 23; memorial, 26; cemetery, 27; barricades, 31; strength, 32; final drive on Berlin, 36; role in WW II, 196–97
Reichgericht, see Imperial Supreme Court
Russia, *see* Soviet Union

Second World War, 21–22, 27, 55, 193–94; German migration resulting from, 27
Seminars, 80, 83–84, 96
Social courts, 46–47, 119, 143–

Social courts (*cont.*)
45, 160, 181, 190–91, 222, 232, 304, 306
Socialism, *see* Marxism-Leninism
Socialist Party of Germany (SPD), 30
Socialist Unity Party of Germany (SED), 48, 96, 109, 132, 136, 137, 143, 157, 170, 179–82, 193, 199, 220, 299; membership pin, 4; formation, 38; control, 39; structure, 41; newspaper, 57
Soviet Union, 8, 22, 75, 78, 95, 101, 102, 129; drawing of occupation zones, 23–28; relation with GDR, 30, 32–33; embassy, 36; influence on office of Procurator General, 46, 155, 157; linked to GDR by constitution, 184; laws studied in GDR, 188; history books on, 190; military in GDR, 194; GDR view of role in WW II, 196–97; cancellation of Honecker's trip to West, 209; influence on Study Plan of GDR, 213–37
Sports, 75, 80
Staat und Recht, 99, 110–11
State Contract Court, 44, 46–47, 103, 118, 159–67, 181–82, 232; *see also* Central Contract Court
State court system, 44, 46–47, 167, 181, 222, 232; organization, 117
State-owned enterprises, 47, 143, 159, 164; *see also* People-owned enterprises
Statistical Yearbook of GDR, 3, 113, 121–22, 144
Stoph, Willi, 41
Streit, Joseph, 157
Student housing: at Humboldt, 58; at Leipzig, 63; at Halle, 68
Study Plan, 73–75, 77, 84–86, 103, 183; text, 213–37
Supreme Court of GDR, 44, 117; library, 58; subject matter organization, 128; cassation, 128, 157; published opinions, 129; issuance of regulations, 130; plenum, 130; presidium, 130, 135; work distribution plan, 130; judges, 135; president, 126, 136
System for the administration of justice, 47, 75

Textbooks, 48, 87–88, 98, 103, 186, 253–59, 269–74
Thälmann, Ernst, 197
Thomasius, Christian, 66–67
Toeplitz, Heinrich, 126, 168, 179
Trade unions, 89, 94, 130, 145, 169, 200

United States, 78, 101, 102, 221; drawing of occupation zones, 24–28; offer of aid to Russian zone, 30; Constitution, 39, 78; local government, 41; structure of courts, 46; GDR parallel to commercial litigation, 47, 160; Supreme Court decisions available, 58; bar associations, 170; groups affiliated with the International Association of Democratic Lawyers, 170; lessons to learn from GDR legal system, 180–81; compared to GDR, 185; history

United States (*cont.*)
books on, 190; seen as fascist, 193; hostility toward, 196; GDR tours advertised in, 198; Library of Congress, 200; affirmative action, 203; religious life, 205; Constitution as seen in the GDR, 275–80
Universities in GDR: under Ministry for Higher Education, 44, 48; professors, 17; publications, 100; newspapers, 110, 194; enrollment by fields, 113–14; theological faculties, 204
USSR, *see* Soviet Union

Weimar, 28, 69, 197
Weimar Constitution, 21
West Germany, *see* Federal Republic of Germany
Wirtschaftsrecht, 102
Wissenschaftliche Zeitschrift, 100
Wünsche, Kurt, 7

Young Pioneers, 137, 179